c20 architecture

THIS IS A CARLTON BOOK

Design copyright © 1998 and 2002 Carlton Books Limited
Text copyright © 1998 and 2002 Jonathan Glancey

This edition published by Carlton Books Limited 2003
20 Mortimer Street
London
W1T 3JW

A CIP catalogue for this book is available
from the British Library

ISBN 1 84222 014 4

Printed and bound in China

CARLTON
BOOKS

C20th architecture

THE STRUCTURES THAT SHAPED
THE TWENTIETH CENTURY

JONATHAN GLANCEY

Contents

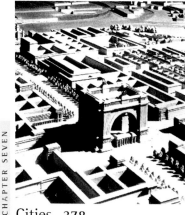

Foreword

THIS IS A VAST SUBJECT and no book can realistically cover the entire history of twentieth-century architecture. If it could, it would either be too heavy to carry or else set in such tiny type that it would be unreadable. This book is meant as an introduction or guide to the riches and sheer diversity of buildings in a century that witnessed mind-boggling change and saw human society rise to peaks of civilization and troughs of savagery and destruction. Human life at the end of the twentieth century was still very much a fight for living space, a space that architects shape and frame. Many of the best architects of the century were practical dreamers who tried to push their art and society to new and civilized heights. They set their compasses and T-squares (computers, too) on the face of the world and tried to create beautiful buildings in perfect towns and cities. People, however, are never as perfect as they are in architectural drawings and, all too often, the architect's dream was diffused or shattered by irrational human behaviour. War – and this was a century of global as well as tribal conflict – was the one great destroyer. Greed, narrow-mindedness and the architect's own inability to communicate ambitious ideas were others. In fact, architects – Le Corbusier first among them – have been accused of trying to destroy civilization in the twentieth century with designs for towers of concrete and steel and ambitions that witnessed the unprecedented demolition of historic buildings, streets and squares. This is unfair, although the architect was, on the whole, a willing collaborator with governments, property developers and the moving spirit of the times. Architects, as Philip Johnson, a very clever US architect said, "are whores": as members of one of the world's oldest professions, they get paid for doing what other people want. And that means the design of banal office blocks and brainless shopping malls as well as beautiful private houses and churches that have the power to reduce the noisiest citizen to silence.

Perhaps the problem for twentieth-century architects was that their talent was spread thinly. They were asked to design an ever-increasing number and range of buildings across the world on an ever-decreasing share of national and global income. Up until the Industrial Revolution, buildings were one of the greatest expenses most societies faced. They were expensive partly because they took a long time to build and required a great deal of skilled manual labour to do so and partly because they were the most visible means society had of expressing its confidence, power and culture. As the twentieth century drew on, there were so many other things for society to spend its money on: sophisticated weaponry, health, education, clothes, food, cars, holidays. Society might have wanted more buildings than it had in the past – and especially housing – and it certainly wanted a far greater range of buildings too – swimming pools, superstores, motorway service stations, airports, bowling alleys, corporate headquarters – but it wanted much more for much less.

Increasingly sophisticated

STEIN HOUSE, P.268.

SETH STEIN, 1995.

technology and new materials enabled modern societies to build with ever-increasing speed. The results could be dire, and the architect was, plinth by cornice, reduced to the role of decorating highly-serviced boxes that might be office blocks, apartment blocks, factories or out-of-town shopping malls. In a century that saw the rise (and fall) of more buildings than ever before, the role of the architect was inexorably marginalized. Architects themselves could not see, or did not like to see, the world this way. And yet, increasingly, their role was being limited and their powers curtailed. Again, this was all but inevitable in a world in which the speed, scale and complexity of so much building construction meant that the architect became simply a part of a team led increasingly by engineers and contractors. In order to preserve their role, architects had to become "imagineers", shaping and guiding the look of buildings and the way they related to their settings.

This was a quantum leap from the architect's role at the beginning of the century. Yet the writing was already on the wall then. The new century required a new type of building, highly serviced machines for making and processing money, sophisticated junction boxes that were a world away from churches and country houses. The sharpest architectural minds could see what was happening, and struggled to interpret and express a new machine age in buildings that were intended to break with the past, but never could. For architecture is an art that seems never to have escaped its roots. Perhaps this is

because in the cultures of East, West, North and South, the earliest architecture was also some of the very best. Throughout the twentieth century, as this book shows, western architects harked back to ancient Greece, where architecture reached a state of near perfection in the fifth century BC. The Parthenon, even in its ruined state (blown apart accidentally by Turkish gunpowder stored there in the seventeenth century), stands as judge of all the architecture that has been built in the cast of its long shadow.

Again, this should not be surprising: architects try in their different ways to create order and would-be perfection from an imperfect world. Each new building by a good architect is a fresh attempt to create a model of perfection. A truly great architect, as you can see in these pages, can get close, but none has ever bettered the Parthenon. In one sense, it was also impossible to do so in a century that demanded so much from its buildings and expected them to be machines for performing specific functions rather than icons expressing the core values, worth, technology and ideals of a society. The Parthenon did all these things. In those sun-bleached, pollutant-etched stones, the patient observer can read the story of Athenian society.

Twentieth-century societies, for the most part, were much more complex (if not better) than that of fifth-century Athens and no one twentieth-century building could tell such a comprehensive tale as the Parthenon does. Our architecture is kaleidoscopic, its

CAPUCHINAS CHAPEL, P.196.

LUIS BARRAGÁN, 1955.

NEUE STAATSGALERIE, P.305.

STIRLING-WILFORD, 1995.

message fragmented and inconclusive. From the end of World War One to perhaps as late as the early 1970s, there was some sort of collective attempt by architects to create a new and comprehensive order: the Modern Movement. This cannot be readily defined, but, without doubt, there did appear to be a more or less collective desire among architects around the world to invent a language of design the equivalent of what Latin was in medieval Europe or that English is in the world today. If there really was such a thing as the Modern Movement, it was doomed to failure. Architecture moves with society (although architects like to believe that it is the other way around) and social change ensured that there could be no one style of architecture that would ever be capable of freeze-framing the world.

To help make sense of the many moods and styles of architecture that emerged over the century, I have divided the 370 buildings illustrated in this book into broad sections. These are not meant to be a perfect fit, but rather compounds into which are herded buildings that would probably get on with each other pretty well if they could meet. It is probably true to say that in the twentieth century architectural ideas were exported and imported with great speed and so you will find many visual cross-references from one style of building to another. All art, said Picasso, is copying and architects, with rare exceptions, have learned from one another and quoted from one another in their designs with pride as well as abandon. In fact, in architecture it is a sign of great sophistication to ensure that your peer group knows that you are making knowing references to past masters. Masters rather than mistresses, of course, for nearly every building shown in this book was designed and built by men.

Because this is an introduction to twentieth-century architecture and because it can only be so big, this book relies almost entirely on photographs of buildings to represent them. To fully understand a building, it is necessary to get behind its façade and to study the way it is built up from a plan. Modern Movement architects saw the plan as a kind of moral as well as practical and aesthetic guideline. A building must be raised up from an "honest" (ie. functional) plan and its final shape should reveal the workings of that plan. In fact, even the greatest Modernists cheated – thank goodness – and very many buildings shown in the following pages are not nearly as rational as their designers claimed them to be. Architecture is as much about emotion as function. Even so, it would have been nice to have had the space to show plans and other drawings. In the event, it is probably better to look at the buildings, to long to see them and to find out more about them. There are thousands of books on various aspects of twentieth-century architects and architecture that will explain in detail most of the buildings shown here. And many monographs are devoted to single designs. What I think this book can offer you is the big picture and the chance to make some sort of sense of an immense and inexhaustible story. If it makes you want to find out more, then it has done its job. If it encourages you to want to be an architect, good luck.

I have visited very many of the buildings shown in the book and have included a number of those I find beautiful, moving or fascinating that have been excluded from previous "pantechnicons" of this kind. There are, however, many buildings that no writer would dare or dream of excluding. Why? Because there are buildings that define a moment, generate a mood, first make use of a new technology that cannot be ignored, not only because they are fascinating in themselves but because they were so influential.

You will find prejudices in the writing. I think this is fair. How can anyone look at every building they meet objectively? I really do not have the stomach for most of the buildings listed in the section sub-titled "Less is a Bore". I find what passed for Postmodernism in architecture, with honourable exceptions, ugly and crass. I do not think that architecture is a particularly funny subject and jokes writ on the scale of a building are embarrassing and even pitiful some years down the line. Buildings, except where land is very scarce and property values exceptionally high, as in Tokyo or Hong Kong, tend to have long lives. There are very few jokes from the nineteenth century that we still find funny. But the Parthenon, Le Corbusier's chapel at Ronchamp and the Farnsworth House by Mies van der Rohe remain things of great and ineffable beauty. They are not remotely funny.

I hope the book, and especially because we have tried to source really good photographs, will also help you see that a beautiful building might well be made from tough modern materials that most people associate with ugliness and even inhumanity. Look again and then go and see how a genius like Le Corbusier or Louis Kahn uses concrete, or of how the play of sunlight on steel beams or weather-boarded concrete transforms what you had imagined to be a brute of a building into an unexpected beauty. As you turn through these pages and begin to visit some of these buildings, I hope you will feel some of the same excitement I felt as a teenager as I began to discover the architecture of the century I was born in, after childhood years spent heaving open the doors of old parish churches and padding the corridors of crumbling country houses. If I was ill or when I was sneaking off "games", I would lie on the floor and pore through old picture books on architecture, dreaming of what the buildings were really like and wondering who designed them. This is a rainy day book – although unfamiliar architecture is generally best for being experienced when the sun is shining.

The book was fun to put together – faster than any building – and I hope it makes you want to discover more: the architectural interpretation of history is, after all, as valid as any other.

Jonathan Glancey
London, 2000

PARC DE LA VILLETTE, P.315.
BERNARD TSCHUMI, 1989.

The Industrial Revolution was a brutalizing experience. For anyone with half a conscience there was something very wrong with the manner in which the wretched of the earth poured into towns and cities looking for work and with the ways they were subsequently treated. For anyone with an eye, the brutal new architecture, if it could be called that, the intrusion of railways, of steam and smoke and choking smogs was nothing

Brotherhood of the Pre-Raphaelites, and William Morris (1834–96) were key figures in the rise of what was to become the Arts and Crafts movement. It began in England and spread its gospel far and wide in the early part of the twentieth century. Its traditions took firm root in Britain and, throughout the radical investigations of the Modern Movement, to which it offered its creed of honest construction and functional

Followers of Morris founded what they hoped would be idyllic rural communities of fellow craft workers and architects. A younger generation, however, such as the fine young architects of the London County Council (created in 1889) took Arts and Crafts ideals into the heart of the city and used them as a basis for improving the lot of those who delved and span for a pittance and lived in squalor. The Boundary Estate in London's Shoreditch (p.14) remains a model of civilized urban housing inspired by Arts and Crafts principles.

Arts and Crafts

THE SEARCH FOR EARTHLY PARADISE

but horror piled upon horror. For high-minded aesthetes there was something rotten in the way that the new machine age could mass-produce goods and architectural details and undermine the work of the skilled craftsmen whose ancestors had once given shape and breathed life into great cathedrals, market crosses and cloth halls.

The Industrial Revolution also meant that ideas could be transported rapidly by train from county to county and country to country so that vernacular traditions were increasingly in danger of being elbowed out from their ancient homes. Artists, writers and architects began, bit by bit, to revolt against these perceived horrors and excesses. John Ruskin (1819–1900), the

plans, and the game-playing of the Postmodern era, the spirit of Ruskin and Morris continued to haunt new architecture, from schools to county halls.

The Arts and Crafts movement was both an aesthetic and a moral crusade. It was part and parcel of a peculiarly English sentiment in which a primitive form of socialism, nostalgia for a medieval world of knights in shining armour and damsels in distress, fear of new technology, love of hand-made objects and a sense of decency and fair play combined to create a recognizable yet informal style of architecture that acted as a rustic stick with which to beat formal artistic decadence.

At first it was more a form of escape from the industrial world than a challenge to it.

Elsewhere in Europe, Arts and Crafts ideas were blended with those of Art Nouveau (or Jugendstijl) with high art colluding with the highest standards of craftsmanship. As well as an idea and a set of ideals, the movement was also, in the hands of many architects, simply another style and one well suited for a new wave of country houses for the newly rich who wished to escape the grubby roots of their wealth by living in romantic "honest" splendour.

The freedom that the Arts and Crafts movement offered architects ensured rich and varied buildings. What they have most in common is their free and "honest" plans and superb standards of construction. At best they are thoughtful and life-enhancing buildings; at worst, they seem gratuitous and ride headlong into the buffers of kitsch.

The Orchard

C. F. A. VOYSEY, 1900

CHORLEYWOOD,

HERTFORDSHIRE, ENGLAND

CHARLES FRANCIS ANNESLEY VOYSEY (1857–1941) was the tiny, bird-like son of a Yorkshire parson who was expelled from the Church of England for denying the existence of Hell. As an architect, Voysey worked tirelessly from 1882 in his own idiosyncratic idiom trying, perhaps, to create a vision of earthly paradise influenced by the socialist Arts and Crafts thinker and designer William Morris and the fiery Gothic Revivalist A. W. N. Pugin.

Voysey's paradise was to be as clean as a new pin: aside from furniture and wallpapers, he designed his own bright blue suits without cuffs or lapels as these gathered unacceptable dust. He lived in a house of his own design, The Orchard, the finest of a group of suburban houses on the northwest fringe of London. Although The Orchard, like many Voysey designs, appears superficially to draw on a mythical Olde-English past, its interior is free-flowing and if not Modern, as has been claimed

by Modern Movement apologists, it has a freedom of plan and clarity of design that made it quietly revolutionary. The house's features – doors, window ledges – are scaled down to Voysey's own miniature scale.

Although The Orchard was to influence the look of England's cosy (and cloying) suburban homes over the next 100 years, it remains at heart – and there are heart motifs to be found throughout its loving detailing – the expression of an architect who wished to create a quiet and ordered domestic heaven on earth under steep roofs and within immaculate white walls.

Hôtel Tassel

VICTOR HORTA, 1900

BRUSSELS, BELGIUM

VICTOR HORTA (1861–1947) studied at the Académie des Beaux-Arts in Brussels after which he began working with Alphonse Balat, a reputable Neoclassical architect. Horta, however, was much taken with the writings of Viollet-le-Duc, the French Gothic revivalist who made great play with the latest industrial materials. The result, when Horta set up on his own, was an exotic flowering of extraordinary houses that manage to combine Baroque and Classical elements with free-flowing plans, serpentine ironwork, tapestries of richly coloured glass and sensuality with common sense. Fitted out in lavish detail by the architect, Hôtel Tassel is probably the most mature of the many houses Horta designed and the one that most fully expresses the ideals of Art Nouveau. The revolutionary aspect of this house, however, lies less in its gorgeous decorated structure and more in its plan and section: these allow rooms to be reached at different levels, in some ways heralding the free use of interior space made by Modern Movement architects after World War One. Yet, what the visitor really feels here is a sense of being inside a three-dimensional illustration by Walter Crane or Aubrey Beardsley.

Horta went on to become a professor at the Académie des Beaux-Arts. He later abandoned curves and decorative sensation for the rigours of straight lines and plain concrete construction.

Boundary Street Estate

LONDON COUNTY COUNCIL
ARCHITECT'S DEPARTMENT,
1900, SHOREDITCH,
LONDON, ENGLAND

UNDER THE DIRECTION of Owen Fleming, the young architects of the London County Council's (LCC) Housing of the Working Class Branch (set up in 1893) designed this, the first and best of several major slum clearance housing projects. Fired by the theories of John Ruskin, William Morris and Karl Marx, the LCC architects created what might truly be called "palaces for the people", bringing art into the life of the artless and downtrodden. More than 5,500 people were housed in the magnificent red and yellow brick Arts and Crafts blocks that form the Boundary Estate. These radiate from Arnold Circus in which an elevated central garden boasts a once fashionable bandstand that lends a festive air to what had long been – and remains in many ways – a grim, down-at-heel quarter of east London.

Many of the details are clearly derived from older masters of the Arts and Crafts movement, and it is easy to spot the guiding hands of Norman Shaw and, more particularly, of Philip Webb, who built a much-copied house for William Morris in Bexley Heath in south London in 1859. Social housing in Britain and continental Europe was rarely to rise to this noble and popular standard again. In the 1990s, the Boundary Street Estate was renovated. It remains a testimony to intelligent city government administration.

Deanery Garden

EDWIN LUTYENS, 1901

SONNING, BERKSHIRE,

ENGLAND

SIR EDWIN LANDSEER LUTYENS (1869–1944) was one of the greatest architects of his generation. Described by his biographer, Christopher Hussey, as "a perfect architectural sonnet", Deanery Garden is the best known of his early English country houses.

The house was radical in its use of space, yet its appearance was a clever contrivance of old English materials and formulas: timber, great windows laced with mullions and transoms and beautifully made, handsomely laid bricks. The house was built for Edward Hudson, the proprietor of *Country Life* magazine and Lutyens' champion. An Edwardian countryside "bachelor pad", it was within easy reach of London via the Great Western Railway. The garden, landscaped by Lutyens and Gertrude Jekyll, is all of a piece with the house as was, when this masterpiece was photographed for a 1903 edition of *Country Life,* the oak furniture and simple decor. The conceit of the house was to create an idyllic domestic setting for the quintessential Edwardian gentleman, a man of great restraint, understated elegance and with a deep attachment to a very English take on history.

The house has worn well over the century, demonstrating the advantage of Lutyens' training in builders' yards: like many of the century's greats, he was not a qualified architect. He built with intuition and love, virtues that can be felt in the construction of this impeccable, inventive English house.

All Saints' Church

W. R. LETHABY, 1902

BROCKHAMPTON,

HEREFORDSHIRE, ENGLAND

WILLIAM LETHABY (1857–1931) is best known, perhaps, as a teacher and theorist. He was the first director of the Central School of Arts and Crafts, London, which was, in many ways, the precursor of the Bauhaus. Lethaby also designed some striking and curious buildings, attempts to bring together Arts and Crafts sensibilities with the use of modern materials.

The church Lethaby built in a backwater of rural Herefordshire is a fascinating attempt to marry ancient and modern technologies and styles. At first glance, All Saints' Church appears to be truly ancient, rooted close to the ground, its muscular stone walls protected by a roof of straw. Inside, it gives up the pretence and we know we have entered not just a very English parish church, but the twentieth century. The roof is made, quite unashamedly, of concrete and its

structure is determinedly like no medieval or Victorian Gothic Revival design. Idiosyncratic window details add to the sense of the strangely new and different.

All Saints' Church is not simply a curiosity – and beautiful, too, in its odd way – but an expression of the tug and tussle so many British architects had, and were to have, with the possibilities and expression of new materials and technologies and with the idea of what exactly constituted the "vernacular" in building design throughout the twentieth century.

Stock Exchange

H. P. BERLAGE, 1903

AMSTERDAM, THE
NETHERLANDS

MASSIVE, ROMANESQUE IN SPIRIT, a modern castle in a city centre, the new Stock Exchange was the greatest work of Hendrik Petrus Berlage (1856–1934). The building's great unbroken brick walls and semi-circular arches recall the work of the Dutch architect's American contemporaries, H. H. Richardson and Frank Lloyd Wright, whose buildings he had known of, yet not seen until a visit to the United States in 1911. Berlage considered himself to be a highly "moral" architect, which appears to imply that the construction of a building should be clearly exposed; so much so that the rooms of the severe houses he designed, such as the Henny House, The Hague (1898), were not allowed plaster over the brickwork. And, as for wallpaper ...

Berlage was reacting against the eclectic free-style architecture of the last two decades of the nineteenth century. In doing so, he helped pave the way for a school or feel for architecture that was to have considerable influence on such later Dutch masters as Willem Marinus Dudok (p.163), who brought together a passion for crafted brickwork and rigorous, Modern elevations.

The Stock Exchange, situated on Amsterdam's busy Damrak, continues to dominate this part of the city and has been beautifully maintained. Its solid, if not entirely austere, exterior conceals a procession of remodelled exhibition halls within.

Hill House

CHARLES RENNIE
MACKINTOSH 1903
HELENSBURGH, SCOTLAND

HILL HOUSE is the largest and
most ambitious of five poetic
homes Charles Rennie Mackintosh
(1868–1928) designed in and
around Glasgow. It was commissioned
by the publisher W. W. Blackie and
caught the imagination of European
observers even though his English
contemporaries thought his designs
decadent. Mackintosh's furniture
designs, shown at the Arts and
Crafts Exhibition of 1896 in
London were widely criticized for
their poor construction and the
Scot was never invited to show
again. Oddly enough, having
designed some of the most
beautiful of all British buildings –
all in Scotland – Mackintosh left
Glasgow for London in 1913 and
took up painting full-time instead.

Hill House is a modern
interpretation of an old Scottish
tower house, its austere walls covered,
like them, in harl (roughcast), and
yet inside it is all whiteness, delicacy
and light. So exquisite is the wilfully
artistic interior that the contemporary
German writer, Herman Muthesius,
author of the hugely influential
Das Englische Haus, 1904, thought
it "refined to such a degree which
the lives of even the artistically
educated are still a long way from
matching ... Even a book in an
unsuitable binding would disturb
the atmosphere simply by lying on
the table." In 1982 the house was
taken into care by the National
Trust for Scotland.

Home Place

E. S. PRIOR, 1905

HOLT, NORFOLK, ENGLAND

"PERHAPS THERE IS SOMETHING in the Norfolk air", wrote the historian Gavin Stamp in *The English House*, 1986, "which accounts for this strange architecture." Home Place is a glorious, wilful Arts and Crafts house designed for the Reverend Percy R. Lloyd by Edward Schroeder Prior (1852–1932).

In essence the house consists of a central range flanked by a pair of "butterfly" wings that flap off at angles of 60 degrees. These are wildly designed with all manner of picturesque detail and, as the architect Roderick Gradidge has observed, Home Place looks "as if it is covered with a very old Fairisle pullover that has been knitted by an imbecile child. Quaintness can be carried no further."

This rather eccentric product of stupendously wealthy Edwardian England became a convalescent home in the 1930s. It still is,

although whether the architecture is restful is debatable. Prior designed some of the most extreme Arts and Crafts buildings in Britain, exaggerating the use of "found" and local materials. He liked, as one of his colleagues said, "to be in a minority of one". He built for the rich, he was an Old Harrovian and a Cambridge graduate, and was pretty much able to do what he wanted. His parish church at Roker in Sunderland (1907), however, was a model of restraint and one of the finest ecclesiastical buildings of its time.

Post Office Savings Bank

OTTO WAGNER, 1906

VIENNA, AUSTRIA

THIS IS OTTO WAGNER'S
(1841–1918) most famous and
brilliant building. The monumental
main façade conceals an ingenious
banking hall at the heart of the
trapezoidal-shaped block. This
features a glass floor, bringing
daylight into the basement, and an
extensively glazed arched roof. This
in turn is protected by a glass roof
at the top of the bank's six-storey
lightwell. The whiteness and
brightness of this space, together
with its brilliant use of glass, means
that it has never seemed anything
other than up to date at any
moment in the twentieth century.
In Wagner's competition entry
for the building, the roof of the
banking hall was to have been
even more radical: a canopy of
glass suspended on cables held by
steel masts. Such detailing might
have been common in the 1980s,
but was almost unheard of outside
the world of structural engineering
in 1904 when the building was
commissioned.

The face the bank presents to
central Vienna is no less daring:
the anchorage points of the marble
panels that form the main façade
are not only exposed, but the
chunky aluminium heads of their
rivets are polished. These proudly
ostentatious rivets take the place
of conventional historic decoration.
This highly distinctive form of
construction was to be much
copied by architects, notably in
Japan, much later in the century.

Scotland Street School

CHARLES RENNIE
MACKINTOSH, 1906
EDINBURGH, SCOTLAND

NOT ALL MACKINTOSH'S BUILDINGS
were as delicate and self-consciously
"artistic" as Hill House (p.18). Scotland
Street School is a substantial building
that has stood the test of time. Its
plan is very simple: two floors of
classrooms divided by a central
corridor behind massive stone walls.
What is special here is the use of
light. Not only are the castle-like
windows vast, but daylight also
floods into the school through the
twin entrance and stair towers. The
building points to a style of civic
and commercial architecture that
could well have been developed into
a convincing alternative to the
slipshod architecture that, under the
misleading banner "Modern", was
to pockmark so many British city
centres in the course of the century.

Mackintosh was, in his lifetime,
much more appreciated in Europe.
He exhibited designs for furniture
and buildings at Munich in 1898 and
the annual exhibition of the Secession
in Vienna in 1900. Mackintosh's
design for an "Art Lover's House"
was entered in a 1901 competition
organized by the German magazine
Zeitschrift für Innerndekoration. It
was built, strangely enlarged as if the
designs had been placed under a
magnifying glass, in Glasgow in the
1990s. Mackintosh lived out his last
years painting sublime watercolours
in the south of France, a long way
in every sense from the rigours of
Scotland Street School and Glasgow.

Hampstead Garden Suburb

RAYMOND UNWIN, ET AL,
1907

LONDON, ENGLAND

THE FIRST GARDEN SUBURB, Hampstead embodied the Garden City concept devised by the planner Ebeneezer Howard in the 1890s and put into practice by Raymond Unwin (1863–1940) at Letchworth (p.380).

Unwin was a Fabian socialist, which meant he looked to change society through steady reform rather than radical upheavals.

Where and how people lived played a key part in this school of socialist thinking, much of which was rooted in the work of William Morris, father figure of the Arts and Crafts movement. The Arts and Crafts influence showed clearly not just in the architecture of Hampstead Garden Suburb but also in the way of life it was designed to engender: arty-crafty. The suburb was designed around a central square, influenced by Lutyens who designed the three highly distinctive buildings that define the spirit of this leafy city annexe: St Jude's Church with its massive roofs and striking spire; the

Free Church – an essay in Lutyens's "Wrenaissance" Baroque; and the Institute, the focal point of life in the new suburb. Around the square Lutyens and others filled in Unwin's plan with large Queen Anne and Neo-Georgian houses. Beyond this grand statement of intent, Unwin's plan unrolls in a sequence of avenues, never less than 12 metres (40 ft) wide that roll with the contours of the land and are lined with smaller Neo-Georgian and Voysey-inspired houses. The effect is neat and green, but more than 90 years on, the suburb still feels remote from the rest of the world; but perhaps that was the idea.

Tempere Cathedral

LARS SONCK, 1907

TEMPERE, FINLAND

THIS APPARENTLY ROUGH HEWN romantic pile represented a significant moment in the history of Finnish architecture. It was at once an expression of the National Romantic movement in Finnish art and culture and at the same time a reaching out from what might have become a culturally isolated era to the world for inspiration. National Romanticism was a reaction, to a large extent, to Finland's fear of being swallowed by Russian imperialism in the late nineteenth century. Artists, musicians and architects sought inspiration in the Karelian heartland of old Finland and a spate of new wooden churches and houses were built in a Karelian revivalist style. Tempere Cathedral sprang from this movement and yet Lars Sonck (1870–1956) was also clearly influenced by the Neo-Romanesque designs of the Chicago architect, H. H. Richardson. The same influence can be seen at work in Sonck's Telephone Company building in Helsinki (1905), although he was also clearly influenced by the English Arts and Crafts movement; this shows in his Eira hospital in Helsinki (1905).

At the time of the building of Tempere Cathedral, Sonck was generally considered to be Finland's leading architect. Like many buildings that were influenced by Arts and Crafts thinking, a busy, picturesque exterior conceals a rational plan.

St Leopold's Church

OTTO WAGNER, 1907

STEINHOF, VIENNA, AUSTRIA

STRIPPED, IN THE MIND'S EYE, of its pregnant dome and exquisite and haunting decoration – grave, beautiful angels and laurel wreaths outside; gold-leaf, mosaics and byzantine panels inside – the church of St Leopold could be an early twentieth-century railway station or exhibition pavilion. This might be an odd way of looking at one of the most memorable of modern churches, yet Wagner's design is fundamentally a secular building with just enough symbolic detail to give it a sacred air. The earliest Christian churches were developed from Roman basilicas and this handsome church is, perhaps, an update of this ancient theme. That it should have a secular character is not surprising.

From 1894, Wagner was Vienna's City Planner. He had already been commissioned to redevelop the heart of the Austrian Empire and was soon busy with the design not just of grand civic buildings, but also with that of Vienna's Stadtbahn – by 1901 he had supervised the design of 31 stations as well as bridges and viaducts – and the re-routing of the River Danube. Wagner had started designing in a grand Classical manner, but became increasingly radical in his approach. He joined the Vienna Secession group of artists in 1899. His later buildings are characterized by the clarity of their plan and organization and by the gorgeousness of their decoration. The church at Steinhof is no exception.

Glasgow School of Art

CHARLES RENNIE
MACKINTOSH, 1909
GLASGOW, SCOTLAND

THIS IS A BUILDING IN TWO
PARTS, both by Mackintosh.
The first wing was built between
1897 and 1899. It is the western
extension of 1907–9 that brings
those who love architecture to
Glasgow School of Art. The library
wing soars from a steep hillside
site, its sheer cliff-like walls
interrupted on the west front by
windows rising in three dramatic
tiers. The trio lighting the library
are 8 metres (25 ft) tall. The library
is a glorious space, its galleries
and ceiling supported by a grid of
horizontal beams and rectangular
pillars that, seen from certain
angles, criss-cross in delightfully
complex ways. Glasgow School
of Art is Mackintosh's masterpiece.
It demonstrates how references to
history – there are Scottish castles
and hill-houses in the mix – can be
translated into a modern architecture
that takes on a powerful life of
its own. Mackintosh, an original
talent, did not know how to copy,
nor did he need to.

Palais Stoclet

JOSEF HOFFMANN, 1911

BRUSSELS, BELGIUM

LIKE SOME LAVISH OCEAN LINER berthed far from its home port, Palais Stoclet is a Viennese house built in Brussels. The client was Adolphe Stoclet, a banker, and the architect Josef Hoffmann (1870–1956). This late-flowering Art Nouveau jewel comes as a surprise still, its white marble walls edged with bronze long since turned vivid green, in striking contrast to the subdued palette of Brussels. Owing something to Mackintosh and lavishly decorated throughout by, among other artists, Gustav Klimt, Adolphe Stoclet's palace is almost too exquisite to bear.

Hoffmann studied under Otto Wagner (p.20) in Vienna where he was one of the founders, in 1897, of the Secession group of artists. Six years later he founded the Wiener Werkstätte (Vienna Workshop), for which he designed much furniture. His interests in art, design and architecture were brought together as a kind of *tour de force* in the Palais Stoclet. Because of its informal plan and pristine whiteness, the house has often been described as being "based on Modern theories"; in fact, rather than looking to the future, it marked the end of an era. Although the European bourgeoisie would continue to demand lavish homes in the 1920s and 1930s, the avant-garde turned to a more rigorous and less overtly opulent style. That was the Modern Movement: Palais Stoclet was *fin de siècle* Vienna in prewar Brussels.

Storer House

FRANK LLOYD WRIGHT,
1912, LOS ANGELES,
CALIFORNIA, USA

FRANK LLOYD WRIGHT (1869–1959)
was a prolific and inspired architect
who, perhaps more than anyone else,
introduced the idea of the open-
plan house. Away with conventional
rooms; in with wide open interior
spaces, one linking naturally with the
rest. The result, especially in the
luxurious houses Wright built in
California, are homes that refuse
to age and are considerably more
modern even at the start of the
twenty-first century than anything
offered for sale by conventional
house builders. The Storer House
also employed exposed concrete
construction, although Wright's use
of concrete blocks here is highly
decorative and designed to give the
building an exotic Mexican flavour.
Wright was never slave to one
material or style: he was eclectic
in terms of form, yet his buildings
tended to be inspired by and
closely rooted to their surroundings:
no matter how inventive, they
seem to belong. Wright was one
of the century's most influential
architects and his concerns – to
do with closeness to Nature, the
passage of the sun, openness and a
sense of freedom – are very much
the concerns of many architects as
they enter the twenty-first century
after two decades of wilful
Postmodernism and the wacky
free-form design of the late 1990s.

Eigen Haard Housing

MICHEL DE KLERK, 1921

AMSTERDAM, THE
NETHERLANDS

THIS WONDERFULLY
IDIOSYNCRATIC housing block is
known locally as "*Het Scheep*" (The
Ship) for the shape of its plan, the
prow of which ploughs into the
Zanstraat district of Amsterdam and
the stern of which is marked by a
tall tower or mast. Commissioned
by the Eigen Haard ("Own Stove")
company, Michel de Klerk
(1884–1923) conjured a courtyard
block from an apparently random
collage of brick elements – towers,
turrets, gables – each highly
pronounced and demonstrating
the art of peerless Dutch brickwork.
Although personal in style, the
decoration – which follows the
principle of Pugin, father of the
English Gothic Revival and a major
influence on Arts and Crafts
architects – is never gratuitous,
instead it enlivens the bold
structure of this building.

De Klerk was a leading light of
the Amsterdam School, a group of
Expressionists whose work occupied
an opposite pole to that of the
De Stijl movement, with its belief
in formal geometry and universal
solutions. The "Eigen Haard" housing
was beautifully built and, with its
steep, tiled roofs and projecting
eaves and gables, well proofed
against wind and rain. Eigen Haard
continues to surprise those who
imagine all twentieth-century Dutch
architecture to be austere and
"rational". It is as pragmatic as it
is romantic: a ship worth sailing on.

Stockholm
City Hall

RAGNAR ÖSTBERG, 1923

STOCKHOLM, SWEDEN

A BEAUTIFUL BUILDING on a
beautiful site, Stockholm City Hall
shows how a skilled twentieth-
century architect could raid history
without getting confused on the
way back to the drawing board or
resorting to pastiche or kitsch.
Here, Ragnar Östberg (1866–1945)
has added to the romantic, nautical
skyline of Stockholm, introducing
a new family of copper-capped
towers, spires and cupolas. What
is intriguing here is the seamless
way that Östberg brings together
a diversity of styles – medieval,
Classical and a current National
Romanticism – and makes them
sit seamlessly and happily together.
    The design, which dates from
a competition of 1903–4, was to
prove widely influential not just
in Sweden, but also in Holland,
Britain and the United States.
Östberg's tower and use of brick
can be seen reworked in buildings
as diverse as Art Deco factories and
metro stations. As an essay in how
to learn from history it merits an
"alpha" grade. Perhaps because
so many architects proved to be
unable to reinterpret history
convincingly to serve their own
times, a clean Modern break
seemed, increasingly, to be the
logical option. The plan of
Stockholm City Hall, behind its
highly crafted and thick skin of
brick and stone, is essentially
Classical in form, order and spirit.
Yet, there is no contradiction here:
the design feels seamless.

Karl Marx Hof

KARL EHN, 1930

VIENNA, AUSTRIA

A COURAGEOUS EXAMPLE of socialist housing, Karl Marx Hof is one of the architectural sights of Vienna. Its powerful Expressionist entrance towers are rendered red and suggest the appearance of heroic industrial workers marching, muscular arms linked, through the city centre. This giant estate was designed under the guiding hand of Karl Ehn (1884–1957), the City Architect who, born in Vienna, had trained under Otto Wagner. The Karl Marx Hof was one of a series of large estates designed for the city by Ehn. He was highly influenced by the work of the socialist architects at the London County Council (LCC) who, at the turn of the century, had produced some of the most urbane and humane slum-replacement housing yet seen.

The ideas of the LCC architects were disseminated across Europe. The principal difference between the London and Vienna estates is the sheer sculptural power of the latter. Where the LCC estates were rooted in the ideals and aesthetics of the Arts and Crafts movement, Ehn's blocks, in purely aesthetic terms, owed much to Expressionist ideas. Although some of the flats are rather dim and pokey, they remain a remarkable example of the way in which mass housing can have a formal beauty of its own. Standing in landscaped gardens, the Karl Marx Hof has been remarkably well maintained.

From 1934 onwards Ehn received little work as Austria moved towards unity with Nazi Germany.

Gruntvig Church

PETER VILHELM

JENSEN-KLINT, 1940

COPENHAGEN, DENMARK

DESIGNED IN THE GUISE of a gigantic organ, Gruntvig Church is a phenomenal work, an unlikely brick masterpiece that can be called neither beautiful nor ugly. Instead, the church has a fairy-tale quality and might illustrate the tales of the Brothers Grimm. The vast brick structure stands at the end of a street of Arts and Crafts almshouses in a Copenhagen suburb; here the world is a quiet place, save for music pealing from the church that Peter Vilhelm Jensen-Klint (1853–1930) built.

Jensen-Klint trained as an engineer, before becoming a painter and architect in his mid-forties. Construction of Gruntvig Church began in 1913, and took 27 years and a number of fits and stops to complete. In the design of the church, Jensen-Klint married a number of his enthusiasms, which at that time were brick architecture of northern Europe, German Expressionism and an exploration of the structural possibilities and limits of brick construction. The church pushes brick technology if not to its limits, then somewhere near them. The Expressionist quality of the building lies in its attempt to represent the notion, sound and force of ecclesiastical music in its outward appearance. The result is unique, memorable and ultimately rather daunting. The church was completed by Jensen-Klint's son ten years after his death.

Classical architecture is the cradle of Western culture. Other cultures talk of classical traditions too, yet Classicism is a style or approach to architecture most closely associated with ancient Greece and Rome. The greatest of the Greek temples was the Parthenon, which has never been bettered and which has inspired architects for the last 2,500 years. In the twentieth century it was an inspiration for the most radical Modern Movement architects – notably Le Corbusier – as well as those who sought either to look at Classicism anew (Gunnar Asplund, Charles Holden) or else to reproduce the Classical architecture of previous centuries takes the elements of Classical architecture, and transforms them through factory mass-production methods and concrete into mass suburban housing.

At its very best, the Classical tradition has been explored and reinvented by architects of the calibre of Edwin Lutyens and Gunnar Asplund who have shown how the design language of Greece and Rome has been far from dead. At its worst, Classical architecture has been used as a sop to the conceits of stuffed shirts – mostly newly rich business people – who think that a veneer of Classical details on a brick box is their passport to high society and culture. Or, as in the case of States, the London Passenger Transport Board (p.46) and the city of Stockholm (p.45). Perhaps it was the trappings of Classical architecture that upset so many of those who adopted a moral view of architecture in the twentieth century. Not only did columns and pediments seem irrelevant to life in an industrial society, but the "dishonesty" of Classical façades, which hide the workings of a given building and do little to express its workaday purpose, seemed somehow wrong.

The Nazis certainly gave Classicism a bad name, but so did those who, most embarrassingly in Britain,

Classicism

OBEYING ORDERS

in one form or another (Albert Speer, Ricardo Bofill), but always harking back through the Renaissance and Rome to Greece and the Parthenon.

The Classical architecture of the twentieth century was rich and varied and proved, in the right hands, to adapt well to modern needs. Peter Behren's AEG factory in Berlin (p.34) is a Classical temple as factory; Pennsylvania Station in New York (p.36) was the Baths of Caracalla transformed into a railroad terminus; Les Arcades du Lac in Paris (p.62) by Ricardo Bofill's Taller de Arquitectura

Albert Speer and Nazi Germany, it has been employed as a very obvious symbol of political and social order. In Nazi Germany, architecture obeyed the orders of Classicism as the German *volk* obeyed those of its dictatorial government.

It was often argued by proponents of Modernism and by libertarians of various aesthetic persuasions that Classicism was inherently anti-democratic. This was clearly untrue: Classicism was as much the language of Hitler's Germany and Mussolini's Italy as it was of Roosevelt's United

sought to revive the outward form of Classical architecture in the 1980s as a reaction to the perceived excesses of Modernism. The results were pitiful and made a mockery of the attempts by an earlier generation of architects who had attempted to revive the spirit of Greece and Rome and not simply their most obvious forms. Classicism may have fallen into many of the wrong hands in the course of the twentieth century, yet the Stockholm City Library stands as a testament to what it could be in the right hands.

AEG Turbine Factory

PETER BEHRENS, 1909

BERLIN, GERMANY

PETER BEHRENS (1868–1940) has a special place in the history of twentieth-century architecture and design. Not only did he design the first modern factory – seen here – and train such future talents as Le Corbusier, Walter Gropius and Ludwig Mies van der Rohe, but he was perhaps the first designer to give a major, modern industrial company – AEG, the German General Electric Company – a convincing corporate image.

Behrens began his career as a painter before turning to architecture and industrial design. From 1907 he worked for AEG, turning his hand and eye to the appearance of cookers, radiators, and lamps as well as the company's packaging, catalogues, posters, letterheads, showrooms and shops. In 1909 he completed his first factory for AEG. It was and remains a masterpiece, a temple to modern industrial technology and production. The temple-like appearance of the turbine hall, however, is a cleverly realized and subtly expressed illusion. What looks at first to be rusticated stonework is, in fact, lightweight concrete serving to fill the gaps in the lightweight steel frame behind. The slim joints in the four corner pylons and the fine metal framing of what passes for a Greek tympanum are highlighted in a way that expresses their artificiality. The Turbine Factory was a brilliant attempt to reconcile Classical culture and history with the new reality of industrial commerce and production.

Admiralty Arch

ASTON WEBB, 1909

TRAFALGAR SQUARE,
LONDON, ENGLAND

THE SUN WAS STILL SHINING
over the British Empire when
Aston Webb (1849–1930), the
most successful and prolific
British architect of the time,
was commissioned to reface
Buckingham Palace in a chaste
Classical manner, to re-address
The Mall, the one truly grand

avenue in London, and to design
Admiralty Arch as a gateway to
the processional avenue and
palace. Admiralty Arch is a
handsome enough gateway, yet
engagingly English in the way
that in any other country it
would be a grandiose monument.

Admiralty Arch was originally
crowded with offices for use by
the Royal Navy, which at the time
was the world's most powerful.
In 1997, the Navy offered to
convert these into temporary
accommodation for the many
thousands of young people who
sleep in the streets of a London

stripped of Empire, ambition and
the idea of social welfare. Webb
was the right man for the original
job because he never seemed to
mind artistic compromise: he
simply built what his clients
wanted. And yet, as Admiralty Arch
proves, it is perfectly possible to
add to the experience of walking
through a city while designing
what in formal terms is a flawed
work of art. Much derided in the
past, Admiralty Arch has become a
much liked gateway to a vision of
Britain that is now more real in
tourists' brochures than in the
minds of its people.

Pennsylvania Station

MCKIM, MEADE AND
WHITE, 1910

NEW YORK CITY, USA

FIRST THERE WERE the imperial baths of Ancient Rome. Then there were the railways. And then Paxton's Crystal Palace (London, 1851), Baltard and Hallet's Central Market Hall (Paris, 1866) and Dutert's Hall of Machines (Exposition Universelle, Paris, 1889). Put these together and the result was Pennsylvania Station,

New York, perhaps the most majestic, romantic and thrilling of all railway stations. And, like the famous Euston Arch in London, wilfully demolished. Today a shabby hole-in-the-ground serves as the entrance to the terminus. What McKim, Meade & White built was a palace of iron, steel and glass that matched the ambition and scale of US railroading at its zenith in the first four decades of the twentieth century.

McKim Meade & White was one of the best architectural practices of its time, its work ranging from superb country houses in the

Shingle Style to grand civic monuments like Pennsylvania Station, Columbia University (1902) and the Brooklyn Museum (1915). The skills of the three architects coaslesced perfectly. Charles McKim (1847–1909) was gifted at monumental design; Stanford White (1853–1906) was decorative and painterly in style; William Rutherford Meade (1846–1928) made it all possible. Drawing its formal langauage from the great baths of Caracalla, Pennsylvania Station was a fitting temple to the mighty age of North American steam power.

Government Offices

JOHN BRYDON, 1912

PARLIAMENT SQUARE,

LONDON, ENGLAND

THIS WAS THE LOOK of the British Empire as it went to war in 1914: pompous, stuffy, civil, correct, yet somehow deeply unsure of itself. These grandiloquent, yet handsome, government offices were the work of John Brydon (1840–1901), a Scot who believed that the one true style was the English Baroque of Christopher Wren, John Vanbrugh and Nicholas Hawksmoor. This style, he said in a talk at the Architectural Association, London, in 1889, was "in some respects superior to even the Italian Renaissance".

The revived Baroque style lasted well into the 1920s even though nominally superseded by the Beaux-Arts French Classicism of architects like Reginald Blomfield, who rebuilt John Nash's Regent Street, and the very talented Mewes and Davis, best known for the delicious Palm Court in London's Ritz Hotel. As for Brydon in Parliament Square, his government offices, although neatly composed and thoroughly well built, are more Palladian in spirit than Baroque. The only real evidence of Baroque design is in the decorative detail such as the twin towers, clearly inspired by Wren, that mark the entrance to the central courtyard. The building has none of the grace of Wren, the dark intelligence of Hawksmoor or the theatricality of Vanbrugh. British Classicism had a long way, however, to descend from this decent and gentlemanly effort.

Grand Central Station

WARREN AND WETMORE,
REED & STERN, 1913
NEW YORK CITY, USA

THE FAMOUS CONCOURSE of Grand Central Station is one of the greatest meeting places in the world. Not only is it lofty and ennobling, but it works supremely well. In a celebrated judgement in 1978, the US Supreme Court declared this greatest of all railway stations a historic landmark and thus saved it from the fate of Penn Station (p.36). The station was planned from 1902 after a serious accident in the old station caused by trapped smoke from steam locomotives. In future all trains in and out of Grand Central were to be electric. Because these could run safely underground, the platforms of the new station were dug under the streets and on two superimposed levels. Altogether there were more than 100 platforms.

The engineering work was by Colonel William John Wilgus (1865–1949). The architecture was initially by the Minnesota railroad specialists Reed & Stern, but the Beaux Arts-trained Warren and Wetmore took over in 1911 and transformed the building into a twentieth-century Roman basilica. The spectacular main concourse measures 36.5 metres (120 ft) by 125.5 metres (375 ft) by 38 metres (125 ft) high. Light pours in from decorated lunettes on high and the eyes of passengers not in too much of a rush are drawn up to Paul Hellau's flamboyant ceiling painting depicting the heavens.

Union Buildings

AFTER THE BOER WARS, South Africa was united under British hegemony. A parliamentary building followed, although it was some time before it arrived, in Pretoria. It was the design of Herbert Baker (1868–1942) an English architect who had come to Cape Town in 1903. Baker had been trained in the Arts and Crafts tradition, but once in the Cape he fell in love with Cape Dutch colonial architecture. When Cecil Rhodes appointed him to design the Union Buildings in 1909, he had arrived at a style that fused Cape Dutch, English Arts and Crafts, and the Baroque style of Wren and Hawksmoor.

Baker sited the Union Buildings in a steep hillside above Pretoria, a great garden tumbling down in terraces from the parliamentary complex to the city below. This elegant building comprises two stone-faced blocks capped with Wren-like domed towers, punctuated by courtyards, linked together by a Baroque arcade. Some commentators have found the central arcade a weakness in Baker's design. Yet Baker's elegant reticence speaks of a quietly confident system of government. The fact that South Africa had to wait 80 years for anything like a decent system of government is another story. Baker worked and fell out with Lutyens (p.47) in India before returning to England. Among other things, he designed South Africa House in Trafalgar Square.

King Edward VII Galleries

JOHN BURNETT, 1914

LONDON, ENGLAND

JOHN BURNET (1857–1938) was a Glaswegian who, after a training at the Ecole des Beaux Arts in Paris, designed many civic and commercial buildings in heroic styles – Greek, Egyptian, Chicago – in London over a period of nearly thirty years. If his most advanced was the Chicago-influenced Kodak Building in Kingsway (with Thomas Tait, 1911), his grandest and best known is the extension he designed at the back of Robert Smirke's Neo-Greek British Museum. Burnet's long building is a steel-frame cloaked with a great screen of Ionic columns, separated by two tiers of decidely modern commercial steel-framed windows. This long facade is interrupted just once with a small entrance, leading to a grand stair, guarded by a pair of imperious granite lions. Burnet's elevation, although Grecian, is very different in spirit from Smirke's entrance block, designed in the 1820s. Where Smirke aimed to be archeologically correct, Burnet's essay in modern Greek owes much to his Beaux-Arts training and would be at home in Washington or Paris. As it is, this was the architecture that saw Britain enter the blood and carnage of the Great War.

Burnet's later work includes Adelaide House (1925), the Neo-Egyptian pile flanking the north-east approach to London Bridge and the Classical sweep of Unilever House (1932), overlooking Blackfriars Bridge.

County Court

GUNNAR ASPLUND (1885-1940) was one of the century's greats. At once Modern and as ancient as the temples of Greece, his buildings approached the elusive goal of timelessness more closely, perhaps, than those of any other twentieth-century architect. Without exception, his buildings are based on clear, symmetrical and deeply satisfying plans that have an elemental appeal.

The plan of the County Court in Solvesborg is that of a circle embedded in a rectangle. The circle is the court room, the focus of this romantic building. Asplund's hand is in evidence throughout the courthouse and includes most of the furniture and the handsome long-case clock that still marks the hours in this remarkably humane seat of justice. From the outside this civic building is in the guise of a traditional Swedish farmhouse; inside it is light, warm and logical. Its sense of authority is simple, yet assured.

At the time of its construction, Sweden was still a predominantly rural country with a population of barely five million. The change in scale and ambition of Asplund's later work reflects the suddenness with which Sweden entered the industrial world. His lively and influential Modern design for the Stockholm Exhibition of 1930 was a clear pointer in the direction Swedish design and architecture would follow as the twentieth century progressed.

Midland Bank

EDWIN LUTYENS, 1922
PICCADILLY, LONDON,
ENGLAND

IF ANYONE COULD KEEP alive the
Classical tradition in the twentieth
century in its original dress it was
Lutyens. Just look at this branch of
the Midland Bank next door to
Christopher Wren's church of St
James's, Piccadilly. A refugee from
Hampton Court Palace, perhaps, it
is a delightful, freestanding brick
and dressed-stone garden pavilion
writ large, punctuated by grand
windows, entered by seemingly
overscaled portals and capped with
a handsome pitched roof. The
quality of the brickwork is superb
and the whole building simply
feels good.

Lutyens knew instinctively that
the Classical canon of architecture
existed to be plundered and
reinterpreted as well as respected,
and because he knew this he was
able to show that Classicism was
far from dead in the age of the
burgeoning Modern Movement.
Perhaps because he refused to act

seriously in public – architects tend
to be very serious folk – Lutyens
was all too readily dismissed by
mid-twentieth century historians.
Tackling a dreary plate of fish
while seated next to King George V
at a banquet, Lutyens leant over
and said "This is the piece of Cod
that passeth all understanding".
At the opening of the Viceroy's
House in New Delhi, he was
introduced to a clergyman named
Western. "Any relation to the
Great Western?" asked Lutyens.
Silly jokes, wonderful architect,
even when put to designing a
small city bank.

Lincoln Memorial

HENRY BACON, 1922

WASHINGTON D.C., USA

UNTOUCHED BY THE HORROR and ravages of the First World War, and by the philosophical and design currents nurtured in its wake, the USA was fairly isolated from Modern Movement ideas until what, from a European perspective, seemed like quite late in the day. The predominant styles of architecture right up until the Second World War were various forms of romantic vernacular and Hollywood-induced Art Deco, together with a grand, Beaux-Arts Classical tradition, nurtured in such influential offices as those of McKim, Meade and White.

Henry Bacon (1866–1942) was one of McKim, Meade and White's many successful graduates. While Erich Mendelsohn was at work on the design of the Einstein Tower, Potsdam, Bacon was at work on the grandiose Lincoln Memorial in Washington DC. Although this massive, white Corinthian monument might have seemed outmoded from a radical European perspective, in the States it represented the celebration and continuance of a democratic tradition and an architectural expression of that tradition rooted in the ideals of the Founding Fathers who themselves were steeped in the ways of ancient Greece and Rome. Far from representing the power of the state, the Lincoln Memorial was a celebration of the strength of US liberty and democracy. If nothing else, this helps to show that architecture can never be "read" in a simplistic way: one style can have several meanings.

Selfridges Department Store

DANIEL BURNHAM, 1926

LONDON, ENGLAND

THIS GRAND twentieth-century Roman basilica is one of London's most famous and grandest retail department stores. It was founded by Gordon Selfridge, a US retailer who had worked for Marshall Field, the famous Chicago department store, before he exported the same idea to London under his own name in 1908. Selfridges was revolutionary in several ways: so much so, that the London building regulations that had kept architecture within certain bounds and bonds for decades were changed to allow the store to rise on the site of what had been blocks of Georgian houses along the north side of Oxford Street.

It was one of the first, and certainly the largest, steel-framed building in Britain. It boasted a dramatic open-plan interior, quite unlike anything seen in Britain before. It was as much a palace of pleasure as it was a shop: there were smoking rooms and places to eat and drink. There were no floorwalkers to begin with: shoppers were encouraged to explore the galaxy of goods on display in their own time and under their own steam.

Although radical in plan and purpose, the store's steel frame was dressed in a grandiloquent Roman toga. The giant Classical order and decoration were the work of Francis Swales, although the plan, structure and overall concept were the work of Daniel Burnham (p.328), who designed Marshall Field. A great central tower was never realized.

Stockholm City Library

GUNNAR ASPLUND, 1928

STOCKHOLM, SWEDEN

THIS IS ONE of the great buildings of the twentieth century. It cannot be called timeless, because no building can be, yet it gets close. It combines the essential elements of Classical architecture, Platonic in their archetypal purity – the cylinder, the cube, the square – bringing them together in a grand, sensual, profound manner. So much depends here on the richness of materials used throughout the building. This, and the quality of light that enters the superior drum and falls in studied shafts across desks and down stairs and corridors. The Library has a terrific sense of being hand-crafted and yet the enveloping architecture is severe. Asplund was only 43 when the Library opened and his most brilliant work was yet to come as he worked towards finding a resolution between the aesthetic and functional demands of twentieth-century architecture and the guiding spirit of Classicsm, reaching back 3,000 years.

55
Broadway

CHARLES HOLDEN, 1929
LONDON, ENGLAND

CHARLES HOLDEN (1875-1960)
was a Quaker who twice refused a
knighthood and, although much
underrated, was one of Britain's
finest architects. He began his
career designing in an Arts and
Crafts idiom, but this changed
when he began to work closely
with Frank Pick (1878–1941), the
brilliant chief executive of the
London Underground in the 1920s.
For Pick's new headquarters near
Westminster Abbey, Holden
designed this unusual steel-framed,
stone-clad office. The design is
cruciform, so that every office is
bathed in sunlight. These offices
are raised above the booking hall
and platforms of St James's Park
station and crowned with a
classical tower.

Stepped back from street level,
55 Broadway has a highly distinct
profile, and yet this friendly giant,
occupying an entire city block, is
almost invisible until you get close
to it. Its stone flanks have sculptures,
representing the spirits of the
winds, carved by such well-known
sculptors as Henry Moore, Jacob
Epstein and Eric Gill. These were
deeply controversial at the time as
architects debated whether
buildings should be vehicles for Art
and, equally, whether they should
be considered artworks in their
unadorned state. Holden went on
to design a sequence of superb
stations for London Underground
and the Senate House tower for
London University.

Viceroy's House

EDWIN LUTYENS, 1931

NEW DELHI, INDIA

BEFORE INDIA gained its independence in 1947, British architectural styles were imposed on the country. Until the 1870s, the style of British Indian buildings reflected fads and fashions in Britain itself. During the Victorian "Battle of the Styles", Bombay became home to Gothic and Calcutta to the Classical. There was a move from the 1870s to mix indigenous styles with those of Britain, leading to a picturesque "Indo-Saracenic" style for official buildings. Although it was quaint, few architects were able to fuse the disparate Indian and European styles. The most successful attempt came late in the day as the sun was setting over the British Empire. It came in the form of Lutyen's imperious and utterly convincing Viceroy's House (now the Rashtrapati Bhavan), the jewel in the crown that is New Delhi. Even Le Corbusier was impressed.

The success of this great domed palace, built in beautiful red, ochre and sandy stone lies in its successful marriage between English Classicism – Lutyens's "Wrenaisance" Baroque under dazzling light – and Indian detailing. It also lies in its almost impossibly grand setting at the end of one of the heroic tree-lined avenues Lutyens and his rival Sir Herbert Baker (p.39) laid out in their creation of New Delhi between 1912 and 1931.

The marble-lined corridors of the Viceroy's residence are wonderfully cool in the Delhi heat, there is at least one room with cornices but no ceiling (to let the heat out and the stars in) and a garden that oozes oriental fantasy. The building has always been faultlessly maintained.

Arnos Grove Tube Station

CHARLES HOLDEN, 1932

LONDON, ENGLAND

THIS EXQUISITE BUILDING brings together the needs of a modern railway station, the Classical architecture of ancient Rome, the modern architecture of Holland and northern Germany, gentlemanly English restraint and bricky British craftsmanship. A heavily corniced brick and glass drum atop a symmetrical glass and brick base, it is a delight to look at and to use. Most of all it is a credit to the vision of Frank Pick (1878–1941), the chief executive of the London Passenger Transport Board, who wanted London to have the world's finest integrated urban public transport system; because of his efforts, for many years it did. Pick teamed up with Holden in 1923. Holden had recently designed some memorable war memorials for the Imperial War Graves Commission (he had served as a Lieutenant in the Royal Engineers during the First World War) and something of their design rubbed off in the first sequence of stations Holden designed from 1925 for London Underground's Northern Line. Arnos Grove was the finest of the stations built for the Piccadilly Line in the early 1930s. Before its design, Pick and Holden made a tour of the latest Dutch and German architecture; they were particularly impressed by the work of Dudok (p.163) and his influence was clearly at work on Holden, though Arnos Grove station also echoes the design of Asplund's Stockholm City Library (p.45).

Sabaudia
New Town

LUIGI PICCINATO,

GINO CANCELOTTI,

EUGENIO MARTUORI,

ALFREDO SCALPELLI, 1933

ITALY

NEARLY SEVENTY YEARS on from its foundation, the Fascist new town of Sabaudia retains its powerful and, given the Roman climate, rather chilling aspect. Designed as an exercise in Rational architecture and urban planning, it was like a De Chirico painting come to life. And yet it is a compelling place, a small town on the Pontine marshes that has a scale and dignity very different from the New Town experience in, for example, Britain, where suburban values tended to hold sway.

Sabaudia was one of four new towns commissioned by Mussolini's government on the infamous, mosquito-infested Pontine marshes. By draining the marshes, Mussolini eradicated malaria. The design of the town was a conscious reaction to the "vernacular" style adopted elsewhere in the Roman new towns. Piccinato (1899-1983) and his colleagues had shown what they intended to do here and elsewhere at the First Exhibition of Rational Architecture held in Rome in 1928. Clear lines, no decoration, a monumental sensibility. The architecture, especially the church at the centre of Sabaudia, is funereal and silent, yet to watch crisp shadows fall across its severe facade and to see the shadow of its tower etched into the piazza below is to be aware of architecture of a high and disciplined order.

The town was planned on an offset grid, its formal rigour softened by the park that opens up to the Lago di Paola at the southern end of its central axis. It was an important achievement and was to inform the work of a later generation of Italian Rationalists centred around Aldo Rossi (p.304).

Olympic Stadium

WERNER MARCH, 1936

BERLIN, GERMANY

THE STIRRING BACKDROP for Leni Riefenstahl's powerful *Olympiad* documentaries, this imposing stadium is a building that reminds us how effective architecture can be as a symbol of political willpower. Architecture has been used as a political tool most effectively by Adolf Hitler's regime. When the Führer saw the first design for the 120,000 seat Olympic Stadium, he was critical of March's (1894-1976) use of exposed steel. March wanted to create a Modern monument: Hitler wanted to recreate the glories of ancient Rome. The upshot was that Hitler's favourite architect, Albert Speer (p.53) intervened. Speer had the structure clad in heroic masonry – granite and limestone – and ringed around with a grand colonnade. The entrance is breath-taking, for although the stadium seems quite big enough from the outside, its perceived height gives no inkling of what is to come. The running track and playing field are set low down, well below the line of the structure as seen from the seemingly interminable avenue that leads visitors here.

Scale aside, this is a remarkably civilized sports building: a ring of restaurants, restrooms and changing rooms is broken only to offer visionary views of the sports fields behind it. The stadium is still very much in use and will no doubt last a thousand years, unlike Hitler's regime which missed this target by 988 years.

Hotel Moskva

ALEXEI SHCHUSEV ET AL,
1936, MOSCOW, RUSSIA

THE OLD JOKE about this monumental hotel is that when Alexei Shchusev (1873–1949) presented Stalin with the plans, he showed him two designs on the same sheet of paper. Stalin nodded, signed the document and that was that: the hotel had to be two designs in one. No one was going to argue with Comrade Stalin's signature. In fact, the Hotel Moskva, one of the first undiluted "Stalinist" designs, looks as if it might contain many more than two buildings. What really happened, and why the building is such a Borzoi's breakfast, is that Shchusev, a distinguished architect who proved able to design in any number of styles, was brought in to tart up a very Modern design by the young architects Savalev and Stapran who appeared to be unaware of the fact that revolutionary Constructivist buildings were no longer acceptable in the Soviet Union.

Shchusev smothered the 17-storey design in lashings of granite, marble, bronze and monumental details. It looked hideous, but fitted the bill and was to be the benchmark for the often pretentious buildings of the Stalin era. The courtyard building is elephantine and was not finally completed until the 1970s when, after a brief "liberal" fling under Nikita Khruschev, the USSR was eeking out its dotage under the ponderous rule of Leonid Brezhnev. The rooms were handsomely appointed and the showy top-floor restaurant was, for many years, the best the comrades had to offer.

Metro Mayakovskaya

ALEKSEI DUSHKIN, 1938

MOSCOW, RUSSIA

THE MOSCOW METRO opened in 1935 and from then on its tentacles spread inexorably across the Russian capital. By 2000, there were ten lines with nearly 150 stations.

The older stations are really extraordinary, lavishly decked out in the richest materials in the guise of palatial Baroque grottoes or underground cathedrals. There were essentially two types: the blisteringly Baroque and the balletic. Metro Mayakovskaya falls into the second category and is one of the most convincing of the early stations. It was designed by Aleksei Dushkin (1904–77), a talented designer and party favourite who won the coveted Stalin Prize three times and managed never to fall out of official favour. The underground concourse of the station is covered with 36 oval cupolas lit by bronze torches and decorated with Soviet stars and hammers and sickles. The cupolas are supported by an impressively turned-out regiment of arches of light and dark marble inset with stainless steel reveals. The platforms are vaulted and lit with Neo-classical lamps. A model of the station was exhibited at the 1938 New York World Fair and won the Grand Prix. Its finest hour came, however, in November 1941 when the German "panzers" of General Guderian were at the gates of Moscow and the city had been partially evacuated. In this glittering concourse deep under the city, Stalin addressed the entire Politburo and effectively began the fight back for Moscow.

Grosse Halle

ALBERT SPEER, 1938

BERLIN, GERMANY

HAD IT BEEN BUILT, the Grosse Halle would have been nearly 300 metres (1,000 ft) tall, seated 180,000 of the Nazi party faithful, and would have been so voluminous that, packed to the gunwhales with a capacity audience, clouds would have formed inside and rain may even have fallen: a suitably Wagnerian environment for the rantings of the Fuhrer. The Grosse Halle was intended to have stood on the site of the Reichstag, which was badly damaged by fire in 1933 and rebuilt by Sir Norman Foster (p.278). It marked the top end of the proposed north–south processional avenue that, lined with Nazi palaces, offices, hotels and cinemas, would have led to a new south Berlin railway terminus and to Tempelhof airport, one of the few surviving buildings of the Nazi era, built by Ernst Sagebiel, 1941.

The architect of the Dome was Hitler's pet Albert Speer (1905–81), who based the design on Hitler's sketches: it was essentially the Pantheon in Rome revisited, but five times taller and with a volume sixteen times greater. Speer rose via the design of Nuremberg Stadium (1937) to become Generalbauinspektor (head of architectural works) of the new Berlin. This was to be called Germania and the intention was to build it in 1948 after German victory. During the war, Speer rose again to become Minister for Mobilization and War Production. Tried at Nuremberg in 1946, he was imprisoned for 25 years. His memoirs were to become world-famous. He died in a hotel bedroom with his mistress in London while filming with the BBC.

Reich Chancellory

ALBERT SPEER, 1939

BERLIN, GERMANY

THE REICH CHANCELLORY was built in a great hurry between 1938 and 1939, using labour and building materials from across Germany. The idea was that this Neoclassical palace, based essentially on the designs of the great nineteenth-century Prussian architect Karl Friedrick Schinkel, represented the spirit and substance of the new Germany under Hitler. Speer's organizational abilities were phenomenal: using a combination of new and tried and tested techniques and materials, the Chancellory was ready for the Führer to move into just before he invaded Poland in September 1939. Hitler's vast study was reached along an attentuated hall of mirrors that had been adapted by Speer from Versailles. The infamous bunker in which Hitler sat out the last four months of the Second World War were below Speer's palace.

At the end of the century, the ruins of the Führerbunker were all that was left of a building that once occupied an entire city block. The building was bombed heavily and demolished by Allied troops after the fall of Berlin in May 1945. As an example of a kind of hi-tech Classicism it had been a fascinating exercise. As a symbol of a cold-hearted regime that was planned to last 1,000 years and, in the event, missed its target by 988 years, it was a fitting monument to the folly of political ambition.

Supreme Court

F. BARRINGTON WARD,

1939, SINGAPORE

THIS WAS ONE OF THE last flings of an Imperial style and owed its inspiration to the work of Sir Edwin Lutyens and Sir Herbert Baker in India and South Africa, who, in turn, owed a well-acknowledged debt to the English Baroque of Sir Christopher Wren (1632–1723). Many buildings for the judiciary were built in this style, notably the Old Bailey in London (Edward Mountford, 1906). Singapore's Supreme Court owes a clear debt to Mountford's precedent. British architects took this "Wrenaissance" style, as Lutyens dubbed it, to all four corners of the British Empire.

By the time Lutyens completed his imperial masterpiece –the Viceroy's House, New Delhi, India (p.47) – the sun was already setting on the world's most expansive empire. And by the time Barrington Ward completed the Supreme Court, the empire was about to be overrun – the Japanese seized Singapore in 1940. The building survived the occupation and is still very much in use: it was clearly built to last for hundreds of years. Although it seems curious to see such overtly British buildings fanned by swaying palm trees and sweating under tropical skies, the substantial structure of the Supreme Court means that the interiors are cool, while vast corridors and lofty chambers allow air to circulate without the tyranny of air-conditioning. The Supreme Court has its place in Singapore.

Forest Crematorium

GUNNAR ASPLUND, 1940
STOCKHOLM, SWEDEN

A WORK OF GENIUS. Standing mournfully, yet beautifully, on a gently sloping wooded hillside, Gunnar Asplund's crematorium is an ancient Greek acropolis for the dead seen through the eyes of a twentieth-century Classicist turned Modernist. The hillside complex at Emskede comprises three chapels, a columbarium (the vault containing funerary urns) and the crematorium itself. The generous entrance is designed for mourners to gather in all weathers. The gas lamps attached to the silent columns holding up the umbrella roof here are dimmed as urns are committed to the vault.

This is a place of great beauty and symbolism that ultimately transcends place and architecture. It is marked by a vast and simple wooden cross and has an elemental simplicity and a power to move that belongs to the very greatest buildings from the pyramids of ancient Egypt onwards. It was also Asplund's swan song. The Swedish architect's genius was to have found a way of bringing the architectural spirit of classical ages into the mid-twentieth century, to demonstrate that there was a way of being Modern that did not deny the past, that architecture was a continuum rather than a *stacatto salvo* of bombastic and radical styles and forms. While the rest of Europe was preparing for war, Asplund had the opportunity to design this *memento mori* that symbolizes eternal rest. He did not fail.

National Gallery of Art

JOHN RUSSELL POPE, 1940

WASHINGTON D.C., USA

ONE WAY OR ANOTHER, the Classical tradition survived into the twentieth century, notably so in the United States. Perhaps this is because Classicism – a certain pure white Classicism – was associated with the democratic values of the ancient Greeks and with the architectural style in vogue immediately after the American War of Independence. Unlike in Germany, Italy or the Soviet Union, Classicism in America has not been linked or confused with authoritarian or fascist dogma and social straight-jacketing. John Russell Pope's (1874-1937) National Gallery of Art is a chaste exercise in Palladian design, yet although far more correct in a scholarly sense than Troost's near-contemporary Munich Art Gallery, it is equally cold, a building to respect grudgingly rather than to admire and certainly not to love.

The inspirations behind the building, from Thomas Jefferson to Karl Friedrick Schinkel, are clear enough, yet the museum took Classicism nowhere new. To outsiders it seems odd that such a gung-ho society as the United States should have aimed to embody its cultural values in such cold-hearted and stiff-shouldered architectural gestures; yet a part of the story of the taming of America is the quest for old-fashioned culture and respectability. Pope's National Gallery remains a very respectable, if lifeless, monument to the United States' cultural ambitions at a time when the country's emigré nuclear scientists were at work developing the atomic bomb.

Lenin Library

VLADIMIR SHCHUKO
AND VLADIMIR GEL'FREIKH,
1941, MOSCOW, RUSSIA

THE BIBLIOTEKA LENINA was built
as a result of a competition for its
design held in 1928–29. It was
completed as the Germany army
moved within sight of the walls
of Moscow in 1941. The library is
a stripped Classical design around
two courtyards and entered through
a dramatic and even aggressive
colonnade: the columns are tall,
square, largely bereft of decoration.
This severity gives way to lavish
lobbies, staircases and reading
rooms (18 of them) designed for
2,300 readers who have access
to more than 36 million volumes
stacked away in this early Stalinist
shrine. The vast building also
contains exhibition halls, lecture
rooms, concert halls, offices, and
an entrance to the Moscow Metro.

At once stark and lavishly
equipped and fitted, the Lenin
Library symbolizes the ambitions
of Stalin's mighty Soviet Union, a
state which, far from withering
into a Communist utopia, was a
massively controlling and often
frightening construct designed
to keep the people firmly in their
place; part of the weight that held
them down was the sheer scale of
official architecture. In Stalinism's
early days, as in the Lenin Library,
the style was heavy-handed yet
crisp; in the years following the
Soviet Union's triumph in the Great
Patriotic War (1941–45), it became
heavy-handed and flamboyant.

Palace of Italian Civilization

GUERRINI, LAPADULA
AND ROMANO, 1942

ROME, ITALY

THE PALACE OF ITALIAN
Civilization was designed as the
architectural showpiece of the
Expositione Universale Roma (EUR),
which was to have opened in 1942.
World War Two intervened and the
exhibition never happened. Instead,
the EUR site became a new focal
point for office, sport and leisure
buildings after the war; thus the

fascist architecture built for the
exhibition was not wasted. The
Palace is a powerful monument,
chaste, formal and a little
frightening. It is a simple building
walled around with glistening
travertine, each floor effectively
arcaded and its interiors
mysteriously hidden from view.
It seems an empty building, a
vacuous momument to a
fundamentally flawed regime. It
is also impressive and memorable:
its simplicity, almost banal, is
its formal strength.

The idea appears to have been
to create an office building from
the design of the Colosseum. The

effect of power and monumentality
is emphasized by the building's
prominent position and by the
muscular sculpture that surrounds
it. The palace is one of a number
of austere and apparently lifeless
buildings at EUR. A Pantheon-
inspired church and the Museum
of Italian Civilization march
alongside the palace, yet they too
seem dead from the pavement up:
acres of marble and big, bold
proportions can only do so much
to create enduring and endearing
architecture. To make Classical
buildings appear cold in the
sensuous warmth of the Roman
sun was quite some achievement.

Lomonosov State University

LEV RUDNEV ET AL, 1953

MOSCOW, RUSSIA

STALIN DIED AS this astonishing building neared completion. It had his enthusiastic endorsement and is widely cited as the symbol of the Communist dictator's unprecedented reign of civil terror. Even so, no one can be unimpressed by this towering wedding cake of Soviet brick and steel. Megalomaniacal it might be: it is also magnificent. Standing on a hilltop 70 metres (230 ft) above the River Moskva, the University dominates many views of the Russian capital. The main building is approached along a great avenue through a stupendous landscaped garden. The 26-storey central tower is topped with an exotic spire that cradles, at its peak, the Red Star symbol of the former Soviet Union. It contains a galaxy of offices, auditoria, club rooms, cafeterias, lecture rooms, offices and laboratories. Virtually every room is kitted out in lavish marbles and mosaics; the standard of finish is impeccable.

The tower is flanked by 18-storey wings (accommodation for students) and the wings by 12-storey blocks (flats for teaching staff). The whole complex is lavishly decorated and peppered with elaborate towers. Behind the main building are two gigantic low-rise blocks; these are the faculties of chemistry and physics. The design of this academic empire was led by Lev Rudnev (1885–1956) who, before the Great Patriotic War of 1941–45, had designed the equally daunting Frunze Military Academy, Moscow (1937) to symbolize the might of the Red Army.

Great Hall of the People

ZHAO DONG-RI AND
ZHANG BO, 1959
BEIJING, CHINA

THE CHINESE REVOLUTION
abounded in contradictions. Was it
for the people or against them?
Were Mao Zedong's "Great Leap
Forward" of the 1950s and Cultural
Revolution of the 1960s well
meaning, if disastrous attempts, to
make life better or to keep a billion,
hard-working people under savage
control, whether by starvation or
brutal "justice"? It is hard to say.
What we know is that architects
were certainly confused. Should they
represent the new Peoples' Republic
in the guise of a revolutionary style
adopted, perhaps, from Soviet or
European inspiration; should they
rework traditional Chinese motifs,
or should they invent a wholly new
way forward? They did none of these.
Instead, mass housing was built
along the grimmest and most
brutally functional lines, while
government buildings tended to
be big, characterless boxes topped
with token Chinese roofs and a
nod, here and there, to the ancient
principles of *feng-shui* –although
this was meant to be anathema in
Communist China, a land in which
all religion and superstition were
officially banned.

The Great Hall of the People is
an example of the overscaled and
dreary architecture of Communist
China built during the disastrous
years of the "Great Leap Forward",
when the economy took a great
leap back and millions starved to
death. This decidely reactionary
building was designed, among
other state purposes, for multi-
coursed official banquets.

Les Arcades du Lac

TALLER DE ARQUITECTURA,
1981

ST QUENTIN-EN-YVELINES,
PARIS, FRANCE

THE IDEA SEEMED to be a good one. Build Versailles for the people. Call in Ricardo Bofill's Taller de Arquitectura and have them run up blocks of flats around a lake in Neoclassical style. Very impressive. Have to make do with prefabricated, pre-dyed panels though. The result is grim indeed.

At the beginning of the 1980s, the Taller de Arquitectura was a *cause célébre* throughout Europe. No one could quite believe what they had been commissioned to do: design and build huge sections of the new Paris suburbs in a grandiose Classical idiom. The drawings looked fascinating on the drawing boards in sunny Barcelona, Spain, but the actual buildings were overpoweringly dreary. Many of the flats that were shoehorned into these highly stylized concrete containers were dark and cramped. Behind the facades, Classical proportion and harmony went by the board. Worse still, the policy of Jacques Chirac, then Mayor of Paris, to decant the poor and wretched into the biggest suburban developments – well away from the chic bourgeois glory of central Paris – ensured that what was meant to be a Renaissance heaven soon became a punky hell. If proof was ever needed that style alone does not make for attractive or desirable architecture, then this was it.

Marne-la-Vallée

TALLER DE ARQUITECTURA, 1982, PARIS, FRANCE

IN THIS DEVELOPMENT of the pre-fabricated concrete classicism of St Quentin-en-Yvelines, the Taller de Arquitectura's idea of a Versailles for the people was taken to an even further extreme. Given the formless nature of the new Parisian suburbs – most are truly hideous and make one almost long for the Mock-Tudor and Neo-Georgian delights of Kingsbury or East Cheam – Bofill's idea of creating a powerful architecture and a sense of place made a certain sense. The problem, though, was largely one of scale. Proportion and light too. And this was just the beginning. The vast central block was kitted out with dreary flats and some of these featured slit-like kitchen windows facing out into Piranesian service routes coursing the depths of the weighty concrete pile above. Not much fun. It seemed as if the architect's efforts had gone into the layout of the development and its chunky facades, and not into individual flats.

In later schemes, notably in Montpelier in the Côte d'Azur, Bofill's classical extravaganzas became notably lighter in spirit and more humane. Classical proportions and a certain amount of detailing were even brought indoors. Perhaps the tragedy of this grandiose approach to suburban housing is that so many of us secretly hoped that it might really work.

National Museum of Roman Art

RAFAEL MONEO, 1984

MERIDA, SPAIN

A FIERCELY DISTINGUISHED building, this one of the best of the wave of new museums that washed over European cities in the 1980s. Here in Merida, Moneo (born 1937) has created a fitting home for a display of Roman art and archaeology, evoking the spirit of Roman architecture without recourse to imitation or pastiche. At first, the museum looks rather like a grand railway terminus of the 1930s, or, from other angles, a particularly impressive factory or power station. Close up, its intention is clear: the entrance pavilion draws visitors in through a muscular brick arch with the legend MUSEO carved in the style of Trajan's Column in a slab of veined white marble. From this pavilion, the visitor is guided across a courtyard and so into the unmitigated splendour of the museum proper. A magnificent brick nave, based on the idea of what a Roman basilica might have felt like inside, runs the length of this cool, calm and collected space. The arches, all built in Roman brick, act as natural divisions between displays, so that the structure of the building does the job that screens do in other museums: Moneo has provided a sense of permanence appropriate to this museum's impressive collection. Beneath the arches is a crypt which houses a major archaeological site. Back upstairs, the brilliance of the design becomes apparent as one realizes that, instead of just the one commanding axis set by the basilica-like nave, there are many axes, criss-crossing the building at an angle, and set askew to the simple rectangular geometry of the building.

Richmond Riverside

QUINLAN TERRY, 1988
RICHMOND-UPON-THAMES,
SURREY, ENGLAND

AS REACTIONARY as it could be revolutionary, the British architecture profession made a number of curious and fanciful diversions in the 1980s that seemed potty at the time, quaint within five years and all but forgotten within a decade. Quinlan Terry (born 1937), the son of very

Modern parents, worked for James Stirling (p305), before setting up a country practice in Dedham, Essex with a God-given mission, or so he himself believed, to convert Britain at least to the strictures of Classicism. A number of villas that resembled dolls' houses was the result and then Richmond Riverside, an annoying confection of pseudo-Georgian offices and shops built alongside the River Thames some 20 km (12 miles) south-west of central London. Annoying, because despite Terry's protestations, Richmond Riverside was a fake in the worst sense. It

might have looked Georgian, but some of the buildings were no more than open-plan offices dressed in wannabe Georgian frock-coats and featured suspended ceilings rather than handsome wooden panelling. Chimneys proved to be air-extractors and, detail by detail, the whole picturesque affair began to stick in one's craw.

For a short while Terry and fellow Classical revivalists enjoyed a brief spell of fame and fortune as the Prince of Wales and his fawning acolytes championed their cause. It soon fizzled out.

Terry's Assorted Villas

QUINLAN TERRY, 1988

LONDON, ENGLAND

WHEN JOHN NASH and his pupils built their wonderful, picturesque villas and terraces around London's new Regent's Park in the 1820s and 1830s, they built rapidly, as if constructing in pen and ink, with cheap brick covered in weatherproof white stucco. The buildings were realized on a heroic scale and the details painted with a broad brush. They were, and thankfully remain, magnificent, urban stage scenery at its very best. Terry's assorted villas – this little one is Gothick, this little one is Venetian – built in the late 1980s alongside the Regent's Canal are quite the opposite. Each is detached, prissy and almost overwhelmed with coy period detail. They seem quite out of character with the park and with the work of Nash. Why? Because they are too self-conscious. They are nervy where Nash was confident, fussy where Terry's predecessor was supremely relaxed. Doubtless, Terry's villas are better made than Nash's: certainly, if you ever peep into one of the basements here, you will be amazed by how much "hi-tech" heating and cooling equipment a pseudo-Georgian house can have when compared to its clean-cut contemporaries.

The problem with such "period" architecture is always much the same; the real talent of any given period is always as the leading edge of design, as Nash was in his day. The best look back to learn, but not to copy.

Paternoster Square

JOHN SIMPSON,

THOMAS BEEBY, ET AL, 1990

LONDON, ENGLAND

THIS PROPOSAL CAME at a very peculiar moment in British architectural history – the peak of the Prince of Wales's influence which was also, by definition, a key moment for the would-be revival of Classical architecture. That it failed was perhaps inevitable. The proposal was for a new range of offices and shops, on a vast scale, flanking the north side of St Paul's Cathedral. These were to have replaced an existing group of dreary Portland-stone clad office blocks erected in the late 1950s and early 1960s on the site of what had once been Paternoster Row, a famous street of booksellers and printers, destroyed by the Luftwaffe during the Blitz. To mitigate their bulk and to please Prince Charles, a would-be pantheon of Classical revivalist architects was brought in to dress the mighty air-conditioned offices and basement-level shops proposed here in antique fancy dress. Critical studies quickly proved that the proposed buildings would be a threat to the integrity of St Paul's Cathedral. The scheme was scaled down and then all but abandoned in the mid-1990s. A new scheme was masterminded by the veteran architect William Whitfield and was eventually announced in 1998. The idea seemed to be to keep the new scheme as quiet as possible in the hope that no one would notice how dull it was. Poor St Paul's.

Poundbury Village

LEON KRIER, ET AL, 1996

DORCHESTER, DORSET,
ENGLAND

ONLY IN BRITAIN could such a thing happen. For some years an excited coterie of tweedy architects sporting bird's nest haircuts and ancient polished brogues sat at the dainty feet of the Prince of Wales discussing a grand new extension of Dorchester, the old county town of Dorset in south-west England. The discussions were dominated by the fiery Leon Krier (born 1946), a lucid theorist who had worked in the 1970s on a number of unbuilt, classically-inspired building and urban design projects with James Stirling. Poundbury – for that was it's name – was intended to be the forerunner of an entirely new way of living, a kind of idyllic "urbs-in-rure" in which houses and shops newly built to look old-fashioned would doff their cornices to renaissance style piazzas. There would be no crime, no nods to fashion and no working-class types. Krier drew up handsome and ambitious plans. The architectural profession bridled. But the Poundbury bubble burst. The reality of planning bye-laws and regulations helped to scupper the plan, so did a general lack of interest.

In the end a few deferential architects turned out some cottages and Dorchester fell asleep again. Clough Williams-Ellis and Francois Spoerry (p.285) had done much better with their holiday villages in Wales and France (Portmeirion and Port Grimaud) years before.

Disney's Celebration

ROBERT STERN,

PHILIP JOHNSON, ET AL,

CELEBRATION, FLORIDA, 1996

CELEBRATION IS "the wonderful world of Disney" made real for all-American families to live, work and play in. By 2010, this squeaky clean, secure, back-to-the-future township will be home to 20,000 people who have chosen to get away from modern city life to settle into the arms of Mickey and Minnie Mouse and in the company of decent, law-abiding, like-minded folk. The white clapboard houses (available in Classical, Victorian, Colonial Revival, Coastal, Mediterranean and French styles) may evoke the spirit of *The Waltons* crossed with *Gone With The Wind*, yet the roots of this urban dreamscape lie as much in the development of the English garden suburb as they do with the handsome US towns of Savannah and Boston. Celebration is built on 4,900 acres of reclaimed swamp land, south of Orlando, Florida. Disney commissioned architects of the undoubted calibre of Robert Stern (born 1939) and Philip Johnson (born 1906) to advise on the project and design its principal buildings.

Although the idea of a Disney town, with a Disney school, Disney maternity hospital and Disney bus to get around may all sound a little too cloying and controlling (curtains and blinds must be white, lawns regularly clipped, no repairing cars on the streets), it is not a "gated" town but a real if highly ordered one. By the mid-1990s, more than four million urban Americans had retreated to "gated" communities, guarded by high walls, razor wire and surveillance cameras and guards. Celebration is a colourful, cartoon-like riposte to this sorry phenomenon, born of collective American paranoia.

At the end of the twentieth century, the word "organic" was being bandied about with incontinent imprecision. Organic vegetables, organic bread, organic toothpaste ... the word was being used as a kind of talisman to ward off the evils of consumer societies in which

growing naturally out of the ground rather than being projected unnaturally into the sky. Gaudí created a form of architecture made up of what appear to be bones and sinews, or tendrils and shoots. Architects like Bruce Goff (p.96) and Herb Greene (p.105) shaped a shaggy

What all the buildings in this section have in common is the sense of being close to nature, either in terms of location or of materials used in their construction. This is why you will find such strange bedfellows as Tadao Ando, Antoni Gaudí and Hugo Häring here. Each of the buildings is highly individualistic, wilful even. obeys conventional rules and is not held back by precedent or convention. They are all in their own way highly emotional buildings, but unlike the architectural expression of Postmodernism, none is cynical, clever-clever or too knowing. Quite the reverse: most have an innocence about them, each an attempt to take architecture into unknown waters.

Organic

"THE STRAIGHT LINE BELONGS TO MAN, THE CURVE TO GOD." (GAUDÍ)

so many things, from what people ate to the homes they lived in, had become mass-produced, unsettling and even unhealthy. Organic architecture is an equally loose term, yet it conveys at least an idea of buildings designed to grow naturally from the ground they stand on. It conjures, too, the idea of buildings that are made of natural materials, that seem somehow to belong in a way that Classical temples or white Modern Movement machines-for-living never do. It also gets over the idea of buildings that make a play on natural forms and employ geometries that have little to do with Euclid and mathematical perfection. And it suggests buildings that are designed to be wide open to the elements.

In extreme cases, as with the work of Antoni Gaudí (pp.75, 80, 81), buildings really do seem to be plants or animals

architecture that might be home for animals and insects as well as human beings. Frank Lloyd Wright, one of the century's most influential architects, left a legacy of Organic buildings that fit into the depths of rural America as they do into the grid-iron of Manhattan (p.102). Imre Makovecz, who founded an entire school of Organic architects and craftworkers in Hungary in the last quarter of the century described his designs as "building beings", and indeed at their strange and haunting best, such as the Mortuary Chapel in Budapest (p.112) or the Catholic church at Paks (p.119), they really do feel as if they are alive and breathing.

There was always, however, a tightrope to be walked in this tradition between inspiration and kitsch and some of the buildings shown here, although intriguing, were always in danger of falling from artistic grace.

This is not to say they lack power or gumption. You can see the energy expressed in the design of the Chilehaus in Hamburg (p.85) and feel the muscle of Stuttgart Station (p.87). As for Arthur Shoosmith's garrison church in New Delhi (p.89) well there is all the might and mystic power of a Mayan temple or Babylonian ziggurat.

Veering between the eccentric and the proudly magnificent, this loose fraternity of buildings includes some of the century's most likeable and most curious. By the end of the twentieth century, with increasing concern for ecological issues and the natural world, it was clear that Organic architecture, in one or other of its many forms, would blossom rather than wilt in the twenty-first.

Westminster Cathedral

JOHN FRANCIS BENTLEY,
1903, LONDON, ENGLAND

THIS MAGNIFICENT BUILDING
with its sky-piercing campanile
and solemn, cavernous interior was
utterly untypical of the work of
John Francis Bentley (1839–1902).
Born in Doncaster, Bentley trained
as a mechanical engineer before
working for a firm of builders,
converting to Catholicism and
launching a successful career as a
church architect designing in a robust
Gothic style. The unexpected move
at Westminster into a Byzantine
style came about when Bentley's
client, Cardinal Vaughan, decided
that it was closer in spirit to the
founding fathers of the Catholic
Church than either Gothic or Classical
style. The cathedral is decidedly
modern; a vast structure infused
with the light of religion. Inside, the
great arched space is capped with
four immense concrete saucer domes.

Until the late 1970s, the
cathedral was hidden at street
level by the grim buildings of
Victoria Street: a piazza has since
been created that allows Bentley's
masterpiece to take pride of place
along this dreary thoroughfare.

Casa Batlló

ANTONI GAUDÍ, 1907

BARCELONA, SPAIN

LIKE SOME MYTHICAL BEAST – a dragon, perhaps, from a medieval fresco – the Casa Batlló still has the power to shock and surprise. Designed for the textile manufacturer Josep Batlló i Casanova, this fantastic apartment block animates the imposing avenue, Paseo de Gracia, that forms the spine of central Barcelona. The waywardness of the exterior – prognathous lower floors in the guise of a gaping jaw, a roof like an armadillo's back and a coating of colourful broken tiles – is carried through into the individual apartments. To stay here is like being Jonah inside the belly of the whale, although the bellies of few whales feature such beautifully finished furniture and fittings. The architect, Antoni Gaudí i Cornet (1852–1926), was one of the most extraordinary architects ever. A devout Catholic, he lived the life of an aesthetic and ascetic monk and was taken for a tramp when admitted to hospital after being knocked down and fatally hurt by a tram while pondering on the construction of his unfinished masterwork, the Expiatory Temple of the Holy Family. In his youth Gaudí was influenced by the "Renaixença", a cultural and political movement that sought to restore Catalonian pride and independence from Spain through the rediscovery of local language and history. Gaudí gave Barcelona an architecture very much its own.

Robie House

FRANK LLOYD WRIGHT, 1910

CHICAGO, ILLINOIS, USA

THE ROBIE HOUSE introduces us to a revolution in domestic design instigated by one of the century's greatest and most controversial talents, Frank Lloyd Wright. Wright's bombast and egomania was cleverly captured in *The Fountainhead* (both the rip-roaring novel by Ayn Rand and the Hollywood movie starring Gary Cooper as the misunderstood architect hero). Although sited in Chicago, the house Wright built for Frederick C. Robie was in spirit the last and finest of the long series of "Prairie" houses he designed from 1894 in the Illinois countryside. Described by Wright himself in a 1900 issue of *Ladies' Home Journal*, the Prairie House was characterized by its wide, deep-eaved roof, its emphasis on the horizontal and a free plan turned around a central hearth. The houses were elegant, well built and as liberating as they were practical.

The Robie House was one of the very first houses anywhere to feature a built-in garage, and in this sense heralded a new era.

Striking today, although overshadowed by clumsy later buildings, the house reveals itself as a low-lying intersection of dramatically elongated planes. The exaggerated overhang of the roof, recalling some ancient Japanese temple mirrored through the lens of early twentieth-century Chicago, is supported by four 30-metre (100-ft) steel beams.

Although finished throughout in a kind of free-flowing and almost streamlined Arts and Crafts manner, the Robie House is also an expression of the new technologies industrial Chicago had to offer by 1910.

Casa Milà

ANTONI GAUDÍ, 1910

BARCELONA, SPAIN

"THE STRAIGHT LINE belongs to
Man. The curved line belongs to
God." Gaudí practised what he
preached: finding a straight line
inside or outside the Casa Milà, a
Surrealist apartment block in the
centre of Barcelona, is harder than
watching a camel trying to pass
through the eye of a needle. This
truly strange building is known
locally as *la Pedrera* (the quarry).
Yet, far from being a heap of stones,
it is a brilliantly resolved stone
palazzo into which Gaudí has poured
sinuous apartments that are like
nothing else you will find on Earth.

The seven-storey building is
grouped around two courtyards
so that each flat, large or small, is
well lit. Outside, the block appears
to stand on the legs of stone
elephants, while balconies and
window mouldings jut out like
strange lips or eyebrows of giants
you would expect to meet in the
grotesque gardens of Baroque Italy.
Adding to the confusion, the
balconies are girdled with bizarre
garlands of encrusted ironwork.
To cap it all, the roof garden is like
a Dalí painting come to life. Casa
Milà has been used by many film
makers. It remains utterly surreal
and yet this is no gimcrack design.
The building is thought through as
all of a piece. Even then, if it chose
to walk off by itself one night to
live in another city, it would have
to come back: only in Barcelona
has architecture of this topsy-turvy
character made sense.

Michelin Building

F. ESPINASSE, 1911

LONDON, ENGLAND

A COMIC-BOOK BUILDING that pops up in London's snooty Fulham Road like a Jack-in-a-box. A florid Art Nouveau design by the French architect F. Espinasse (1880-1925), the Michelin Building was a kind of strident and witty advertisement for the French tyre company. The exuberant façades are decorated with colourful glazed bricks, white faïence tiles, a pot-pourri of flowery Classical references and, inevitably, representations of pneumatic rubber tyres. The corners are capped with the bulbous stacks of tyres that form the torso of the Michelin Man (add a head, legs and arms in your mind's eye).

The building was bought by the retailer, publisher and restaurateur Terence Conran and publisher Paul Hamlyn in 1984 and was lovingly transformed into an oyster bar, restaurant, shop and offices. The one jarring note is the extension behind and alongside which has none of the grace or humour of the original building. What makes the building special, aside from the fact that it is genuinely funny – a rarity in architecture, much though architects like to talk about "wit" in their designs – is its luminous quality; it glows in sunshine and shines in the rain, proving the durability and surprisingly good urban manners of its fancy dress.

Goetheanum

RUDOLF STEINER, 1913

DORNACH, BASEL,
SWITZERLAND

RUDOLF STEINER (1861–1925) was the founder of Anthroposophy, which, aside from being hard to say, was a part educational and part religious movement aimed at "developing the faculty of cognition and the realization of spiritual reality." The movement led eventually to the construction of an increasing number of highly expressive and idiosyncratic schools across Europe, rated highly for their notably humane methods of education. The Goetheanum was the first headquarters, or meeting hall, of Steiner's movement. It was to have been built in Munich, but Steiner was refused permission. In 1913 the bulbous, exotic domes of the Goetheanum rose in the hills above Basel. The style of the building could be described, loosely, as Organic. Or, it could be labelled under the heading Expressionist. The truth, however, is that for buildings designed by mavericks, no ready label is particularly helpful. The plan of the building, and to an extent its form, have, however, echoed down the century and found new roots in the work of architects such as Reima Pietilä (born 1923) in Finland and Imre Makovecz (p.112) in Hungary. In effect, the plan of the Goetheanum was like a cross-section of the human womb, and the female form of the covering architecture supported this. The idea behind this was one of warmth and shelter. The building was short-lived: it burned down in 1922 and was replaced by an equally unusual design, by Steiner with Herman Ranzenberger, this time in concrete. It is still there.

Centennial Hall

MAX BERG, 1913

BRESLAU, GERMANY

A MIND-BLOWING BUILDING realized on a truly heroic scale by Max Berg (1870–1947), the city architect of Breslau. Built to commemorate the centenary of the local uprising against Napoleon, the Jahrhunderthalle was, in 1913, the most ambitious concrete building yet attempted. So stupendous was the achievement that Berg's decision to leave the concrete exposed went all but unchallenged. The reinforced concrete structure is in the form of a 65-metre (213-ft) dome made up of 32 ribs stretching up from four giant arches to a central lantern. The spaces behind the arches form four apses that can be closed off from the central space. As contemporary glass technology was not up to creating curved walls of glass over the ribs of the concrete dome, Berg designed a sequence of four concrete rings around it and fixed the biggest windows he could into them.

There were few precedents for Berg's hall and in its day it was looked on as a kind of twentieth-century Hagia Sophia. Nevertheless, the structure had to be much heavier and more substantial than Berg might have liked as the properties of reinforced concrete on such a scale were, as yet, largely unknown. The building survived World War Two and remains almost exactly as it was built and still serving its original purpose.

Helsinki Station

ELIEL SAARINEN, 1914

HELSINKI, FINLAND

ELIEL SAARINEN (1873–1950) was a bridge between the architectural concerns of the nineteenth and twentieth centuries, between art and architecture and between the Old and New Worlds. Born in Rantasalmi, Finland, he trained as a painter and architect at the same time, flitting between Helsinki's University and Polytechnic. In 1904, he won the competition for the design of Helsinki Station. This imposing and theatrical monument represented Saarinen's breakaway from the National Romantic movement he had been a part of, in company with Jean Sibelius, the composer, the artist Akseli Gallen-Kallela and the architects he initially teamed up with, Herman Gesellius and Armas Lindgren. The station, famous for the sculpted granite giants that bear the great lamps to light the main entrance, was a rational, logical design, wrapped in a cloak of monumental, sculpted granite. The profile of the clocktower is almost streamlined and its influence was soon to be seen in railway and other civic buildings in America, the country to which Saarinen emigrated in 1923. Working with his son, Eero, Saarinen went on to design some of the most trendsetting mid-century Modern buildings, including the General Motors Technical Center, Warren, Michigan (p.194). He had journeyed a long way from Finnish National Romanticism and Helsinki Station.

Parc Güell

ANTONI GAUDÍ, 1914

BARCELONA, SPAIN

ONE OF THE MOST LOVED of all city parks was laid out on a steep hillside at the edge of Barcelona between 1900 and 1914 by Antoni Gaudi for the industrialist Eusebi Güell i Bacigalupi. Güell had originally planned a model new town on the site but this fell through. The park, however, remains. Its glory is a hall or cavern of massive fluted Doric columns supporting a serpentine balcony on which the stone benches, coated in a brilliant mosaic of broken tiles and glass fragments, are an integral part of the parapet. This is a wonderful place to sit, not just to meet people, but to look out across one of the world's most charismatic and idiosyncratic city centres.

Elsewhere in the park, sinuous paths lead through grotto-like tunnels supported by rough-cut columns that slope at what seem like wayward angles, yet, in truth, express the natural forces at work.

Gaudi lived for many years in a small house of his own design at the bottom of the park. It has long been a Catalonian shrine. The architect's narrow cot is a moving sign of his monastic way of life; his, however, was a monasticism that in no way denied beauty or sensuality, as the magical design of Parc Güell proves. Although clever in concept and colourful in execution, the design of Parc Güell shows how clearly Gaudi felt for and understood the order of Nature to be found beneath its gorgeous skin.

Santa Coloma de Cervelló, Colonia Güell

ANTONI GAUDÍ, 1914

BARCELONA, SPAIN

THIS IS ONE of the most idiosyncratic buildings of the twentieth century, a chapel designed by Gaudí to be the spiritual heart of the ideal industrial community commissioned by his great patron Eusebi Güell i Bacigalupi. Strange enough seen from the outside with its vulva-like windows and mysterious porch, the crypt is absolutely extraordinary. Four massive columns,

leaning at improbable – yet, from the point of view of natural physics, entirely rational – angles support a nave ribbed with determinedly hand-made bricks. Two of the columns are made of rudely cut stone, their counterparts of brick only partly covered in a cement render. Worshippers sit on or kneel at wooden benches that appear to have been designed by an insect or with insects in mind. Even so, the crypt has a wonderfully calm atmosphere and the logic of its construction grows clear.

Gaudí's was a highly individual attempt to reconcile Architecture to

Nature. If God was in his details, it was the God who created birds, plants, insects and fish. The truly remarkable thing about Gaudí's work is that it is always logical in its own wilful manner; he may have looked at the world in a way very different from the majority of twentieth-century architects, yet he is never gratuitous, and although he steers close, never sinks into kitsch. So demanding is the alternative logic of Gaudí's sense of structure that it is obvious why he left no real followers. Or, at least, no one competent enough to take the risks he did.

Grosses Schauspielhaus

HANS POELZIG, 1919

BERLIN, GERMANY

THE BUILDINGS OF HANS POELZIG'S later years were designed in a monumental, stripped Classical style, an idiom that found much favour in Nazi Germany. Just after World War One, he indulged in a number of remarkable Expressionist projects, one of which – the Grosses Schauspielhaus – was actually built. Sadly, only fragments of this fantasy, designed for the flamboyant theatre director, Max Reinhardt, exist today in what is now the Friedrichpalast, Berlin. This cavern of Expressionist stalactites was a conversion of the old Schumann Circus building, housed in a steel-framed market hall. Poelzig (1869–1936) refaced the exterior in an imposing arcaded Roman style, but saved his best for the braggadocio interior. An Egyptian-style foyer led into the 5,000 seat auditorium which, to heighten the sense of exoticism and mystery, was painted blood red. The Nazis altered this haunting interior, which was later all but destroyed in the Allied assault on Berlin. The Grosses Schauspielhaus remains, in photographs, one of the most heightened examples of Expressionist architecture, a loose-knit philosophy of design that emerged in Germany in the lead up to World War One; there were no hard and fast rules, though it seems as if the Expressionists were seeking to break away from the formal, geometric bounds of architecture and the restraints imposed by all too solid building materials.

Einstein Tower

ERICH MENDELSOHN, 1921

POTSDAM, GERMANY

THIS CURIOUS BOOT-LIKE
BUILDING was designed to test
Albert Einstein's theory of relativity.
It was instigated by Einstein's
assistant, Erwin Finlay-Freundlich
and went into operation in 1924. A
telescope in the observatory caught
cosmic rays that were reflected by
mirrors to the "spectrographic"
equipment housed in the basement
laboratories. Erich Mendelsohn
(1887–1953), recently returned
from fighting on the Russian front,
was the architect.

Before and during World War One,
Mendelsohn, who was fascinated by
the cosmos, drew superb sketches
of fantastic buildings – streamlined
designs that appeared to owe nothing
to conventional architectural logic
or to the constraints imposed by
existing materials. He was certainly
the right architect for the Einstein
project, although it could not be
built as he had hoped of a single
material with highly plastic
properties: the material didn't really
exist and an exhausted German
construction industry was hardly in
a position to help. The result is a
building made of crude brick and
concrete, rendered to look as
streamlined and otherworldy as
possible. Although much smaller in
reality than it appears to be in
photographs, the Einstein Tower
remains a captivating architectural
experience and a pointer to a
direction in which mainstream
twentieth-century architecture
might have gone.

Church of the Sacred Heart

ALBERT VON HUFFELL, 1922

BRUSSELS, BELGIUM

THIS VAST DOMED BASILICA rises
alongside the busy tramlines in
central Brussels, dominates most
views of the city and yet, as though
everyone were ashamed of it, is
barely ever mentioned in
architectural histories. Perhaps this
is because what was designed as a
National Memorial or a kind of
sacred pantheon to the glories of
Belgium, was not completed until
1970, by which time its curious
architectural style – National
Romanticism of the 1880s meets
Art Deco on a trip via Christopher
Wren's St Paul's Cathedral – was
as old-fashioned as it was
unconvincing. And, yet the
presence of the building and its
idiosyncrasy make it unforgettable.
The sheer scale of the basilica is
impressive, yet its interior – awash
with daylight – feels cold and
unengaging: there is no sense
of mystery or piety.

Although Albert von Huffell's
design appears to have lead him up
a stylistic cul-de-sac, the idea of a
great domed building dominating
a city centre was far from dead. It
was to be revived soon afterwards
by Edwin Lutyens in his unbuilt
design for a Catholic cathedral in
Liverpool and by Albert Speer in his
design for a giant assembly hall in
Berlin (the Red Army put paid to
that). What von Huffell's design
lacks, however, is the sense of
awe or womb-like enclosure that
Lutyens and Speer promised in their
remarkable, if overbearing, designs.

Chilehaus

FRITZ HÖGER, 1923

HAMBURG, GERMANY

FRITZ HÖGER (1877–1949) was born
in Holstein and made his name in
Hamburg from 1907 with the
design of a number of small houses
in an Arts and Crafts style rooted in
the work of Herman Muthesius who
imported many of his designs from
England. The Chilehaus is his
masterpiece, a magnificent
Expressionist office block anchored
in the city centre like a giant,
barnacle-encrusted liner. It was
commissioned by Henry Brarens
Sloman who had made his fortune
exporting saltpetre from Chile.
Designed around two courtyards,
the building forms a complete city
block. Shops are incorporated into
the Chilehaus at street level. Above,
the offices follow the curve of a
wave-like plan, that climaxes at the
eastern tip or "prow". Offices step
back from the street line above the
sixth storey, and the windows gain
arched tops.

A Wagnerian (Richard rather
than Otto) *tour de force*, the
Chilehaus is proof that the
twentieth-century office block was
able to develop in several directions
and the Miesian model was far
from being the only one. Höger's
brilliance was to design a highly
original and truly memorable city
building that is urbane and well
mannered from the perspective of
those walking by. In Hamburg,
pedestrians walk alongside Höger's
rhythmic arcade: the age of
walking past extractor fans and
service entrances had yet to come.

Cow
Shed

THE MODERN MOVEMENT was
essentially an urban phenomenon.
Hugo Häring (1882-1958), however,
took it not just to the countryside
but to the farmyard itself. This
Expressionist cow shed is a
wonderful oddity. The brick
substructure conceals a uterine
arrangement of concrete portal
frames; the spaces between house
40 cows waiting to be serviced by a
bull who is restrained in his own
pen. The weather-boarded
superstructure houses the haylofts.
It all works very well and the cow
shed has been in constant use since
it was built. Of course it is a little
scuffed, but one can only pray that
in the age of artificial insemination
it retains its seminal purpose and is
not converted in to an art gallery
or architecture centre. The year
the cow shed was finished, Häring
became one of the founder
members of Der Ring, a group
of architects including Erich
Mendelsohn (p.83) and Ludwig
Mies van der Rohe (p.152),
dedicated to fighting the stuffy
attitudes of the planning
authorities in Berlin. The group was
disbanded by the Nazis when they
were elected into power in 1933.
Häring remained in Germany
teaching at a private art school
until 1943 and then retired to
Biberach where he was born. It
seems curious to remember him
for the design of a cow shed, yet
at Gut Garkau he showed how
local needs, local materials and
even animals could benefit from
a radical rethink of their treatment.

Stuttgart Station

PAUL BONATZ, 1927

STUTTGART, GERMANY

TO DRINK A COFFEE in the arcade of this great railway station is to enjoy German city making at its best. Catching a train from here is a delight too. Although clearly derived from Saarinen's terminus at Helsinki, this station has a memorable presence, its style a kind of stripped classicism shot through with a late-flowering National Romanticism. It has a wonderful "trains run on time" feel about it. It was designed by Paul Bonatz (1877–1956) in partnership with Friedrich Eugen Scholer. Bonatz was born in Lorraine, but studied in Munich, becoming a professor at Stuttgart's Technische Hochschule in 1908. Later, he worked with Fritz Todt on the design of the Nazi autobahn network, and continued to work throughout and beyond the Hitler era. He designed traditional houses and severe modern factories, yet it was in the monumental form and presence of Stuttgart Station that, like other architects of the interwar period, he found his voice. Work on the building began in 1911 in Imperial Germany, but was not completed until 1927, six years before the collapse of the Weimar Republic. With its great clock tower, severe colonnade and grand structural simplicity, it offered a distinctive vision of the way more twentieth-century architecture might have progressed had Classicism not become associated all too directly with Nazism in the 1930s.

Frielingsdorf Church

DOMINIKUS BÖHM, 1927

COLOGNE, GERMANY

THIS MAGNIFICENT CHURCH was an attempt by the Bavarian architect Dominikus Böhm (1880–1955) to reinvent the plan of the traditional Catholic church. His approach was prescient, although it was many more years before the deliberations of Vatican II dictated that congregation and priest be brought close together in the manner Böhm's church provided for. The Frielingsdorf church is essentially one large, dramatic space inside, Böhm doing away with the conventional hierarchy of spaces – nave, aisles, choir – that once characterized Catholic churches. The concrete vaults soar from floor to roof, as if wings of angels enfolding the faithful. The pronounced spring of energy in these vaults creates the sense of a space devoted to prayer rising to Heaven. The clarity of the vaults and the great expanse of window create a sublime, if ascetic interior that must rank as one of the finest of its type.

Böhm was born in Jettingen, Bavaria and like Paul Donatz who designed Stuttgart Station (p.87), which was completed the same year as the church, studied under Theodor Fischer in Stuttgart. In later years, although he continued to specialize in church design, his approach became less individual, as he gave up his Expressionist tendencies and came to adopt a more rigorous and less emotional Modern Movement approach. German church design, however, saw some of the very best architects following in Böhm's footsteps, including his son, Gottfried, who took this specialist branch of architecture to new heights in the 1950s and 1960s.

St Martin's Church

ARTHUR GORDON
SHOOSMITH, 1930
NEW DELHI, INDIA

FOR MANY HISTORIANS and architectural critics, this is one of the finest British buildings of the century. Shoosmith (1888-1974) was an assistant of Edwin Lutyens. As Lutyens was extremely busy elsewhere in New Delhi, Shoosmith was allowed a free hand with the design of St Martin's. Partly to keep the heat and rain at bay, and partly because the material was cheap and easy for a largely unskilled labour force to utilize, he shaped his church from bricks, creating what amounts to a monumental and virtually impermeable brick sculpture. Although the form of the building is taken from Lutyens (the Cenotaph war memorial in London's Whitehall springs to mind), Shoosmith's masterpiece is free from all decoration. It somehow manages to combine the new industrial aesthetic of the 1920s with Classical geometry and the plan of a traditional English parish church: no mean achievement, although an odd one. The roof is made up of a series of concrete vaults. The interior is simple, lofty and deeply atmospheric. On sweltering summer days, it provides a cool, calm refuge from the city. The church was built for the military, which is why it has something of the look of a fortress. Today, it serves the Northern Diocese of the Church of India. Through the help of readers of the *Independent* newspaper in London, it was restored in the mid-1990s.

Church of the Holiest Heart of Our Lord

JOSIP PLECVNIK, 1932

PRAGUE, CZECH REPUBLIC

JOSIP PLECVNIK (1872-1957) was one of the most distinctive of all central European architects working in the twentieth century and yet for many years his contribution was all but ignored. Even in what was once Czechoslovakia it was all but impossible to find anything written about him, much less to see his buildings listed and described in guide-books. There must have been many visitors to Prague who stumbled across this extraordinary church, rising from the gardens of George of Podebrady Square. The Church of the Holiest Heart clearly straddles two centuries of design. On the one hand it appears to date from the time of mid-nineteenth century Classicism, and yet the large, Surrealist clock punched through its shibbolethic tower suggests it must be from the 1920s or 1930s, which, of course, it is.

Plecvnik owed no loyalty to any school or style: he was very much his own designer, and the curious form of this unforgettable church was an attempt to evoke the power and spirit of the very first Christian basilicas in a contemporary manner. The body of the church measures 26 by 38 metres (85 by 125 ft) and is 13 metres (43 ft) high. The lower two-thirds of its walls are faced with vitrified bricks punctuated by cubic stone protrusions. The upper third is finished in snow white plaster. Above the pedimented hall, or nave, rises a mostly curious clocktower, the whole caboodle adorned with pylons and obelisks. All very curious and almost a precursor of Postmodernism.

Santa Maria Novella Railway Station

GIOVANNI MICHELUCCI,
1936, FLORENCE, ITALY

GIOVANNI MICHELUCCI (1891–1991) lived long enough to see his masterpiece – Santa Maria Novella Station – go in and out of fashion and back again. The building is a marvel, one of the finest of the Italian Rationalist buildings of the period. It cannot be crudely described as Fascist because it was commissioned and built during Mussolini's regime; it is much too fine a building for that.

Still a busy railway station, Santa Maria Novella is also an urban landmark and a public meeting place that has been looked after with great care and sensitivity by the Ferrovia Statale (FS) and the city of Florence.

In essence, the station is a Roman basilica shorn of decoration, but clad in marble and looking as noble as any imperial courthouse. Its massive walls act as thermal barriers in the hot Florentine summer: it is always cool here, a perfect place to sit and drink coffee and watch the world hurry by whether on its way to Sicily or Salzburg. Of all the sights in Florence, the Santa Maria Novella station ranks among the finest, and yet tourists rush out in search of Brunelleschi and Michelangelo as if Michelucci meant nothing.

Later on in his long career, Michelucci designed far freer and more overtly expressive buildings – notably the Church of San Giovanni Battista (1963) alongside the Autostrada del Sole near Florence, but these seemed forced and restless in comparison to his peerless railway station.

St Andrew's House

THOMAS TAIT, 1936

EDINBURGH, SCOTLAND

ST ANDREW'S HOUSE is the home of the Scottish Office, the government bureaucracy that changed its spots as Scotland gained its own political assembly at the end of the century. Positioned on a magnificent site between the heights and Classical follies of Calton Hill and the historic grandeur of Holyrood House and Edinburgh's Royal Mile, St Andrew's House is an impressive office block that demonstrates how large buildings of its type can contribute positively to a historic and sensitive cityscape. Thomas Tait's (1882–1952) genius was to incorporate new ideas arising from the Modern Movement in a building that was not only clad head to foot in local stone, but which had a formal air that suited the grand city below it. In many ways, St Andrew's House shows how later generations of Scottish architects might have gone about renewing and adding to Edinburgh; instead of large, featureless concrete shoeboxes – Edinburgh boasts some of the blandest and ugliest British buildings of the 1960s and 1970s – these might have been realized imaginatively in stone and glass. It took until the 1990s before new buildings in Edinburgh gained anything of the urban grace and good manners of St Andrew's House. This is not a great building, yet its intelligence shines through its formal reticence and even stiffness in much the same way as, say, Charles Holden's Senate House in London.

Casa Malaparte

CURZIO MALAPARTE AND
ADALBERTO LIBERA, 1942
CAPRI, ITALY

THE FASCIST WRITER and
adventurer Curzio Malaparte
(1898–1957) entertained
Field Marshall Erwin Rommel,
commander of the Afrika Corps,
at his new house on the edge of
Capri, shortly before the Battle of
El Alamein in 1942. The Field
Marshall asked if Malaparte had
designed the exquisitely beautiful
house himself. No, lied the writer,
he had found the house as it was,
but had designed the landscape.
That landscape, or seascape,
remains one of the world's most
desirable. Malaparte, with an initial
helping hand from Aldalberto
Libera (1903–63), chose the site for
his house with infinite care. It sits
on a rock jutting into the sea and
was designed to represent the mind
and body of Malaparte himself. In
this sense, the Casa Malaparte is an
intensely personal design and owes
precious little to contemporary
architectural currents.

A leading light of the Italian
Fascist movement, although he was
also imprisoned by it, Malaparte
was later a Communist and on his
deathbed a Catholic. Malaparte
was a writer and journalist of great
imagination. The house was as
much a mausoleum as it was a
seduction pad and writer's retreat,
an image, Malaparte said, "of my
own nostalgia." The plan of the
house is distinctly unusual: the
Acropolis-like stair leads on to the
roof of the house – for sunbathing
and views – rather than to the
entrance which is all but hidden
below. Bedrooms are like cells. The
living room is vast and washed in
the shimmering light of the sea.
The building is now owned by the
Casa Malaparte Association. No
one else has lived here since
Malaparte's death.

Church of
St Francis of Assisi

OSCAR NIEMEYER, 1946

PAMPÚLHLA, BRAZIL

THE EXUBERANT SWOOP of the
roof of the Church of St Francis of
Assisi echoes the waves crashing on
the nearby Brazilian coast. It is a
wonderful conceit and must have
been a challenge to the concrete
technology of the mid-1940s. Oscar
Niemeyer's engineer, Cardozo, was
clearly up to the job and the
complex sequence of parabolic
arches seems as inevitable as it is

easy and assured. The result is a
poetic and Organic building that
uses its roof like a great umbrella
to keep the sun at bay. What light
there is in the church filters through
vertical louvres set above the
entrance and the main altar. The
campanile and entrance porch are
freestanding: the wave of the roofs
is completely uninterrupted. The
rear wall of the church is covered in
blue and white tiles by the artist
Portinari. The overall effect is of a
sea-shell washed up on a beach
and a wave washing over it.

Niemeyer's quest, unlike that of
his European contemporaries, was

not to create a rational, functional
architecture with precise rules and
hard edges, rather he sought a form
of poetry that an imaginative use
of concrete made possible. Perhaps
buildings like the Church of St
Francis can be seen as the
architectural equivalent of the
poems of Pablo Neruda, or the
novels of Gabriel García Márquez:
they set out to be lyrical and to
stretch our sensibilities. To be
Modern, Niemeyer (born 1907)
seems to say in the design of this
voluptuous seaside church, is not
the same thing as being austere
and passionless.

Gourna Village

HASSAN FATHY, 1947

LUXOR, EGYPT

HASSAN FATHY (1900–89) tried harder than almost any other twentieth-century architect to reconcile Modern and traditional worlds and to create an architecture that was as ecologically correct as it was a delight for those it served. Not that he was always successful. Fathy's attempt to create a new village, or small town, on the edge of Luxor from the late 1940s was beset by petty local politics

and even pettier local rows. Nevertheless, at Gourna, he managed to give shape to houses and other buildings that were rational in plan and built entirely of hand-baked mud bricks. The idea was partly to prove that housing in poor parts of the world could be built without expensive imported materials and without structures and techniques that would either overstretch or be beyond local skills.

Fathy was born in Alexandria; he later moved to Cairo where he was to become the genial head of architecture at the city's university. Fathy's mission was never less than

a struggle; even as he was encouraging and developing a low-cost, environmentally aware architecture, the cities of north Africa and the Middle East were prey to banal, sub-Modern design that appeared in the guise of flamboyant, air-conditioned offices, hotels and, ultimately, shopping malls that required huge amounts of power to run, ignoring the power of the Sun, and which are a part of a system of latter-day imperialism that makes poor countries more and more, rather than less and less, dependent on the rich. Fathy's struggle continues after his death.

Samuel Ford House

BRUCE GOFF, 1949

AURORA, ILLINOIS, USA

BRUCE GOFF (1904–82) built houses that looked as if they were designed for fairy-tale animals rather than refrigerator-age Americans; yet, despite their pronounced eccentricity – Goff was a pupil of Frank Lloyd Wright – houses like the Samuel Ford residence in Aurora, Illinois were rational, intelligent and likeable homes.

The Ford house comprises a large 50.5-metre (166-ft) diameter dome made of steel and covered in shingles. A central lantern supported by an almost Gothic latticework of steel beams brings daylight into the very heart of the house, which boasts a spectacular galleried interior.

Goff was among the most expressive of North American Organic architects and, far from being a philosophical cul-de-sac, his ideas were to be echoed in the pioneering and experimental houses built by many Americans from the 1960s. They were searching for a way of life that was ecologically sound and which represented, in twentieth-century guise, the pioneering spirit of early settlers.

Goff was born in Kansas and began working in Chicago. He later moved to Oklahoma where he was professor of the School of Architecture at the University of Oklahoma at Norman between 1947 and 1955. Most of his designs were for houses; he was fortunate to find clients willing to take the necessary leap of faith and imagination that enabled them to break away from conventional homes.

Johnson Wax Building

FRANK LLOYD WRIGHT, 1950

RACINE, WISCONSIN, USA

AN OFFICE LIKE NO OTHER, the Johnson Wax Building was developed in two phases between 1936 and 1950. The exterior of the complex – a streamlined flow of bricks – is apparently impenetrable; it is impossible to imagine the nature of the idiosyncratic, Martian interior that flowers inside. The extensive offices are divided by a bizarre forest of lofty and unlikely mushroom-topped concrete columns that reach up from the linoleum floors as if standing on tip-toe. Around and between them, Johnson clerks toil from desks designed by Wright. They have no view out; daylight reaches them from the roof supported by the mushroom columns and from a near continuous 34-kilometre (21-mile) strip of Pyrex glass tubing that snakes around the tops of the walls. The inward-looking character of the building is pronounced. Wright was asked to add a research laboratory and this he did between 1944 and 1950 in the form of a rounded, 15-storey brick and glass tower rising above the mushroom offices. Even here, Wright was unable to do the conventional thing. Each alternate floor is a circular mezzanine. All floors are cantilevered from a hollow, reinforced concrete core, housing the lifts and stairs. The result is a very special office tower that offers those who work here more light and space than offered in conventional high-rise buildings, designed for the most part like giant filing cabinets, in which each floor is a self-contained world and the others might as well not exist.

Breda Pavilion

LUCIANO BALDESSARI, 1951
MILAN, ITALY

THE "ECONOMIC MIRACLE" that saw Italy get back on its feet in the 1950s, after a shameful and destructive war fighting on the side of Nazi Germany, was founded to a large extent on the brilliance of the country's designers. Italian manufacturers put their trust in the talents of architects and designers to a degree unprecedented outside the United States. One of Italy's biggest and most dynamic manufacturers was Breda, famous for its railway locomotives and transport equipment. For the 1951 Milan trade fair, Breda commissioned Luciano Baldessari (1896–1982) to design its stand. Treating concrete as a sculptor might, Baldessari produced a sensational pavilion – great folds of white concrete through which visitors could walk on elevated gangways, meeting the latest Breda designs on the way. By making the stand an adventure in itself, Baldessari created something that, far from being worthy, was much like a fun-fair ride.

Baldessari, a Milanese architect, had cut his teeth working with Expressionist designers in the theatre and cinema in the early 1920s: he worked on the fantastic sets of *The Cabinet of Dr Caligari* (p.391) before making a name for himself as an exhibition, furniture and lighting designer. He lived just long enough to see his playful and adventurous approach to form return to favour. Compare the Breda Pavilion with the Guggenheim Museum, Bilbao (p.321).

Dome
House

PAOLO SOLERI (born 1919) was born, brought up and studied in Turin, but left Italy in 1947 to work with Frank Lloyd Wright at the master's studio at Taliesin West. He began working on the design of the Dome House with Mark Mills in 1949. It remains a truly radical habitation. The main body of the house is dug like a cave into a hillside and lined with masonry walls. The rooms are warm in winter, cool in the blazing Arizona summer. Daylight and air feed down into this man-made cave from a glass dome. Mounted on rails, this reacts to heat and light, opening up to the elements whenever it makes sense to do so. This makes the Dome House one of the first constructions to be truly concerned with notions of low energy and sustainability. It has been copied in many different ways since by hippies, New Age settlers and others looking for an escape from irresponsible energy gobbling and city life.

Soleri went back to Italy between 1950 and 1955, returning to the USA in 1956 to set up the Cosanti Foundation in Scottsdale, Arizona, dedicated to the pursuit of new forms of urban living. These included a series of what Soleri called "Arcologies" (Noah's Arks for an age concerned with the ecology), which were megastructures in the desert capable of housing up to six million people. In 1970 he began the long process of building a trial "Arcology" for 150,000 people, in the Arizona desert.

Church of the Miraculous Virgin

FELIX CANDELA, 1955

MEXICO CITY, MEXICO

SOON AFTER COMPLETING his studies at the Escuela Superior de Arquitectura and the Academia de Bellas Artes de San Fernando in Madrid, Felix Candela (born 1910) was fighting Franco, the future Spanish dictator, as a soldier in the Republican Army. He survived to reach Mexico via the refugee camps of the French Pyrenees in 1939 where he teamed up with his brother,

Antonio, to work as builders and jobbing architects. Candela's study of concrete shell structures during this time stood him in good stead. Not only was concrete a cheap material – Mexico was, and remains, a poor country – but it could be used to create original and even flamboyant forms without over-taxing the skill of local labour. Candela proved the point with the design, assisted by Enrique de la Mora, of this spectacular church. The double curved concrete vaults (hyperbolic paraboloids) could be formed, odd though it sounds, with the use of straight boards, making

its apparently difficult construction remarkably easy.

Candela acted as his own engineer on the project and, typically, said the design and construction of the vaults were all down to intuition. It certainly was not – Candela is a fine and imaginative engineer. The exterior of the church is essentially a simple concrete rectangle; the interior comes as a mesmerising surprise. In a country in which Baroque architecture, brought here by the Jesuits, has long been appreciated, Candela has offered a new way of designing and building with passion and drama.

Chapel of Notre Dame-du-haut

LE CORBUSIER, 1955

RONCHAMP, FRANCE

CONCRETE POETRY. Le Corbusier's pilgrimage chapel at Ronchamp stands on a site of ancient worship high on a hill in the Vosges. The chapel was a radical and, for many

architects and critics at the time, shocking departure from the apparently rational Corbusier of the past 30 years. Yet, Ronchamp has its own logic. It is a deeply spiritual building and one that has most people praying, in whatever fashion, as they step inside its haunting interior. Before going inside, however, visitors need to understand that this is a church that works, from a ritual point of view, inside and out. The thick, white, roughcast concrete walls are a frame for outdoor masses and worship; the great overhanging shell-like roof acts as a sounding board for hymns sung, prayers said and sermons given outside the walls.

The extraordinary form of the chapel, said Le Corbusier (1887–1965), was inspired by a shell he picked up on a beach. The interior, protected by thick walls, is lit through an apparently random placing of tiny windows – some filled with coloured glass, others with plain glass – and by a ring of daylight that shines through the glazed gap between walls and roof. This device comes as something of a shock when thought about. What supports the roof? The answer is slim steel columns set into the thickness of the concrete walls; the roof itself, despite its apparent bulk, is a hollow shell and so very light. Ronchamp is unique and very special, an escape from the machine age into the realm of the spiritual.

Solomon R. Guggenheim Museum

FRANK LLOYD WRIGHT, 1959

NEW YORK CITY, USA

THE GUGGENHEIM MUSEUM is quite simply one of the world's most famous buildings. Wright's winding, gyrating, twisting Martian snail of a gallery is wonderfully mad, endearingly potty. There are many people who still find it a bad joke: a spiralling ramp that requires gallery-goers to peer at pictures while standing at an angle that makes one leg feel shorter than the other. One imagines the Surrealists must have loved it. So too must most New Yorkers and visitors to the Big Apple.

Although low for a Manhattan building, the Solomon R. Guggenheim Museum cannot be missed: its pillbox-like profile juts out into Fifth Avenue and ropes visitors into its spectacular interior. This consists of little more than a giant drum, tapering outwards as it rises, around which a ramp spirals. The roof is covered in a shallow glass dome. Visitors are encouraged to take the lift to the top of the museum and to walk slowly back down. Most spend a good long while leaning over the balustrades and watching other visitors as they wind round and round this artful climbing frame.

Wright had been toying with spiral designs from the mid-1920s, and began work on the Guggenheim as early as 1943. Various delays, not least World War Two, held progress back. His crowning and most popular achievement, the museum finally opened in the year Wright died. It has since been extended, yet the purity of the original experience – and what an odd one it is – remains.

José Marti Memorial

VARIOUS ARCHITECTS, 1959

HAVANA, CUBA

HAVANA AT THE END of the 1950s and immediately before the Cuban Revolution led by Fidel Castro, Raul Castro and Che Guevara, was a sweltering hotbed of decadence and corruption. The Caribbean island was under the heel of the posturing dictator Fulgencio Batista, a former army sergeant, and its coffers were filled with ill-gotten revenue from prostitution, gambling, extortion, illegal trade of all sorts, as well as from rum, sugar and tobacco. This was a sad state of affairs for an island that had won its independence from Spain the hard way some 60 years earlier. Cuba's national hero, José Marti, died fighting the Spanish troops in the Cuban War of Independence. This bizarre memorial was finally erected to his memory in a new and highly planned government district of Havana in 1958. Its distinctive profile was adapted from a design taken from a contemporary whiskey advertisement, a rum thing to do given the reverence in which Marti is held in Havana.

The monument protrudes from the heart of the vast Plaza de la Revolucion where Fidel Castro has made many of his famous speeches. The limestone-clad tower rises from a star-shaped base and narrows to viewing platforms reached by a lift 80 metres (250 ft) above the tropical Havana skyscape. Today the monument is open to the public and is a kitsch shrine to both Marti and the Cuban revolution.

TWA Terminal

EERO SAARINEN, 1961

IDLEWILD (NOW JFK)
AIRPORT,

NEW YORK CITY, USA

YOU WOULD HAVE TO BE a
miserable sort not to get a kick out
of this effortlessly entertaining,
stylish and decidedly upbeat airport
building, and not least because so
many buildings associated with air
travel are so mind-numbingly dull.
The TWA terminal really looks as if
it might fly; its theatrical structure

is made up from four intersecting
concrete vaults, or wings, each
supported by swooping Y-shaped
buttresses. The gaps between are
glazed, meaning that, unlike the
vast majority of airport buildings,
it is beautifully lit night and day.
The interior lives up to
expectations. The roofs soar up,
and a gallery is gained by a suitably
rousing stair. Every last detail was
shaped for visual pleasure. You
can't help feeling that the architect
and his client had a lot of fun here,
although the structure must have
been demanding to get set out and
to get right. The TWA Terminal, at
what is now New York's "JFK"

airport, demonstrated how what
had become a long tradition of
showy, advertising-induced US
buildings could happily meet new
ways of buildings and some of
the latest ideas in avant-garde
architecture.

The TWA Terminal was a
glorious match for US airliners and
luxury automobiles of the time: it
pleads for a Lockheed Super
Constellation to land alongside
and for passengers in pencil-skirts
and mohair suits to be picked up
in '59 Cadillac El Dorados. A more
ambitious Saarinen design at Dulles
Airport, Texas, partially collapsed in
1980. It has since been rebuilt.

Greene House

HERB GREENE, 1961

NORMAN, OKLAHOMA, USA

IS IT A BIRD? Is it a buffalo? Can it be a house standing out there on the lonesome Oklahoma prairie? Who knows. Even Herb Greene (born 1929) is unsure. This curious shingle house, standing alone in the middle of nowhere, is meant to evoke any number of responses. It is, of course, a home, although a very peculiar one, and it does look at first like a buffalo the US Cavalry forgot to slaughter, grazing mournfully on the great mid-western plains. Close up, its shingles hang like the feathers of a bird of prey, a vulture perhaps. Even closer up – inside, for instance – the puzzle goes on. The interior is much like the outside, hung wall-to-wall with cedar shingles, lit from unaccustomed angles and explored by wooden ladders.

Herb Greene was clearly influenced by Bruce Goff (p.96) who in turn was a disciple of Frank Lloyd Wright (p.102). In the latest turn of events, Greene had a considerable influence on the school of Organic architects who grew up around Imre Makovecz (p.112) in Hungary.

A "natural' or "Organic" approach to architecture has always been an alternative to the rigours and rules of formal design. All too often the results are awkward and rather embarrassing: a building is not a living creature and cannot satisfactorily represent a bird of prey or a buffalo. It can, however, evoke the spirit of a natural, rural way of life, refuting the certainties of civil architecture. In these ways, the Greene House is an unexpected and breath-stealing jab in the ribs.

National School of Art

RICARDO PORRO, ET AL,
1965, HAVANA, CUBA

THE CUBAN REVOLUTION spawned little in the way of new architecture. This was not for want or lack of ideas, but because the island's economy was never able to take off after Washington imposed a petulant and spiteful economic embargo on what it regarded as an American colony after US-backed armed forces lost to Cuban troops at the Bay of Pigs in 1961. This failed attempt at counter-revolution was a moral triumph for Cuba but led, via the Cuban Missile Crisis of the following year, to economic pain despite financial support from the Soviet Union. This was hardly a climate in which architecture could thrive.

The distinctive and sophisticated National School of Art, set in urban parkland at Miramar, a western suburb of Havana, was the glorious exception. The five buildings housed the faculties of Fine Arts, shown here, by Ricardo Porro (born 1925), a Cuban architect; the Music and Ballet Schools, by Vincent Garatti and the School of Scenic Arts, by Roberto Gotardi. Each architect brought their individual style to the complex, while maintaining the formal similarities – the connected series of bricked domes and the links with Nature – that result in a campus that is at once Organic and Modern.

The Shrine of the Book

FREDERICK KIESLER AND
ARMAND P. BARTOS, 1965
JERUSALEM, ISRAEL

THE DEAD SEA SCROLLS and other precious Biblical manuscripts are housed in this striking Israeli monument. What Kiesler (1890–1965) created here was a form of inhabitable sculpture. Certainly, it comes as a surprise to be able to walk into what appears, at first, to be a silent and solid monument in the guise of a shallow white brick dome rising from the depths of one of the world's most ancient and intriguing cities. The bulk of the building – museum and archives – is, in fact, below ground: the dome is very much the tip of an architectural iceberg. The space beneath the dome is contemplative and haunting: it's hard not to think of Jonah trapped in the belly of the Biblical whale.

Kiesler considered his work to be sculpture. He was born in Vienna and after working briefly for Adolf Loos (p.129) made his name principally as a stage designer; he went to New York in 1926 where he became Director of Stage Design at the Juilliard School of Music. He later taught at Colombia University before setting up an architectural office with Armand Bartos at the age of 67. Their work was mostly concerned with the theatre. The Shrine of the Book was Kiesler's last major work.

Pilgrimage Church

GOTTFRIED BÖHM, 1968

NEVIGES, GERMANY

THE PILGRIMAGE CHURCH is a building type that was pursued with remarkable vigour in Catholic countries during the twentieth century. The pilgrim movement has given us such gems as Le Corbusier's peerless chapel at Ronchamp (p.101). Also in the top league is this astonishing church in Neviges, Germany, which rises above a new settlement for pilgrims designed by Gottfried Böhm (born 1920). A stepped walkway winds up and around a snaking twist of pilgrims' hostels up to Böhm's imposing church. This is a triumphant mountain, or more accurately a giant crystal, represented in concrete. Not only is the building very moving, as well as surprising – much like the Baroque and Rococo churches of eighteenth-century Germany which are far more spiritual in feel than photographs depict – but it demonstrates the possibilities of concrete as a building material. Symbolically, Böhm's masterpiece appears to be the mountain pilgrims have to climb to reach the Celestial City and to meet God face to face. Even if you are not a believer, it has great power and a haunting majesty without once giving way to the conventional decorative trappings of lesser or more flamboyant Roman Catholic churches. An overlooked treasure.

Brasília Cathedral

OSCAR NIEMEYER, 1970

BRASÍLIA, BRAZIL

DESIGNED BEFORE Frederick
Gibberd's Liverpool Cathedral
(p.221) the cathedral at Brasilia
represents Modern architecture as
uncompromised sculpture. It is all
of a piece and if you don't like it
there are no pretty details or nooks
or corners for you to explore to
take your eye off the main feast.
The reason for this is that the
cathedral is designed as much as a
place of worship as an Organic and
florid counterpart to the daunting
geometrical abstraction of the
Congress and ministry buildings
Niemeyer had completed here
previously. The cathedral represents
the Crown of Thorns placed on
Christ's head before his crucifixion.
It is composed of swooping concrete
buttresses that rise almost sensually
from the ground and are held
together almost invisibly at their
apex by a ring of steel and concrete.
The spaces in between are entirely
glazed. The drama of the cathedral
is enhanced by the fact that the
church is entered from ground level,
from a narrow defile or passageway
that descends before it climbs in near
darkness up into the light of the
Crown of Thorns. It is a breathtaking
experience. Inside, the cathedral
appears to be much bigger than it is
from outside. This is because the
circular floor is set below ground
level and because furniture and
worshippers offer a sense of scale
that is almost impossible to grasp
when walking among the heroic
civic monuments of central Brasilia.

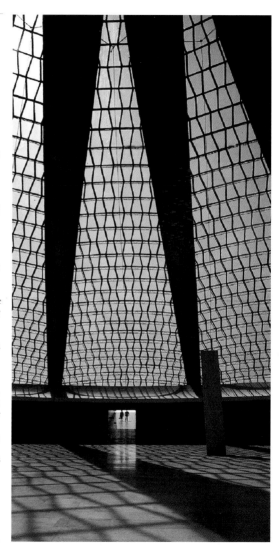

Brion Cemetery

CARLO SCARPA, 1972
SAN VITO D'ALTIVOLE,
TREVISO, ITALY

CARLO SCARPA (1906–78) worked very much in his own personal idiom, and his designs, if never self-effacing, were often a reworking of existing buildings such as the Accademia in Venice (1952), an annexe to the glorious Gipsoteca Canoviana in Treviso (1957) and the influential remodelling of the Castelvecchio at Verona (1964) into a museum (p.213).

Brion Cemetery is one of Carlo Scarpa's finest designs and here, for once, he was given a free hand. Cemetery design in Italy has long been a fine art and Scarpa added to a legacy of proud architecture for those who have moved on – hopefully – to the City of God blissfully free of shopping malls and Postmodernism.

Brion Cemetery has been described as a celebration of death. In actual fact it is difficult to define or categorize. Scarpa has grouped together what appear to be fragments of buildings belonging to no era and yet to all eras. These fragments, like the ruins of ancient Rome as they would have been when first rediscovered by the artists and architects of the Renaissance, are overgrown with rich foliage. The cemetery is alive with birds, insects and creeping things.

Brion Cemetery is a curious place and not a little unsettling; however, it is moving, all the same. Scarpa built his architecture from fragments and these are curiously – and even mysteriously – often as powerful and as telling as entire buildings.

Sydney Opera House

JØRN UTZON, 1973

SYDNEY, AUSTRALIA

IT'S FAIR TO SAY that this highly memorable building put Sydney fairly, if not squarely, on the international map in a way that it never had been before. In truth, the Sydney Opera House is both brilliant and frustrating at one and the same time. No one can doubt the thrill of its roofline – whether you see in those remarkable roofshells the beaks of seagulls, shark fins, waves or wimples – and the fascinating story there is to be had of its construction. The latter was left largely to Peter Rice, a very young Irish structural engineer, working for Ove Arup, who was to be awarded the Royal Gold Medal for Architecture before he died in 1992. The interiors of the building, though, are rather pedestrian: the thrill of the exterior fails to survive the long haul through the lobbies to the auditorium itself. This is probably because Jørn Utzon (born 1918), the Danish architect, resigned – or was pushed off the project – in 1966 and the building was completed without his special, if wayward, genius.

Rather like Gaudi, Utzon continued to work on the design of his buildings as he went along, so that we do not know quite how he would have finished his most ambitious work. His other buildings, mostly in his native Denmark, are all inventive and combine an intriguing marriage of experimentation with new materials and technologies with Organic forms.

Farkasrét Mortuary Chapel

IMRE MAKOVECZ, 1977

BUDAPEST, HUNGARY

THE EXTRAORDINARY and moving interior of this building is a representation of the human rib cage. Coffins are placed where the heart would be and mourners sit on either side in carved wooden stalls that themselves resemble mourners: the chapel is never empty. Dug into the side of a hill in the extensive Farkasrét cemetery in the Buda hills, a winding tram ride from the centre of Budapest, the chapel was the first work of Imre Makovecz (born 1935) to gain international attention. Makovecz is the undisputed leader of an ever-growing band of architects who, like Robin Hood and his Merry Men, were all but outlaws during the Communist era, but since 1989 have been national heroes. Not everyone, of course, appreciates the Organic architecture Makovecz has nurtured since the early 1970s, yet in the 1980s it became a symbol and rallying point for dissent in Hungary; it was significant that Makovecz was chosen to design the memorable Hungarian pavilion for Expo '92 in Seville.

The son of a carpenter, Makovecz trained as an architect in Budapest. Arrested and tried during the Hungarian uprising of 1956, he was often in trouble with the authorities and was only able to find work designing for the forestry commission and in some of Hungary's remoter villages. With limited materials he developed a style of architecture drawn from the ideas of Frank Lloyd Wright, Bruce Goff and Rudolf Steiner which, at the time, he was able to see only in prohibited books.

State Library

HANS SCHAROUN, 1978

BERLIN, GERMANY

IT IS HARD to get turned on by this lumbering great library designed by Hans Scharoun (1893–1972) and completed by his one-time partner Edgar Wisniewski. The building straddles what was once Potsdammer Strasse and appears to be all over the place with no guiding strategy or form.

The interior, though, is a revelation and in parts more than exceedingly good. The main reading room is a wonderful space in which to while away a rainy afternoon, and was used to great effect by Wim Wenders, the German film director, in his poetic film *Wings of Desire*.

The library is one part of a trio of cultural buildings – the other two are the Philharmonic Hall (1963) and the Chamber Music Hall (1987) – all designed by Scharoun who lived long enough only to see the first completed.

All share the same wibbly-wobbly look and do not, from the outside anyway, feel like city buildings. Scharoun, however, was the director of building and housing in Berlin after World War Two and perhaps his Organic style was a deliberate reaction against the militaristic Neoclassicism, so beloved by the Nazis and the Prussian kings and emperors before them. His Berlin interiors, however, are a triumph as were the fine villas he built in Germany in the 1930s.

Liverpool Cathedral

GILES GILBERT SCOTT, 1978

LIVERPOOL, ENGLAND

THIS ECCLESIASTICAL EVEREST was 75 years in the making. It is one of the biggest buildings in the world and a gloriously disdainful design that makes anyone who dares to enter it feel utterly insignificant. The cathedral is 100 metres (330 ft) high, but seems much taller because of its magnificent, if weather-beaten, site on a hill commanding the city stretched out along the River Mersey below.

Giles Gilbert Scott (1880–1960) was just 21 years old when he won the competition to design the cathedral. The building committee insisted he work with an older architect, George Frederick Bodley (1827–1907), which is why the first part of the cathedral to be completed, the Lady Chapel in 1910, is so much fussier and, frankly, Victorian than the red sandstone grandeur that came afterwards.

After Bodley's death, Scott let rip, redesigning the main body of his great masterpiece several times.

His genius was to create a vast space beneath the principal crossing quite unlike that of a medieval English cathedral. The sense of space here is daunting. Throughout, the building is masterful and proof that the Gothic tradition was far from exhausted. Construction continued throughout World War Two, during which time the cathedral was bombed.

The west front was finally completed by Frederick Thomas in 1978 with more than a little help from tons of concrete and other modern materials. These have been carefully hidden.

National Assembly Building

LOUIS KAHN, 1983

DHAKA, BANGLADESH

LOUIS KAHN (1901–74) worked on the design of this highly original building – a cluster of covered spaces linked together – for the last 11 years of his life, and in the event it took 20 years to complete. A remarkable fusion of the religious and political spheres, it is first and foremost a superb meeting place.

The programme is complex with assembly chamber, mosque and offices appearing to wrap around and even circle one another as one walks its watery perimeter. The essential architectural components are the cube and the sphere, worked and reworked until the repertoire is all but exhausted. The red brick walls are lined inside with concrete and marble and, as one would expect of Kahn, washed, dappled and adorned with beautiful shafts and beams of daylight playing from slits and

chutes, arches and skylights. Interior and exterior play complementary games and the whole complex can be experienced as a thrilling architectural puzzle. The construction is well able to hold back the wall of heat that leans against Dhaka much of the year.

The Assembly Building is located on the edge of the Bangladeshi capital in a city extension known as Sher-e-Bangla Nagur or "the city of the Bengal Tiger". Kahn's powerful design ensures it lives up to its formidable name.

Lowengasse and Kegelgasse Housing

FRIEDENSREICH

HUNDERTWASSER, 1985

VIENNA, AUSTRIA

SOCIAL HOUSING like no other. Artist and architect Friedensreich Hundertwasser (1928–2000) broke away entirely from the constraints of conventional city apartment blocks with this madcap design. Future residents were engaged in a dialogue with the architect who interpreted their needs and desires in a wilfully loose-fit manner. The end result is a building that looks like a big bit of knitting or weaving that has gone askew and in which every last colour of wool or thread in the basket has been used up to get the job finished. These houses might not be to everyone's taste and it does help to look at them when wearing sunglasses, yet Hundertwasser's popularity should not be in doubt. He listened to people and, in a very literal way, brought colour into the lives of those who previously have had little say in where and how they live. But, is this a real improvement on, say, Vienna's Karl Marx Hof (p.30)?

The 1980s were a time in which some of the big questions relating to social housing were addressed. In Britain, the solution was to stop building altogether. The French got Ricardo Bofill and the Taller de Arquitectura (pp.62–3), the Genovese Renzo Piano (p.256) and the Viennese Hundertwasser. Many mistakes were undoubtedly made during this decade, but architects were being forced to learn how to discuss their work and to engage with those who had to live in their designs. If they didn't want to listen, then the likes of Hundertwasser would.

Church of the Light

TADAO ANDO, 1989

IBARAKI, OSAKA, JAPAN

SET IN A BUILT-UP DISTRICT of Osaka, Ando's Church of the Light transforms the congregation of the Ibaraki Kasugaoka Church (a branch of the United Church of Christ in Japan) into an otherworldly realm. The building is simple: a rectangle of concrete panels is cut through with a freestanding wall to create an opening sense of drama. The interior is immensely powerful. Behind the altar the wall is a cross of light. Ando (born 1941) wanted this to be unglazed so that the congregation would feel the spirit of God move upon them. But as this would have been more like the spirit of Azrael, the angel of death, in the cold winter months, he thought better of this. The light from the cruciform opening reflects on the concrete roof: the symbol of the cross feels omnipresent and there is no need for any religious art to reinforce this bold message. The blackened cedar floor slopes down to the altar, the Church believing that as Christ moved among his people, the priest should do the same.

This building is another reminder of how architecture can be free of decoration, yet rich in symbolism and even spiritual power. Much of this, as Ando knew better than perhaps any architect at the end of the twentieth century, is to do with the manipulation of light and shadow. The twentieth century was one that tried to banish the shadow and thus one of the key expressions of the realm of the spirit.

Phoenix Library

WILL BRUDER, 1992

PHOENIX, ARIZONA, USA

WILL BRUDER (BORN 1946) trained as a sculptor, but as an architect he was self-taught. A modern disciple of Frank Lloyd Wright, he is part of a US tradition that generates local colour and form while adapting to and taking up with new materials and building technologies. The result, as can be seen in this impressive library, is an architecture that seems relaxed and informal despite its monumental scale and strong sculptural form. On its sunny side, the library presents a tall and solid wall faced in local stone, coloured concrete and corrugated steel. On its shady side it presents an almost sheer wall of glass to the world, although this is tempered by a grille of steel mullions and transoms. The effect is dramatic, particularly so at night when the building casts strong shadows. The interior on several levels is ultra-modern in a laid-back version of "Hi Tech". The lofty steel roof of the topmost reading room is held up by tapering masts that sprout struts like branches from a machine-made tree.

In effect, Bruder's library is rather like a modern barn. This is a reasonable comparison, not least because it was built cheaply and has none of the pretensions, delays and precious aesthetic foibles of the Bibliothèque Nationale (p.318) or the British Library (p.271). The library incorporates an abundance of new computer technology and is living proof that the rise of the home computer and the Internet is not a reason to suppose that the big public library will soon disappear.

Church of the Holy Spirit

IMRE MAKOVECZ, 1992

PAKS, HUNGARY

PAKS, A SMALL TOWN on the Danube south of Budapest, is famous for two modern buildings: Hungary's only nuclear power station and, this, the Church of the Holy Spirit, designed by Imre Makovecz. Local children call it the "devil's church" because of its rather Transylvanian look. It is one of Makovecz's most distinguished buildings. The womb-like body of the church is contrasted with the detached bell tower and its three spires. These are capped with symbols representing the sun, moon and crucifixion. The church – a superb example of the skill of Makovecz's roving band of carpenters – is meant to be a representation of the opposites of dark and light, earth and sky, male and female, sun and moon. Its symbolism is pagan and Catholic at one and the same time, and is all the more realistic and powerful for being so. The interior is lit from the top by a stained glass ceiling shaped like an ancient Celtic symbol, often used in jewellery, representing eternity. Daylight filters down into a nave and chancel that flow naturally into one another and are realized throughout in timber. Makovecz says that his mission is to reconcile Heaven with Earth and in his highly personal and moving buildings he gets a long way in recreating what must have been the sentiments and aesthetic expression of the early church at a time when the pagan tribes of the Hungarian plains took to Christianity.

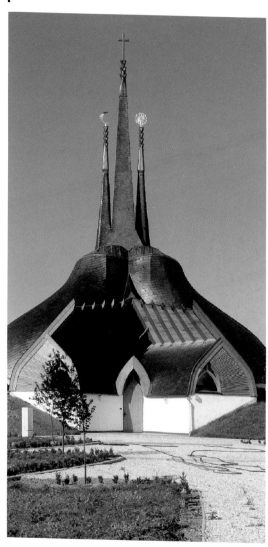

American Heritage Center

ANTOINE PREDROCK, 1993

LARAMIE, WYOMING, USA

ANTOINE PREDROCK (BORN 1936) is keen on UFOs, which figures when you come across the American Heritage Center: it looks as if it might have landed from outer space and be full of "greys". Stuck out in a deserted landscape, it can certainly look rather sinister. This museum and heritage centre is one of those buildings visitors enjoy attaching labels to: it's a flying saucer; no, it's an Indian tepee, and so on. In fact, the architect enjoyed this game too – while pointing out that it was also intended to reflect the nearby Medicine Bow mountains. Its location is a fascinating landscape of mountain, forest, desert, hot springs and the graveyards of dinosaurs: these natural riches and historical depths are reflected in the building.

Predrock is a master of the dramatic architectural image and it is not a surprise to learn that he was also one of the architects of EuroDisney. The patinated copper dome of the main body of the Heritage Center rises from a podium along which are ranged a variety of stone-clad outbuildings that, although blocky and more strictly geometrical than the dome, are as equally enigmatic. Like the buildings of Frank Lloyd Wright, the Heritage Center creates a man-made drama out of a big landscape that would swamp a neat little something by a city architect.

Truss-Wall House

EISAKU USHIDA AND
KATHRYN FINDLAY, 1997
TOKYO, JAPAN

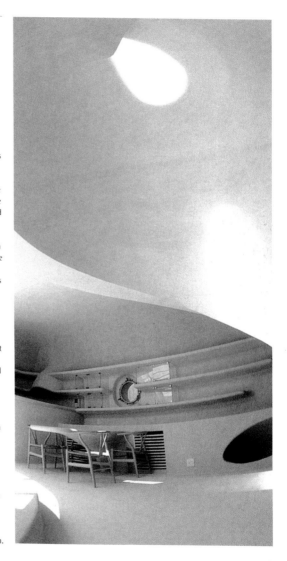

THROUGHOUT THE 1990s, young architects began to rediscover the Modernism that had been buried under layers of Postmodern and other stylistic conceits in the previous twenty years. For many, this meant the pursuit of a soft Modern style that was more concerned with pure appearance or style, rather than the concerns that the first Moderns had with plan and purpose. The upshot was a creamy smooth and polite white architecture, beloved by fashion magazines, that could travel anywhere and be accepted everywhere. There were exceptions to this rule such as this clever and endearing house in Tokyo by Eisaku Ushida and Kathryn Findlay. Its soft, flowing, Organic style mirrors an intelligent plan that allows for a relaxed way of living in one of the world's most intense cities. Delightfully, for a collaboration between a British and a Japanese architect, it makes no play on national traditions but has a character entirely of its own. The sweeping forms adopted by Ushida and Findlay were part of a move in the mid-1990s to more Organic forms in interiors, fashion and furniture. If there was a bit of the Space Age in the design mix, then this reflected the optimism of the architects who clearly believed that Postmodern irony (or defeatist decadence) was dead and that the Modern house was still a worthy subject for research and celebration.

Hindu Temple

VARIOUS MASONS, 1997
NEASDEN, LONDON,
ENGLAND

ONE OF THE MOST CHARMING new buildings in London at the end of the twentieth century is this Hindu temple on the North Circular Road in Neasden, a suburb best known as a standing joke in the satirical fortnightly *Private Eye*, but here reinvented as a larger-than-life slice of life in India. Unlike previous Hindu architecture in Britain – which since the mid-eighteenth century had been used as a style for follies, rococo interior decoration, the Royal Pavilion in Brighton and the odd romantic country house like Sezincote – this is the real thing. The Hindu population in Britain has grown as thousands of Indian people previously settled in various parts of the world, notably East Africa, have come to Britain in search of security, education and freedom of religious expression. In Neasden, this freedom is expressed in a gloriously frothy white marble architecture that was cut and shaped, carved and decorated almost entirely in India with the numbered pieces being shipped over as and when needed. In this sense, this is certainly no fake and is part of a religious tradition that sees no need to reinvent the fundamentals and certainly not the details of the design of its temples. Rising in a wave of exuberant domes and filigree details above the red-tiled roofs of Mock Tudor Neasden, it is truly a sight to behold, a welcome addition to a hit-and-miss townscape.

Thermal Bath

PETER ZUMTHOR, 1997
VALS, SWITZERLAND

PETER ZUMTHOR (BORN 1943) won international acclaim for this unexpected and beautiful thermal bath in southern Switzerland. Part of an old hotel that had run to seed and was in need of new life, the bath is reached by a tunnel. The ascent, through the various changing rooms, steam rooms and plunge pools, is thrilling and relaxing at one and the same time. At the top, a steaming pool opens up into the mountainscape where in winter the mix of snow, steam, hot water and icy air is intoxicating. The quality, invention and touch of Zumthor's architecture lifts the experience into that of the sublime. Every material that a hand or foot touches is a pleasure, whether it is stone, terrazzo, timber or leather. The bath is a feast for the senses and not least the eye.

The building itself is dug into a hillside leaving one handsome flank exposed and the rest a secret well worth discovering. Zumthor is a craftsman as well as an architect and this shows clearly throughout the building in which every join has been treated with a Zen-like care. Because of this and the fact that he worked with his own building team, Zumthor's output is small and largely confined to a corner of his native Switzerland. To find an architect of such quality and originality working within such a tight confine was unusual at the end of a century of hurriedly consumed images.

This is the core of the book and the fast-spinning hub around which so much twentieth-century architecture turned. The Modern Movement had many sources, and these were debated, confirmed and denied many times over the last quarter of the century. At this distance what still seems to hold true is that, like the Arts and Crafts movement, Modernism was a moral force in the idea of a crisp, clinical, machine-like aesthetic that brooked no decoration and suffered no poetry. On the other, there were those who saw in Modern design a new form of lyrical expression. Among these were architects like Le Corbusier or Oscar Niemeyer who may have spouted all the right words about the creation of new forms of decent architecture for the masses and yet ended up is how it was. What began as a recognizable creed with a clear message of health, light, openness and honesty after the blood and mud of World War One became a diaspora of contradictory and even warring ideas after half a century of relentless experimentation. The difference between the concerns of Ludwig Mies van der Rohe and a local authority architect toiling on the design of a housing estate in London could hardly have been more profound, even though both would mouth many of the same formulas and Modernist mantras.

Yet, in whatever shape or form Modern architecture arrived, two things are clear. The first is that Modernism was not simply a style, but more of an attitude, a determination to break with the past and free the architect from the stifling rules of convention and etiquette. The second is that at the very same time architects were celebrating the Modern building's machine-like qualities, so they began to lose out to armies of engineers and contractors; for if form must play second fiddle to function, who needs an architect? The wisest Modernists – Mies perhaps above all – knew that the architect could create and shape an aesthetic of minimal form aiming for a state of perfection that no one but an artist would be likely to find. Less in Mies van der Rohe's case was indeed more, yet for many architects, the Modern building meant less is less.

Modernism

"LESS IS MORE." MIES VAN DER ROHE

and a philosophical investigation as much as it was revolution in aesthetic sensibilties. Of course looks mattered – although you will find some real brutes here – yet one of the principal ideas driving Modern architecture was that buildings should be first and foremost functional machines for performing various programmes; and if this makes them sound like washing machines ... well, some of them are. Le Corbusier, the greatest of the Modernists, tired quickly of the word "functional". He wished to create a form of architecture that was truly of the century, a celebration of the machine age and yet poetic. And here lay a struggle or contradiction within Modernism. On the one hand there were puritanical architects who revelled designing one-off monuments as if they were the successors of Michelangelo and Borromini rather than the social scientists architects were meant to be in the mid-twentieth century.

As the century progressed this contradiction and division in the ranks became increasingly clear. Even as the certainties of the Modern experiment were crumbling at the end of the 1960s and the beginning of the 1970s, there were those architects who thought systems, prefabrication and no concessions to appearances was the one true path and those who plunged deeper into the unfathomable waters of formalism. If this makes Modernism sound like a religion that had begun to split into factions, then perhaps this

Apartment Building

AUGUSTE PERRET, 1903

PARIS, FRANCE

THE ROMANS made extensive use of concrete in their buildings 2000 years ago; but reinforced concrete, the material that made possible so many of the most adventurous buildings of the twentieth century, was almost another 2000 years in the making. Available from the 1890s, it captured the imagination of the young French architect Auguste Perret (1874–1954) and his brothers Gustave and Claude with whom he set up a construction firm, Perrets Frères Entrepreneurs, after completing his studies at the Ecole des Beaux-Arts in Paris. The apartment block, overlooking a park in rue Franklin, Paris, was Perret's first significant building and much impressed the youthful Le Corbusier when he worked with the brothers in the winter of 1908–9.

The block comprises a simple reinforced concrete frame, almost unheard of at the time, infilled with concrete panels. In the spirit of the time, Perret had these decorated with floral Art Nouveau designs; whether this was a response to fashion or a polite way of disguising the unfamiliar brutality of concrete construction is hard to say. Either way, the building marked the beginning of a trend for concrete apartment blocks boasting large windows and generous, airy interiors. The block was topped with a roof garden. The Perret brothers themselves used the ground floor as an office for several years.

Carson, Pirie and Scott Department Store

LOUIS SULLIVAN, 1904
CHICAGO, ILLINOIS, USA

ORIGINALLY THE Schlesinger and Mayer store, this 12-storey commercial block in downtown Chicago did much to shape the modern office block, although it was and remains a grand and glittering shop. Only the first two floors of Sullivan's building are decorated – and very lavishly so – while the upper ten storeys rise cleanly and clearly with their big, picture windows to the architect's signature "attic" at the very top. The floorplans are those of almost any mid to late twentieth-century high-rise, city centre office block. Even then, the building clearly follows Sullivan's base-central shaft-capital approach to the design of tall buildings: the clean-cut, straight up and down was still a long way in coming.

Sullivan (1856–1924) trained at the Massachusetts Institute of Technology, Chicago and the Ecole des Beaux-Arts, Paris. In many ways, he was the link between nineteenth- and twentieth-century architectural forms and sensibilities. He is best remembered, aside from his superb buildings, for the conclusion to his 1906 essay: "It is the pervading law of all things organic and inorganic, of all things physical and metaphysical, of all things human and all things superhuman, of all true manifestations of the head, of the heart, of the soul, that the life is recognizable in its expression, that form ever follows function. This is the law ...".

Larkin Building

FRANK LLOYD WRIGHT, 1905

BUFFALO, NEW YORK, USA

THE LARKIN BUILDING was demolished in 1950. Its brief life, however, is no measure of its immense importance: this was the first truly modern office block, a building designed inside and out to match purpose and function in a near-scientific manner. It was also the very first air-conditioned office and the first to be based around a central atrium.

The Larkin brothers more or less invented the mail order business; they needed a large supply of well-educated, diligent clerks to process a huge number of intricate orders. Lined in serried rows at the smart desks designed for them by Frank Lloyd Wright (1867–1959), these early office workers were in certain ways no more and no less than the victims of the revolution in organizational thinking led by Frederick Taylor (1856–1915), father of the school of Scientific Management that led to Henry Ford's mass-production techniques, time and motion men and lifelong tedium for the twentieth-century white-collar worker. Whatever the limitations and inhumanity of Taylor's findings, the Larkins' fast turnover business or Wright's design, the Larkin Building remains as radical a concept today as it was in 1905 when just 5 per cent of the US population toiled in offices compared with over 50 per cent by the end of the century.

Steiner House

ADOLF LOOS, 1911

VIENNA, AUSTRIA

THE STEINER HOUSE was often used to illustrate stripped-bare Modern design in books promoting a revolutionary approach to architecture in the wake of World War One. Yet, it was only the back of the house that was ever shown: the front was compromised by the insistence of the local planning authority that it must have a pitched roof. Canny Loos gave the Steiner House a roof that curved up from the ground floor front and on to a severe back that looked like the front he had wanted to begin with. In this sense the Steiner House is a curiosity. However, in intent this reinforced concrete house was among the very first buildings hinting at what an up and coming generation of Germanic architects might do and did.

Adolf Loos (1870–1933) was the son of a stonemason; he studied at the Technische Hochschule, Dresden, before spending three years in the United States where he worked as mason, floor-layer and dish-washer, before settling in Vienna in 1896. An early commission, the Museum Café in Vienna, was known as the Café Nihilismus because of its stark lack of decoration. In 1908 he published his famous essay, "Ornament and Crime", which equated decoration with decadence and criminality; Loos had inspected criminals in Vienna's prisons and found they were often tattooed, something no civilized, law-abiding citizen could possibly condone. He admired the notion of the decorous "English gentleman" and was always impeccably dressed.

Goldman and Salatsch Building

ADOLF LOOS, 1911

VIENNA, AUSTRIA

"MODERN MAN, the man with modern nerves", wrote Loos in "Ornament and Crime", "does not need ornamentation; it disgusts him." Unhappily for Loos, it was the very lack of ornamentation that set the press, public and planners against the Goldman and Salatsch Building when the scaffolding was first taken down. The Viennese, with their passion for opera and baroque cakes, were aghast at the nakedness of this supposedly refined tailors' store. The owners, Leopold Goldman and Emanuel Aufricht, took fright and a second competition was held to complete the building which, in the event, Loos won as he had the first. The result is a handsome and well-polished corner block in the heart of Vienna that marries a neatly tailored cleanness of line with lavish materials.

The base of the building is granite and its lower floors are lined with green Greek Cipollino marble. The pillars bestriding the mezzanine windows were cast in zinc and wrapped in bronze. The interior of the shop was fitted out with every extravagance possible behind the label "austere". Above the shop, a plain, stucco façade is punctuated with windows, some of which appear to rest on bronze window-boxes. The Goldman and Salatsch building is not just a lovely thing; it announces the junction elegantly and commandingly. It has worn its age like a well-pressed suit, cut from the finest cloth.

Fagus-Werke

WALTER GROPIUS AND
ADOLF MEYER, 1914
ALFELD-AN-DER-LEINE,
GERMANY

IN THE QUEST as he saw it to "wrest the impression of corporeality from unsubstantial materials", Walter Gropius (1883–1969) designed one of the first buildings that we associate with the look and style of Modern Movement architecture. While working in the office of Peter Behrens, Gropius, the future founder of the Bauhaus, met Adolf Meyer (1881–1929), a cabinet-maker turned architect. The two designed a brick, steel and glass factory for making shoe lasts that abandoned the apparently solid structure of architecture to date. The corners of the famous administration block were realized almost entirely in glass. In fact, here, for the first time, the core of a building was effectively surrounded in an envelope of glass.

There had been much discussion in Germany in the previous decade – and certainly since the setting up of the Deutsche Werkbund in 1907 – about the contribution architecture could make to the public image of industrial manufacturers. Behrens had pointed the way with the AEG Turbine Hall in Berlin (p.34); Gropius, whose influence was to become international and all-pervading in the coming decade, took the next step and created a factory that was not simply elegant and refined but overtly Modern. This was Gropius's first independent commission. It could hardly have been more significant, and was to set the style of modern factories worldwide.

Holland House

H. P. BERLAGE, 1914

CITY OF LONDON,

ENGLAND

BERLAGE DESIGNED this colourful, Jacob's coat of an office block for Muller, a Dutch shipping company, in one of the City of London's typically narrow streets. It was his only work in Britain and remains as much a curiosity as it was at the time of its construction, a pointer towards the office of the future. Holland House might look as if it is made from solid masonry walls, but beneath its green glazed tilework and polished black granite plinth, it is no more and no less than a steel-frame, housing some of the earliest open-plan offices complete with moveable partitions. The granite plinth appears to frame the building, rising over its doorways and forming giant flat pilasters at either end of the Bury Street façade. The lobby is highly decorated, although the logic of the steel frame construction is openly, or "honestly" as architects liked to say, expressed.

If Holland House shows Modern tendencies, Berlage nevertheless thought of himself as a traditionalist; he attended the very first meeting of Congrès Internationaux d'Architecture Moderne (CIAM) in 1928, but declined to join this fertile seedbed of young radicals. Holland House has since been extended unsympathetically; Berlage's design, however, remains intact and a genuine surprise to anyone who thinks of British architecture of the period as "Wrenaissance" domes and columns.

Model Factory, Werkbund Exhibition

**WALTER GROPIUS AND
ADOLF MEYER, 1914
COLOGNE, GERMANY**

JUST BEFORE GROPIUS went off
to fight in Kaiser Wilhelm's army,
he produced this hugely influential
design for a model factory. Although
the core and roofline of the
administration block are clearly
influenced by Frank Lloyd Wright,
the twin stair towers – streamlined

glass structures – were a new
device that was to influence
countless architects, beginning in
Germany, after World War One. The
factory was very much a model for
future industrial buildings around
the world, with its swish office
block fronting a simple workshop
separated by a courtyard behind.
Here, the clearly expressed intention
was that the factory itself would
be one of the key expressions of
a manufacturer's image. No longer
a "dark, satanic mill", the modern
factory was to be shown off not
just to visitors, but in advertising

and publicity campaigns.

The Werkbund Exhibition itself
was an important event, architects
divided between those, like Gropius,
who believed that modern buildings
could be all but mass-produced
like cars and domestic goods, and
those who insisted that the architect's
role was to give each new building
a distinctive character of its own.
The glazed rear elevation of the
office block was to influence the
self-conscious "machine aesthetic"
of a wide variety of building types,
from schools to railway stations,
in the 1920s and 1930s.

Henny House

ROBERT VAN'T HOFF, 1919
UTRECHT, THE NETHERLANDS

ROBERT VAN'T HOFF (1887–1979) was so taken by the writings of Frank Lloyd Wright that he went to the United States to work with the master for a year (1913–14). On his return he designed what must be one of the very earliest Modern houses in Europe. Although clearly influenced by Wright – it has much of the look and overall design of, say, Wright's Gale House in Oak Park, Illinois (1909) – the Henny House is more restrained than anything Wright built. Its reinforced construction is severely expressed and the house has a determinedly elemental character, without fuss or frills. The concrete slabs are painted grey to identify the logic of the construction.

The house was begun almost immediately after the end of World War One. It sits on an immaculately groomed lawn entirely separate from the world around it; it must have seemed quite shocking when first built. For van't Hoff and his client, at least, the age of decadent, bourgeois European architecture, whether Neo-Baroque or Art Nouveau, was over. The Henny House was an early attempt to show that not just architecture but even the home could be freed from egotistical individual expression and reinterpreted in an objective and universal manner; that was the idea, anyway.

Van't Hoff joined the De Stijl group of artists and architects gathered around Theo van Doesburg in Leiden, but broke away in the early days. From 1937 he lived in England, although spent as an architectural force.

Notre Dame de Raincy

AUGUSTE PERRET, 1922

PARIS, FRANCE

ALTHOUGH BORROWING some of the basic elements from Gothic parish churches – the soaring bell tower, long nave and aisles – Perret's Notre Dame was a demonstration of the liberating properties of reinforced concrete. Inside, all is light, reason and decidedly Modern. The barrel-vault above the nave is supported by tall (11-metre/35-ft) and slender (35.5-cm/14-inch) concrete pillars that also mark the division of the barrel-vaulted aisles into twelve bays. The effect is magnificent and comes as a complete surprise after the conventions of the bell-tower and the massive construction of the west front. So sparing is the construction of the nave that the walls are almost all glass, an effect medieval architects all but obtained with stone, a much less yielding material than Perret's concrete. The interior of this impressive church had a profound influence on much twentieth-century architecture. It showed, aside from the new possibilities of concrete construction, how new materials and new ways of designing were not incompatible with a sense of immateriality and the spiritual dimension of life.

After World War Two, Perret was involved in the reconstruction of Le Havre; many visitors find his vision of the city too severe, even if they are usually transfixed by one of his very last designs, the Church of St Joseph, which takes up where Raincy left off.

Schindler House

RUDOLF SCHINDLER, 1923
LOS ANGELES,
CALIFORNIA, USA

RUDOLF SCHINDLER (1887–1953)
left his native Vienna for California
shortly before the outbreak of
World War One. He saw the West
Coast as virgin territory for Modern
architecture, saying "I believe that
climate and character, in company
with a further genuine development
of spatial architecture, will make
Southern California the cradle of a
new form of architectural
expression." This it did and
especially when Schindler built
this remarkable single-storey,
timber-framed house in West
Hollywood. Hidden by a bamboo
screen that sounds like the sea as
it sways in the wind, the house
occupies just about all of its
garden site, with the interior and
exterior blurring into one another.

The house is made up of four
studios, a guest wing and garage.
Doors are sliding screens, light
filters through canvas walls, and
the whole house has an air of
modern informality that is quite
remarkable for its time. The
minimal interiors with their
concrete floors, and elemental
furniture and fittings were to
influence architects and designers
much later in the century. The
rooms interlock with the garden
so that with the screens open it
is difficult to tell where one ends
and the other begins. After
Schindler's death, the house
was lived in by many well-known
artists and writers, including the
musician John Cage and the
architectural historian Charles
Jencks. By the end of the century
it had become a museum and
shrine to this revolutionary and
bohemian architect.

Le Roche–Jeanneret House

LE CORBUSIER AND
PIERRE JEANNERET, 1923
AUTEIL, PARIS, FRANCE

LE CORBUSIER was arguably the century's greatest architect. A profound and original thinker, a brilliant polemicist and equally inspired self-publicist, he tried harder than almost anyone to give a new shape to what he saw as a new age. Like Picasso, he moved through many stylistic phases and the great works of his sixties seem far removed from the radical, yet exquisite white villas of his thirties.

The Le Roche–Jeanneret House established Corbu's early style: a first floor (or *piano nobile*) raised on *pilotis* (free-standing columns), double-height living spaces, internal ramps and roof gardens. Proportioned according to a strict geometry, this modern urban "semi" proved the extent to which classical geometry could give rise to a new architecture free from the corsetting restraints of traditional Beaux-Arts thinking. Not only was the house a "machine for living", to use Le Corbusier's famous phrase, but it was also an expression of his idea of architecture being the "masterly, correct and magnificent play of masses brought together in light."

Le Corbusier was born Charles-Edouard Jeanneret at La Chaux-des-Fonds in Switzerland where he trained as a metal engraver before setting out on a tour of Europe, during which he learned to become an architect partly by sketching and partly by working in the offices of Auguste Perret in Paris and Peter Behrens in Berlin. His pseudonym is a play on an old family name Lecorbesier and the nickname Corbeau (crow) because of his physical and, as he saw it, psychological resemblance to that solitary bird.

Schröder House

GERRIT RIETVELD, 1924
UTRECHT, THE NETHERLANDS

THIS IS A MONDRIAN PAINTING transformed into a house by Gerrit Rietveld (1888–1964), a cabinet-maker and jewellery designer who joined the De Stijl group of artists and architects in 1918, a year after its foundation. Influenced as much by their puritanical Calvinist backgrounds as by radical notions of what art and architecture could be, the members of De Stijl aimed to frame the strict fruits of their imagination within the strictures of the 90-degree angle. So much so, that when you open a window in Rietveld's jewel-like house in Utrecht, it can only be held open at – you guessed – 90 degrees.

The Schröder House is built on a series of frames, based on the cube, which project in and out of the main structure like a sequence of Mondrian canvases grouped tightly together. Despite (or because of) the rigour of the plan and elevations, the house is gloriously light and enjoyable to be in. Inside, sliding partitions can be moved aside to create smaller or larger rooms. The furniture was designed to be all of a piece with the house, while the colour scheme – flat planes of red, white, yellow and blue – was taken directly from Mondrian's restricted palette. Perhaps because the client, Truus Schröder-Schräder, was involved very closely with the design, the house is remarkably practical – a painting for living in. The only low note is that the house is sited on a dreary avenue and tacked uncomfortably on to the end of a row of dull hipped-roof brick houses.

Pavillon de L'Esprit Nouveau

LE CORBUSIER, 1925

PARIS, FRANCE

THE SENSATION of the 1925 Exposition Internationale des Arts Décoratifs et Industriels Modernes, this striking pavilion was intended to represent a typical flat from an apartment block of the future. Le Corbusier had prepared the idea some three years earlier, working in collaboration with the painter Amédée Ozenfant. Together they launched and edited their own magazine, *L'Esprit Nouveau* (1920–25) in which Corbu wrote the essays that made up his famous polemic *Vers une Architecture* of 1923. "We have acquired", wrote Corbu in *L'Esprit Nouveau*, "a taste for clean air and full sunlight ... the house is a machine for living in, bathrooms, sun, hot and cold water, temperatures which can be adjusted as required, food storage, hygiene, beauty in harmonious proportions." Much of this has come to pass, despite the fact that Le Corbusier is still accused of masterminding hideous, low-rent public housing at the end of the century by those who know him only by his mysterious name.

To see the pavilion in 1925 was something quite as shocking as a glimpse of stocking had been ten years earlier. The pavilion was rooted around a mature tree which appeared to grown up through the "roof garden". It boasted a double-height living room complete with sleeping gallery, avant-garde artworks and furnishings. It still looks new 75 years on. Hidden behind a screen for the opening ceremony by the exhibition's organizers for reasons of good taste, the pavilion won the top prize.

Soviet Pavilion

KONSTANTIN MELNIKOV,
1925, PARIS, FRANCE

LESS THAN TEN YEARS on from the design of this pavilion, along with Le Corbusier's the most original at the "Arts Décoratifs" exhibition of 1925, Konstantin Melnikov's (1890–1974) career was effectively at an end. His Constructivist style was rejected by Stalin and his cronies as Social Realism, and an exotic Classicism came to dominate architectural design in the Soviet Union. Until then, Melnikov's own red star had been very much in the ascendant; he was chosen to represent the radical young Communist nation (Lenin had died the year before) at Paris. His design was one of the first built expressions of revolutionary Constructivism and was extremely impressive. The structure was built of timber. What was radical was the plan, a rectangle riven through as if by bolts of lightning in the guise of long, diagonal entrance stairs. These passed under what looked like steel beams crossed liked swords embellished with graphics that drew on the Constructivist revolutionary slogans of the previous eight years.

Although this style of architecture reached a dead end in the Soviet Union, it became a kind of visual folklore among designers seeking forms of radical expression throughout the twentieth century. In fact, it was to enjoy its finest hours in the capitalist West during the 1990s in the work of such architects as Zaha Hadid (p.395) and Daniel Libeskind (p.323).

Café
De Unie

J. J. P. OUD, 1925

ROTTERDAM,

THE NETHERLANDS

JACOBUS JOHANNES PIETER OUD (1890-1963) was made City Architect of Rotterdam when he was just 28. This explains why such a lofty-sounding public servant was engaged in the design of what was the city's most fashionable hang-out, the Café De Unie. Oud's major work was in public housing, at which he excelled. The Café De Unie represented an early phase in his career when he was a part of the De Stijl group and, like Rietveld, attempting to turn what were essentially two-dimensional images into three-dimensional buildings.

The Café De Unie succeeded in part because the interior was very simple, but also because what the café needed to draw attention to itself in a long and regular avenue was a striking façade. The front was much like a giant Mondrian painting. Or, as Oud said himself, "modern architecture will increasingly develop into a process of reduction to positive proportions, comparable to a modern painting." The façade – which is really all that Oud designed himself – was also intended to be a provocation, making no attempt to fit in with the buildings on either side of it. The café was destroyed in 1940, but has since been rebuilt and is just as striking to look at today as it must have been in 1925.

Bauhaus

WALTER GROPIUS, 1926
DESSAU, GERMANY

"THE BAUHAUS", said Walter Gropius
the school's founder-director in its
first prospectus in 1919, "strives to
collect all artistic creativity into a
unity, to reunite all artistic disciplines
– sculpture, painting, design and
handicraft – into a new architecture."
The new architecture came in 1926
when this radical art school moved
from Weimar, where it had fallen
from political favour, to Dessau,
a small provincial German capital.
Here, Gropius and Adolf Meyer
were able to design a building that
expressed their artistic ideals. The
severe yet glamorous concrete and
glass complex comprised workshops
(behind the famous curtain wall),
the City of Dessau Technical School
(on the other side of a road bridge;
the road was never built),
administrative offices and Gropius's
studio (located in the bridge), a
student housing block (complete
with gym) and a canteen and hall
(in a single-storey link between the
students' rooms and the classrooms
and workshops). The building was a
powerful advert for the school
which, hugely influential worldwide,
was always beset by problems,
either academic (what to teach
and how) or political (it was always
seen as leaning too far to the Left).

The school's graduates did much
to spread the Modern Movement
gospel. Gropius resigned in 1928;
the school was closed by the
Nazis in 1933. It has since
reopened and the buildings have
been thoroughly restored.

New
Ways

PETER BEHRENS, 1926

NORTHAMPTON, ENGLAND

BEHRENS WAS 58 YEARS OLD when he designed New Ways for Bassett-Lowke, the man who designed and built model railways that were as popular in Germany as they were in their native England. Behrens was at the height of his powers, successor to Otto Wagner as head of the Vienna Academy of Arts and architect of the magnificent IG-Farben chemical factory in Hochst. His attempt at designing a Modern house was fairly lame and by the standards of, say, Le Corbusier, rather tired. In England though, the Basset-Lowke house appeared to be avant-garde. This was not surprising at a time when Basset-Lowke's contemporaries considered the

Arts and Crafts housing of Letchworth and Hampstead Garden Suburb a little too radical for comfort. Nevertheless, New Ways proved that it was possible to import the new European architecture to England, albeit in a soft-focus guise.

Much like the Steiner House in Vienna by Adolf Loos, it is the rear, or garden elevation, of New Ways that is always shown in the progressive press; the front of the house was less radical still, as it had to make some concessions to its tweedy neighbours. As a bridge to Continental Europe, however, New Ways had a significance beyond the less than stunning impact of its design.

Lovell Beach House

RUDOLF SCHINDLER, 1926

NEWPORT BEACH,

CALIFORNIA, USA

THIS FAMOUS BEACH HOUSE for Dr Lovell was much criticized at the time of its building by young US moderns for being too "tricksy". It was excluded from the seminal International Style exhibition curated by Philip Johnson and Henry Russell Hitchcock held at the Museum of Modern Art, New York, in 1932. In fact the house is as ingenious as it is delightful to live in. Based around a large, double-height living room overlooking the Pacific Ocean, it is raised on five exposed concrete frames. This raises the living accommodation above the beach and the street and provides a covered, open area complete with fireplace for barbecues. The second storey is cantilevered into the double-height living space, providing a balcony, bedrooms and a way of handling space that continues to delight and intrigue today.

Schindler was a loner, and the houses he designed offered a freedom to their owners that was not always appreciated by contemporary critics. In his own house in West Hollywood he liked to sleep on the roof. This was daring in the early 1920s when beach culture was just beginning to be enjoyed by the professional classes. The combination of a complex structure and a plan that offered a way of life that had yet to come into its own made the Lovell Beach House hard to understand for East Coasters and those raised on Victorian mores.

Hook of Holland Housing Estate

J. J. P. OUD, 1927
ROTTERDAM, THE
NETHERLANDS

OUD'S CAREER WAS METEORIC.
Having studied in Amsterdam, Delft
and Munich, he became one of the
founders of the De Stijl movement
in 1917. The next year he became
City Planner for Rotterdam and
designed a series of remarkable
housing estates. Severe, logical and
functional, these low-cost housing
schemes were also elegant and
humane. They have matured well
and survive today.

Perhaps the most approachable
of Oud's three major schemes is the
Hook of Holland housing. The
two-storey buildings run in low
and emphatic horizontals along
the new streets; although the
blocks read as single entities from
a distance, close up each house is
clearly identifiable with its own
separate entrance and walled
garden. The two main blocks are
characterized by rounded ends that
provide accommodation for small
shops. What Oud showed in this
exemplary scheme is that the new
style of mass housing could be
rigorous and yet realized on a
notably humane scale. The houses
face on to conventional streets and
are easy to identify, unlike those of
later Modern housing estates. Oud
went on to build much-praised
show housing in the Weissenhof
district of Stuttgart (1927), but
thereafter appears to have slowed
down and almost disappeared from
practice. He turned down the chair
of architecture at Harvard
University, having left his official
post in Rotterdam in 1933, and
built little for the rest of his life,
with the major exception of the
rather formal and heavy-handed
Shell Building, The Hague (1942).

Rue Mallet-Stevens Housing

ROBERT MALLET-STEVENS,
1927, PASSY, PARIS, FRANCE

THE GRAND RUE Mallet-Stevens is a bravura expression of Cubism applied to architecture, although its blocky concrete houses and apartments have often been labelled Moderne, a faintly patronising tag suggesting whimsy rather than substance, rigour or Modern. This Paris street remains a surprise: it is all of a piece and a rare example of Art Deco urban planning.

Mallet-Stevens (1886–1945) studied and later taught at the Ecole Spéciale d'Architecture in Paris. With Pierre Chareau, he founded the Union des Artistes Modernes. Much influenced by Josef Hoffmann and Charles Rennie Mackintosh, his architecture was almost backwards looking by the late 1920s when Le Corbusier was coming into his own with a radical approach to the design of the home. Unlike Le Corbusier's, the plans of Mallet-Stevens nominally Modern houses and apartments were traditional. Nevertheless, Rue Mallet-Stevens stands out as a memorable and convincing composition. In the event, it was a short-lived cul-de-sac in the history of architecture. Cubism, a form of painting devised by Georges Braque and Pablo Picasso between 1905 and 1910, aimed at depicting a sense of three-dimensional space without the use of perspective. It was a difficult concept to translate into architecture; Mallet-Stevens and his Czech contemporaries adapted the style mostly in terms of surface appearance.

Weissenhofsiedlung

LUDWIG MIES VAN DER ROHE
(DIRECTOR), 1927
STUTTGART, GERMANY

THE CREATION of the Weissenhof housing estate on the edge of Stuttgart, under the direction of Mies van der Rohe (1888–1969) was a significant achievement. Here, for the first time, Modern Movement architects were able to plan a part of a city on new lines and attempt to prove that it was possible to build beautiful, airy,

functional, low-cost urban housing for those on low incomes. The cast of designers involved in the project included Le Corbusier (with Pierre Jeanneret), Walter Gropius, J. J. P. Oud, Peter Behrens and Hans Scharoun. Although each architect had a recognizable approach of his own, this arrangement of simple white houses and apartment blocks had a unity of design: the young turks of the Modern Movement could clearly work together.

The exhibition was sponsored by the Deutscher Werkbund and left a legacy of what were to have been 21 permanent houses – some since much changed, others

demolished – and Mies van der Rohe's impressive apartment block, a design that was to set the tone for much European and US housing in subsequent years.

The Weissenhofsiedlung gave ordinary Germans an opportunity to see what a Modern city might be like. However, when the Nazis were voted into power six years later such light and airy Modern housing went by the board. When Modern housing made its reappearance in Germany after 1945, it was never able to be quite so delicate and idealistic. Its lessons had still to be learned at the end of the century.

Schocken Department Store

ERICH MENDELSOHN, 1928

STUTTGART, GERMANY

AFTER THE DESIGN of the sensational Einstein Tower (p.83), Mendelsohn was heavily involved in the design of factories and private houses in various parts of Germany. Yet, it was the design of a department store for Schocken that pushed his style further towards a convincing fusion of Expressionism and Modernism. The Stuttgart store was rooted around a central courtyard in the city centre. The two dominant façades, one to the main street the other following the drop of a steep side street, were linked by a striking stair tower cantilevered from the main body of the building and striated with steel bands to give an impression of exaggerated height as well as the intensity of a compressed spring. Mendelsohn also imbued this energetic building with further drama by designing vast letters spelling out the name of the store. Finally, the magnificent theatricality of the Schocken store was set brilliantly against the grand and fussy nineteenth-century buildings without undermining their stately presence.

Mendelsohn had the ability of introducing radical architecture into city centres without undermining their character or integrity, and – quite the reverse – of raising their sights and souls. All this with a department store. It was demolished in 1960.

Bata Shoe Shop

LUDVIK KYSELA, 1928

PRAGUE, CZECH REPUBLIC

IN THE 1920s Czechoslovakia was noted for its highly accomplished and progressive architecture. The Bata shoe shop by Ludvik Kysela (1883-1960) looked up-to-the-minute sixty years after it was built as it was ahead of the clock in 1928. Essentially it is a simple building of the sort that became almost routine in European cities over the next three-quarters of a century; at the time it must have been a revelation. Its very clarity is what made it special both in the 1920s and at the end of the century. This clarity is achieved by facing the seven-floor concrete structure with a wall of what is as far as possible sheer glass, offset by minimal bands of white opaque glass. As evening falls, the building lights up in contrasting layers of clear and milky tungsten and fluorescent. The building was designed for the Bata shoe company, which was to open shops in many parts of Europe selling cheap but decent footwear. The company had its own design and architecture department with whom Kysela worked closely.

The Bata shop has become an icon of Modern design, its clarity and more than bearable lightness of being a rebuke to the formal excesses of late-flowering Modernism and the excrescences of what generally passed for Postmodernism. This, then, is a good example of a simple building that acted as a benchmark for design that came after.

Zuyev
Club

I. A. GOLOSOV, 1928

MOSCOW, RUSSIA

THE ORIGINAL SKETCHES of this
Moscow club were by Konstantin
Melnikov who proposed a
building composed of five glass
cylinders. The design was handed
over to I. A. Golosov (1883–1945)
who retained just one glass
cylinder. Even so, this has a
dramatic impact on Lesnaya
Street at it thrusts up from
the pavement through the
rectangular bulk of the
building. The plan of the club
is directed at all points to this
distinctive corner tower.

This was one of several large
factory clubs built in Moscow in
the 1920s. Apart from the social
function they performed, their
designs encompassed the stylistic
battles Soviet architects fought in
that difficult decade as the early
ideals of the October Revolution
gave way to Stalin's Terror.
Revolutionary architects fell
out with one another as they
struggled between the more
rational designs of
"Constructivists" like Vesnin
and Ginzberg, and the more
expressive or flamboyant work
of (to make matters complicated)
the so-called "Rationalists"
including Melnikov and Golosov.
The battles were effectively ended
by Stalin's adherence to a Soviet
Classicism from about 1935.
Golosov's other notable designs
(none built) included those for
the Palace of Labour (1923) and
the Palace of Soviets (1934).

Silver End
Housing Estate

THOMAS TAIT, 1928

CHELMSFORD, ESSEX,

ENGLAND

THIS WAS A VERY ENGLISH
introduction to Modern architecture.
Tait's houses look Modern at
first glance, but are in fact rather
conventional brick suburban villas
treated to a hint of European
Modernism with flat roofs, horizontal

windows and a lick of white paint.
Nevertheless they were a beginning.
The estate was commissioned by
the Crittall window company, which
established itself in the 1920s with
steel window frames that were
designed to match the aspirations
and needs of contemporary architects.
Silver End was designed as a model
estate for Crittall's employees. The
inhabitants were to act as guinea-
pigs to see how the new windows
coped with damp and deleterious
English weather over time

The houses are laid out on

Garden City lines, in picturesque
rather than formal groups. Most
are built of brick and painted
white. Their plans are conventional.
Nevertheless, Silver End proved that
it was possible to drip feed new
ideas from continental Europe into
Britain, although the bulk of private
housing built in Britain throughout
the rest of the century tended to
be in faux historic styles such as
Georgian and Tudor. Silver End
continues to be well looked after
and Tait's quixotic would-be Modern
houses have stood the test of time.

German Pavilion

LUDWIG MIES VAN DER ROHE,

1929

BARCELONA, SPAIN

LIKE LE CORBUSIER, another twentieth-century giant, Ludwig Mies van der Rohe had no formal architectural training. Born the son of a mason and stone-carver in Aachen, Mies was to bring Neoclassical architecture bang up to date with what appeared to be a seamless sequence of cool, masterful and – for the most part –

beautifully crafted buildings in Europe and the United States. The first of these was the hugely influential German Pavilion designed for the International Exhibition at Barcelona. Mies had built and designed much before, yet the Pavilion was the first of his temple-like structures and very much a symbol of the new European architecture.

Restored to its original state, the Pavilion is disarmingly simple. It comprises a concrete slab (the roof) supported by slim, cross-shaped and chrome-plated steel columns. Underneath the slab and between the column, Mies has slid flat

planes of glass and polished travertine; the panels both enclose and expose the space beneath the roof. Sunlight reflects off the Pavilion's twin pools and dapples from the glass and travertine panels of onyx and marble. Although there is nothing but space inside the Pavilion, it feels deeply luxurious. Mies provided a few of his new and soon-to-be famous Barcelona chairs inside for rest and contemplation. "Along this path", said Mies, "industry and technology will join forces with the forces of thought and culture". And, who, cooling off inside this Pavilion on a sunny day, would dare to disagree?

Seaside House E.1027

EILEEN GRAY AND
JEAN BADOVICI, 1929
ROQUEBRUNE-CAP MARTIN,
FRANCE

EILEEN GRAY (1878–1976) was born into a landed Irish family, but rather than doing the right things by her family – marrying a decent chap, breeding and ordering servants about – she went to Paris and became a successful, if unsung, designer. From the mid-1920s she produced furniture, lamps, rugs and mirrors that have become classics of twentieth-century design. Although not an architect, she also designed this summer house for herself and her lover Jean Badovici: together they were "E.1027", their initials translated into numerals. Standing on stilts and overlooking a beautifully shaped bay, the house was much admired by Le Corbusier, who stayed here frequently, and drowned in the sea nearby in 1965. Inside, the house was designed as a Modern *gesamtkunstwerk*, although Gray herself was always a free spirit and never aligned herself with an artistic or architectural movement. Her designs were made from costly materials and so her clients had to be wealthy. This is something of a shame, as in the two houses she designed, Gray displayed a warmth and grace that was all too often lacking in Modern Movement mass housing. E.1027 boasts many details that, for Gray, were no more than common sense, but which seemed new to visiting architects who were rarely as practical as their manifestoes liked to claim. Her furniture later achieved "classic" status.

Le Marbeauf Showroom

ALBERT LAPRADE AND

L. E. BAZIN, 1929

PARIS, FRANCE

CONTEMPORARY PHOTOGRAPHS of this extraordinary Citroën car showroom never fail to delight. Perhaps this is because the brand new cars with their vertical radiators, headlamps on stalks, voluptuous wings and exposed running boards seem so much older than the glass-fronted building. Laprade and Bazin stacked the cars on a sequence of cantilevered concrete galleries overlooking a six-storey void (or atrium) faced with sheet glass from floor to ceiling. A door on the other side of the great window allowed motorists buying a car to drive in to the garage at the back of the showroom in their old car through one door and to drive out in a spanking new model through the other. Cars and Modern architecture had been closely connected by Le Corbusier in his hugely influential work *Vers une Architecture* (1923) and photographers like Frank Yerbury, who made the Marbeauf Showroom world-famous with his striking glass-plate images, played up this relationship between the fruits of the machine age and the new architecture that served them. Sadly, the showroom has long gone, which is a shame because it would have been fashionable again by the end of the century and perfect for the display of modern cars.

Melnikov House

KONSTANTIN MELNIKOV,
1929, MOSCOW, RUSSIA

THIS WAS THE ONLY PRIVATE HOUSE built in Moscow during the Soviet era. The authorities were so taken with Melnikov's extraordinary design that they even bailed him out when he ran out of money during construction. The house comprises two intersecting cylinders, one taller than the other. The cylinder facing the street, close to Arbatskaya Metro station,

is faced with a wall of glass topped with a roof terrace; the second cylinder contains the architect's studio and bedroom, designed rather mysteriously as a "sonata for sleep". These remarkable rooms are 5 metres (16 ft) high and lit by beehive-like hexagonal windows. These are not randomly placed but are a part of the complex geometry of the structure of the house, based on 200 hexagonal "modules", 140 of which are infilled with brick and 60 of which are windows. You could try drawing the grid for yourself, but it might tie your brain in knots.

Melnikov filled the house with ingenious gadgetry, including speaking tubes, a waste-disposal system and sliding doors that served two openings. The house was partly restored in 1990–91 and at the end of the century was still lived in by Melnikov's son. Although decidedly eccentric and not a house that every family would find easy to live in, the Melnikov house was a brave attempt to rethink domesticity and the architecture that frames it. That it has survived intact and longer than the USSR is a fact more remarkable than the design itself.

Schocken
Department Store

ERICH MENDELSOHN, 1929

CHEMNITZ, GERMANY

CHEMNITZ WAS TO BECOME Karl
Marx Stadt when Germany was
split in two in the 1950s and this
Prussian city found itself under
Communist rule. Of all the buildings
that best expressed the values of
capitalism and the consumer
society, Mendelsohn's Schocken
store in Chemnitz was surely the
most impressive. Completed in time

for the Wall Street Crash and
Weimar Germany's fall into
Nazidom, it was the most brilliant
streamlined building in Europe,
fusing Modern razzmatazz with
the rigours of German Modernism.

The manner in which the clean
bands of the street front sweep
round in a smooth and uninterrupted
curve is quite breathtaking. The
top three floors were zoned back
to meet local planning regulations;
this gave the store the feel of a
great modern ocean liner at
berth in the city centre. This was
appropriate, as Le Corbusier had

been championing the ocean liner
in his writing (notably in *Vers une
Architecture,* 1923): the liner was
the Parthenon of Modern times.
The Shocken store also demonstrated
how effective Modern architecture
could be at night, with its elongated
bands of glazing lit up and giving
the street an energy appropriate for
the speed and (perhaps spurious)
glamour of the motor age. The
store was badly damaged by Allied
bombing during World War Two.
It has long proved that the most
striking Modern building has its
place in city centres.

Lovell House

THIS IS ONE OF THE CENTURY'S most glamorous and desirable houses. What Dr Philip Lovell, the client, described as a "demonstration health house" was designed by Richard Neutra (1892–1970) and built on a steep hillside with magnificent views. From the street the house appears to be single-storey; appearances can certainly be deceptive, for once inside it drops several storeys down the hillside, its breathtaking balconies held in place by a lightweight steel frame that was erected in just 40 hours. As well as a house for Lovell, the Neutra building was also an experimental open-air school. This was the era of sun-worship and the new clean, white, open architecture. If it looks more German than 1920s Californian, this is because Neutra was an Austrian who trained with Adolf Loos in Vienna and then worked with Erich Mendelsohn in Berlin. He moved to the USA in 1923 and worked with Frank Lloyd Wright, and from 1925 with his fellow Austrian Rudolf Schindler in Los Angeles.

The Lovell House was proof that standardized factory components could be used to create radical and beautiful homes. The design makes extensive use of identically sized glass and concrete panels. Its interior is fitted out to a very high standard. Always a star, the house played a leading role in the Hollywood movie *LA Confidential* in 1997.

Wittgenstein House

PAUL ENGELMAN AND
LUDWIG WITTGENSTEIN,
1929, VIENNA, AUSTRIA

"WHEREOF WE CANNOT SPEAK,
thereof we must be silent." This
is the famous conclusion of the
Tractacus Logico-Philosophicus
(1921) by Ludwig Wittgenstein
(1889–1951), a classmate of Adolf
Hitler's and one of the greatest, if
most misunderstood, philosophers
of all time. Having published the
Tractacus and decided that it solved
all problems of philosophy,
Wittgenstein abandoned the
subject, broke down, and became
a teacher in an Austrian backwater.
In 1929, his sister Margarethe
Stonborough–Wittgenstein wooed
him back to his native Vienna with
a promise of work with her architect
Paul Engelman (1891–1965) on the
design of her new house. Engelman
had been a student of Adolf Loos
(p.129) and this is evident in the
look of this severe, geometrical
structure. The Modern exterior
belies the bourgeois interior: the
Wittgensteins were a very grand
and wealthy family and Margarethe
enjoyed entertaining. Her brother's
contribution was to refine and
re-refine the proportions of the
rooms – he had a new ceiling torn
down because it was a millimetre
or two out as far as his piercing
eye saw it –and in the loving
engineering-based details that give
the house its unbalanced character,
at once puritanical and hedonistic.

Wittgenstein trained as an
engineer before turning to
mathematics and philosophy.
Working on this house caused
him to return to the latter. He
was always fascinated with
architecture, but once the house
was complete, remained all but
silent on the subject.

Siemenstadt Housing

WALTER GROPIUS, 1930

BERLIN, GERMANY

THE TWO APARTMENT BLOCKS, one four-, the other five-storey, Walter Gropius designed for this factory estate were to be repeated in one form or the other across the world in the ensuing 60 years. This is what Modern apartment blocks tend to look like. The idea behind them was essentially humanitarian. While working and teaching at the Bauhaus, which he left in 1928, Gropius was exercised with the question of how to rehouse industrial workers in modern homes that could be built in city centres at the same density as traditional urban housing yet with a maximum of sunlight and air. When Siemens asked him to plan and supervise the design and construction of their new factory estate in Berlin, he had his opportunity to solve the problem.

Sited on parkland lawns, Gropius's pure white blocks packed a great density of housing into clean-cut blocks aligned on a north–south axis to benefit from as much daylight as possible. Each landing gave access to just two flats to rid the plan of corridors and to give residents a sense of having a private entrance of a sort. The whiteness of the blocks and their rather antiseptic quality was perhaps a statement of intent by the architect: those who toiled in industrial factories came home to escape fumes and dirt and to clean themselves mentally and physically in preparation for the next day's toil.

Hilversum Town Hall

WILLEM MARINUS DUDOK,
1930, HILVERSUM, THE
NETHERLANDS

INFLUENCED TO AN EXTENT by
Frank Lloyd Wright and the Amsterdam
School, Dudok (1884–1974) was a
military engineer turned architect
who developed a complete, bricky
and monumental style of his own.
Whether designing a school, public
baths or town hall, he approached
the brief with a surety of form that
he was never to stray from. Hilversum
Town Hall is the grandest and most
evolved of Dudok's heroic essays in
powerful and unrelieved brick verticals
and horizontals. It has the curious
quality of appearing to be a cathedral,
a factory and a crematorium all at
once. There is nothing likeable here,
yet the effect is deeply impressive
and the rigour with which the
building is carried through – both
in terms of plan and in the quality
of construction – exemplary.

Dudok was born in Amsterdam,
trained at the Royal Military Academy,
Breda and became director of
municipal works at Hilversum
(1915–27) and municipal architect
then on. His work was to influence
Charles Holden, the British architect,
who softened the Dutch master's
monumentality in such designs as
Arnos Grove Station (p.48) on the
London Underground. The style was
then used for municipal works in
Britain, and the influence of Hilversum
can also be seen in Sir Giles Gilbert
Scott's transformation of Bankside
Power Station, Southwark, London
into a grand, if unlovable, civic temple.

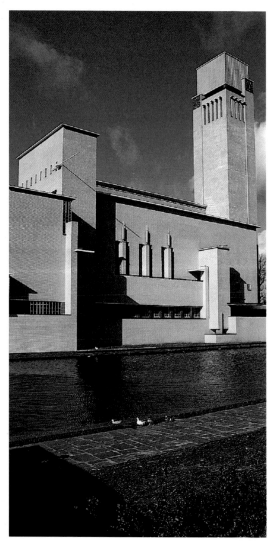

Villa Savoye

LE CORBUSIER, 1931

POISSY, FRANCE

"THROUGH THE BALCONY-LIKE projection of the floor over the *pilotis*, the entire façade is extended beyond the building skeleton. It thereby loses its loadbearing character ... and thus has freedom of composition." The Villa Savoye marks the climax of a sequence of perfect, white, freestanding villas Le Corbusier built on the suburban fringe of Paris from 1922. The Villa Savoye is at once the most delicate and ethereal and as magical and as satisfying as the best of Palladio's villas of the sixteenth century.

Appearing to have landed on stilts as if from outer space, the Villa Savoye offered a truly revolutionary way of living. Visitors arriving by car from Paris parked out of sight in a garage reached between *pilotis* (stilts or columns). They entered the house though a glass box beneath the main floor, washed at a prominently located basin and then climbed by ramp or stair to the main living floor. The miracle of this is that what was outdoors and what was indoors was unclear: the villa is a homage to light and air as well as to a complex geometry and plan that can be quite baffling on first encounter of even the closest kind. The roof is a terrace for sunbathing.

This special house was left for many years to run to seed. However, it has since been restored and is open to the public.

Royal Corinthian Yacht Club

JOSEPH EMBERTON, 1931,
BURNHAM-ON-CROUCH,
ESSEX, ENGLAND

THE ESSEX TOWN OF Burnham-on-Crouch is not the sort of town in which anyone would expect to encounter modern architecture of any distinction, if at all. Yet, the Royal Corinthian Yacht Club still goes about its comfortable work in this east coast English town with great distinction.

Designed by Joseph Emberton (1889–1956), it was one of the first Modern buildings of any noteworthy scale in Britain. Emberton himself designed in a number of fashionable styles and cannot be considered a dedicated Modernist along the lines of his Dutch, French, German and Austrian contemporaries. The Yacht Club is not even as Modern as it first appears: it is built largely of brick in the English way, although a certain degree of steel in the construction allowed for its distinctive cantilevered balconies. From an English point of view in 1931, a building might look Modern if its setting warranted it. As Emberton's design was clearly "nautical" in spirit, it was quite acceptable and even to be welcomed. Elsewhere, such a clear, open and elegant building would have been frowned upon.

It is significant that when the building won an award soon after its completion, this was given in view of its nautical character and not because of its modernity.

Bijenkorf Department Store

WILLEM DUDOK, 1931

ROTTERDAM,

THE NETHERLANDS

SADLY, THIS FORCEFUL BUILDING was badly damaged in a bombing raid in 1940 and demolished when Rotterdam was rebuilt after World War Two. The loss is particularly poignant as Rotterdam is, from a strictly architectural and urbanistic point of view, now one of the most Modern cities in the world. Dudok's Bijenkorf Store was the most overtly Modern of his creations. The design is based on the idea of a store being made up of a number of street markets superimposed on one another and enclosed in glass. These highly glazed markets expressed as relentless horizontal elements are brought together at the vertical, slab-sided entrance tower. At one and the same time, each separate element of the store is clearly expressed in the transparent architecture, and they are joined by the horizontal bands held in check by the tower. Thus, the design had immense visual strength, combining a sense of freedom of plan within a powerful, if abstract, order. Even if you have little interest in shopping, this is one of those stores you would want to visit time and again just to watch the play of light on its façades and to see that wonderful abstract clock marking the hours. Soon after the store's completion, Dudok moved to The Hague where he became the Town Planner.

Trade Union House

MAX TAUT, 1931

FRANKFURT-AM-MAIN,

GERMANY

MAX TAUT (1884–1967) was
highly influenced by the reaction
to Impressionism referred to as
Neue Sachlichkeit (New Objectivity),
a label that was coined by the art
critic G. F. Hartlaub in 1924. What
did a *Neue Sachlichkeit* architecture
do to counteract Impressionism?
Build in the clearest cut way with
powerfully expressed concrete
frames, that's what. This was Taut's
– who saw Impressionism as soft,
woolly and unfocused – new
objectivity, and it is seen at its
most extreme and convincing in
the design of the Trade Union
House in Frankfurt.

A highly controlled and rational
structure, the Trade Union House
is composed of identical
symmetrical elements and forms a
very determined picture of German
logic. The building made its mark
right up until the end of the
twentieth century: countless
office buildings were designed
along the same severe lines.

Although strict, the Trade
Union House is not without its
poetry. As for Taut, he was
effectively banned from
architectural practice throughout
the Hitler years. At the end of
World War Two he returned
to prominence as one of the most
important teachers of the time;
he was based at the Hochschule
für Bildende Künste in West Berlin
between 1945 and 1954.

Daily Express Building

ELLIS CLARKE, RONALD
ATKINSON, OWEN WILLIAMS,
1932, FLEET STREET,
LONDON, ENGLAND

BRITAIN'S NATIONAL NEWSPAPERS
abandoned Fleet Street, their
traditional home, at the end of the
1980s as new technology enabled
them to separate journalists from
printers. In 1989, the *Daily Express*
deserted this glorious Art Deco
headquarters, an unforgettable
words-factory, with one of London's
most famous, popular and dazzling
interiors. The main body of this
concrete-framed, glass-wrapped
building was designed by the
engineer Owen Williams (1890–1969).
For what is essentially a factory,
the building is very glamorous.
Sited in one of the City of
London's busiest streets and in the
shadow of the dome of St Paul's
Cathedral, perhaps it had to be.
The distinctive black glass façade
gave it its popular, if satirical,
nickname – the "Black Lubianka".

The entrance hall, designed by
Ronald Atkinson, is like a still from
a Busby Berkeley extravaganza. The
approach to the Hollywood stair is
based on the entrance to Cleopatra's
tomb, complete with chrome-plated
snake handrails. Electric light dances
from steel stalactites hanging from
the cha-cha-cha ceiling. Ritzy metal
relief sculptures depict jingoistic scenes
of imperial enterprise. The total effect
of the building is one of immense
verve, reflecting the confidence of
newspapers at the very height of
their success in the 1930s.

Maison de Verre

PIERRE CHAREAU AND
BERNARD BIJVOET, 1932
PARIS, FRANCE

THE MAISON DE VERRE is no lie:
aside from its filigree steel frame,
it is built almost entirely from glass
and is one of the most
extraordinary houses of the century.
Hidden from view in a courtyard, it
is an outgrowth of an old house
and capped by its top floor – the
old lady who lived here refused to

move and so the Maison de Verre
was unable to grow to its full
height. Even so, it is a thing of
light and grace and the
imagination, perhaps the most
perfectly realized *machine à habiter*.
It was designed by Pierre Chareau
(1883–1950) and Bernard Bijvoet
(1889–1979) for Dr Dalsace, an
eminent Parisian gynaecologist and
was meant to represent the notions
and virtues of hygiene and medical
efficiency. Despite this, it is also
very beautiful.

The most impressive part of the
house is the spacious, double-height
living room, which boasts floor to

ceiling windows, exposed steel
columns and a gallery. This style of
"loft living" took another 50 years
to become popular among middle-
class professionals, and, even then,
few have created such a radical and
liveable home from this very open
arrangement of space and from the
unabashed use of industrial materials.
The glass bricks that Chareau made
such extensive use of were brand
new in 1932. Chareau emigrated
to the United States in 1940
where he was to build a second
special house, this time for the
painter Robert Motherwell at
East Hampton, Long Island.

Boots Factory

OWEN WILLIAMS, 1932

BEESTON, NOTTINGHAM,
ENGLAND

OWEN WILLIAMS, the structural engineer, designed this great factory at a time when few architects could have managed the brief with such confidence. Boots the Chemists was and is a hugely successful high-street chemist. At the beginning of the 1930s, the company decided to pull its manufacturing and distribution arms into one building on the edge of Nottingham. Williams came up trumps with a spectacular and airy design based on a widely spaced forest of mushroom-headed concrete columns. The building is arranged on four storeys, with galleries penetrating the floors at frequent intervals. The result is one of the sunniest factories of its time and a building of great and simple logic that, more than 65 years on from its completion, is still serving its original purpose extremely well.

Owen was educated at London University and worked in railway and aircraft design before moving on to architecture. After Beeston he designed the swimming pool at Wembley Stadium (1933), a pioneering Health Centre in Peckham (1936) and the Synagogue at Dollis Hill (1938). Until the arrival of the Danish engineer, Ove Arup, in the early 1930s, Williams was perhaps the only British-based engineer who understood intuitively the relationship between the forms of Modern architecture and the possibilities of new structural techniques.

New Farm

AMYAS CONNELL AND
BASIL WARD, 1932
HASLEMERE,
SURREY, ENGLAND

THE MODERN HOUSE came to
Britain much later than elsewhere
in Continental Europe. This was due
as much to Britain's island mentality
and endemic nostalgia as it was for
a lack of architects with new ideas.
New Farm, by Amyas Connell
(1901-1980) and Basil Ward (1902-

1976) was a brave stab at
Constructivist design in rural Surrey,
a gentle English landscape better
known for its houses by Lutyens
and gardens by Jekyll than for
cutting-edge Continental design.

New Farm is characterized by
the severe planes of its thin
concrete walls and by its glazed
stair-tower. When completed, the
house was photographed for the
Architectural Review as part of this
influential magazine's late coming
to the Modern Movement. When
the glass plate negatives arrived,
the editors – then under the
inspired direction of Hubert de

Cronin Hastings (1902–84) – were
disappointed by the patchy quality
of the concrete walls. They had
their art editor paint them white
on the glass plates so that, when
published, they gleamed smooth
and whiter than white. This was
proof that the Modern Movement
was as much a tool of propaganda
as it was a new way of designing,
building and living. Since then,
New Farm has settled happily
into life in a most English country
garden. Most recently it has been
bought by a car designer and his
family who wish to rescue it from
65 years of Surrey sleep.

Paimio
Sanatorium

ALVAR AALTO, 1933

PAIMIO, FINLAND

ALVAR AALTO (1898–1976) is one of
the greats of twentieth-century
architecture. His ability to reconcile
natural forms with machine-age
design remained pretty much
unchallenged at the end of the
century. He got off to a flying
start, working on the design of this
pristine sanatorium in the remote
forests of southwest Finland when
he was just 30. The building
expressed the hopes of more than
50 local Finnish communities who
paid for its design and
construction. What they got for
their money, and confidence in a
brilliant young architect, was a
model hospital, the plan of which
– and to an extent its style – has
been copied around the world ever
since its completion. The slim and
elegant buildings comprise separate
accommodation for patients and
staff. The former occupy the
famously photographed block that
ends with ship-like balconies
projecting out into the forest
landscape. Patients' rooms are
awash with daylight for as much of
the year as possible and, although
simple throughout, the building is
beautifully detailed. It is built
of concrete and painted white.

Throughout its design,
Aalto worked closely with the
sanatorium's doctors. The result
is a very successful building both
formally and functionally. It is
still very much in use at the start
of the twenty-first century with
the spectre of tuberculosis
haunting Europe afresh.

Isokon Flats

WELLS COATES, 1934

LAWN ROAD, HAMPSTEAD,
LONDON, ENGLAND

ALTHOUGH RATHER UNGRACEFUL, the Isokon Flats (named after the furniture factory of Jack Pritchard, the model Modern client who commissioned them) are important as the first of a type of residential building that never quite got going and yet could be successful again in the twenty-first century. The "existenzminium" flats grouped here on four floors and giving on to heavily defined exterior galleries, were designed for a new generation of highly mobile intellectuals and artists. People would come and go on short leases when they needed to be in London and to walk and talk on Hampstead Heath.

The idea had its roots in the Swiss Pavilion, Paris (Le Corbusier, 1930) and the Narkomfin flats, Moscow (Moisei Ginzburg, 1929). The block boasted a club room and bar designed by the Bauhaus architect Marcel Breuer. Its architect was the flamboyant Wells Coates (1895–1958), born in Tokyo, raised in Vancouver and who worked for several years as a journalist for the London *Daily Express* before turning to architecture and design. Coates was, perhaps, to become better known in the public eye as a designer of what were, for their time, very successful wireless (radio) sets rather than buildings. Nevertheless, the Isokon Flats were a notable attempt to establish a new way of life beyond the confines of the standard city flat and the English suburban semi. Neglected for many years, the Isokon Flats were restored at the end of the century.

Penguin Pool

BERTHOLD LUBETKIN AND
TECTON, 1934
REGENT'S PARK ZOO,
LONDON, ENGLAND

LUBETKIN (1901–90) was a Russian émigré who came to London via the October Revolution of 1917. Feisty, mercurial, charming and a great storyteller, he soon made his mark with the English intellectual elite. One of his earliest commissions was from the Director of London Zoo. A penguin pool might sound a very modest proposition, but in Lubtekin's hands it became one of the iconic architectural designs of the 1930s. Working with the brilliant Danish engineer, Ove Arup, Lubetkin shaped the pool around a balletic spiralling of concrete ramps above the blue pool. The penguins seemed happy and this romantic, rational, structure continues to serve its original purpose, delighting both visitors and penguins. It was restored by Lubetkin and Avanti Architects in 1985. Lubetkin went on to design other animal pavilions at Regent's Park and Whipsnade Zoos as well as some of the best accommodation for the human zoo in Highgate and the old London Borough of Finsbury. A lifelong Communist, he gave up architecture in the 1950s over a row over the design of Peterlee, a New Town for miners, and retired to become a pig farmer. He was chivvied from his lair by fans in the 1980s and awarded the Royal Gold Medal for Architecture duly, if late in the day.

Highpoint 1

AFTER WORKING BRIEFLY with Jean Ginsburg in Paris (1927–30), Lubetkin came to London and established Tecton, the cooperative practice he effectively dominated. Tecton's first major venture into housing was Highpoint 1, a block of 64 flats set on eight floors of a gleaming white, double-cruciform tower on Highgate Ridge. From this suburban eyrie, residents commanded the sort of views Le Corbusier had dreamed of in his plans for ideal modern cities in which professional people would live in airy, gracious flats each with a balcony and magnificent views and set above urban parkland. Highpoint 1 comes pretty close to fulfilling Corbusier's dream. In fact, the legendary French architect came to visit when the flats were new and gave them his approval. The design was originally considerably more substantial than the block that was built. Before the concrete was poured, Lubetkin had met up with Ove Arup, the émigré Danish engineer, who showed him how Highpoint did not need a substantial concrete frame: the walls could be designed to carry their own weight.

The block became home to many famous figures in the Modern Movement, not least the landscape gardener, Geoffrey Jellicoe, who lived here until his death in 1995. Looking out from his apartment across miles of wooded landscape, Jellicoe said he didn't need a garden of his own.

Hoover Building

WALLIS, GILBERT AND
PARTNERS, 1935, PERIVALE,
LONDON, ENGLAND

THE GERMAN ÉMIGRÉ historian Nikolaus Pevsner described this Art Deco palace of labour as "perhaps the most offensive of the modernistic atrocities along this road [Western Avenue] of typical by-pass factories." That was nearly 40 years ago; tastes have changed. In a later history of London architecture, Edward Jones and Christopher Woodward describe the Hoover Factory as "a serious attempt to dignify the workplace". And indeed it was.

The Hoover Factory survived several threats of demolition in the 1970s and 1980s; it is now a Tesco superstore. Hoover is the world-famous maker of vacuum cleaners and other household appliances; in London, its workers were treated to a splendid cinematic entrance, a bright and breezy top floor canteen (its design adopted by the Van Nelle Factory, Rotterdam, p.333), and a Modern cornucopia of architectural details drawn from such diverse sources as Mendelsohn's Einstein Tower at Potsdam, Hoffman's Palais Stoclet in Brussels and Mackintosh's Glasgow School of Art. Whatever, the building has become a favourite London landmark over the years, celebrated in song by Elvis Costello and a happy distraction from the horrendous traffic jams that build up morning and evening on this main western exit from the city. Even the great Professor Doctor Pevsner could be wrong.

De La Warr Pavilion

THIS DELIGHTFUL SEASIDE pleasure palace was designed by Erich Mendelsohn, after he left Nazi Germany and before he went to Palestine, and Serge Chermayeff (born 1900), the Russian-born, Harrow-educated dancer and window dresser, who graduated to architecture in time to work for three years with his famous Prussian partner. Mendelsohn and Chermayeff won an open competition to design the pavilion, their prize £150. They were immediately attacked by members of the British architectural profession in a display of vicious chauvinism and anti-semitism that encouraged Mendelsohn to move from what he imagined to be the liberal sanctuary of Great Britain, home of fair play and decency.

The De La Warr Pavilion is both fair and decent, a design of great clarity and a building of lightness and delight. It faces the sea in a swirl of stairs, walls of glass and shining white concrete. It contains and frames a sun-lounge restaurant, library and an auditorium that was to have a major influence on the design of the Royal Festival Hall, London (1951). The pavilion is all the more surprising for being set, on its roadside, against a decidedly unquiet sea of harsh red brick and brittle terracotta Victorian apartment blocks. In fact, it is quite remarkable to find such a distinguished Modern building in this south coast gerontocracy. Yet, it is much loved by local people, and in the latter part of the 1990s was the subject of an extensive restoration by the architects Troughton McAslan.

Casa del Fascio

GIUSEPPE TERRAGNI, 1936
COMO, ITALY

A BREATHTAKING BUILDING.
Giuseppe Terragni (1904–41) was
just 28 when he was commissioned
to design this meeting hall and
local headquarters for Benito
Mussolini's Fascist Party in the
lakeside town of Como. He had
already designed a superb block
of pristine white flats elsewhere in
Como (Novocomum, 1928), but this
still owed something to the Russian

Constructivism the young Terragni
abandoned as he discovered, in the
design of the Casa del Fascio, a
remarkably effective and compelling
middle way between Classical and
Cubist architecture. The result is
a building that, if not timeless,
has the qualities of a de Chirico
townscape brought to haunting
life. The building, which faces
Como's cathedral across a
sun-bleached piazza, is a
travertine-clad, concrete-framed
box: the centre is a floor to ceiling
glass courtyard entered from the
cathedral side through an
impressive parade of 16 glass

doors. Each side of the building,
however, is arranged differently, the
concrete frame exposed or closed
in a complex play of geometry.
Here the building appears to be
impermeable; there, it is possible to
see into its core. This is a game the
architecture enthusiast can never
tire of. Yet, the building is also icily
calm and dignified. It has a very
special presence and is surely one
of the century's top ten buildings.

Since the fall of Mussolini in
1943, it has been the Casa del
Populo, but although open to the
public, it is the local headquarters
of the Carabinieri.

Falling Water

FRANK LLOYD WRIGHT, 1936

BEAR RUN, PENNSYLVANIA,

USA

THIS IS THE ENIGMATIC, eclectic and long-lived Frank Lloyd Wright at his very best. Falling Water never fails to surprise and delight visitors who trek here through the prolific woodlands of rural Pennsylvania. It was designed as a romantic retreat for the publisher Edgar Kaufmann. Having found the site – a waterfall roaring over ancient rocks – Wright anchored the house as closely as he could to the water. In effect, the house is a series of great horizontal trays pivoted around and held up by a central tower, which is also a chimney. So, although Wright claimed that the section of the house was adopted from an ancient Mayan temple, Falling Water is also like a great tent realized in concrete, timber, steel and glass rather than canvas or buffalo hides.

The architect's determining hand is seen everywhere, in every last detail. And yet, far from being precious, the house is liberating. How does Wright manage this? Perhaps, because from anywhere in the house, there are views out taking in unexpected vistas of the building as well as the primordial landscape. This is one of the most photographed and most famous houses in the world and it deserves to be. It is at its best out of season when you can have the place almost, if not quite, to yourself: the ghost of Frank Lloyd Wright is always looking over your shoulder.

Peter Jones Store

WILLIAM CRABTREE, 1937

CHELSEA, LONDON,

ENGLAND

CLEARLY OWING A DEBT to Mendelsohn's Schocken stores (pp.148, 156), Crabtree's Peter Jones is one of the few Modern buildings in London that knows how to turn a corner. For most architects, this simple and graceful act is something quite beyond them. And, yet it is this simple device that makes Peter Jones such a well-loved shop. Crabtree swept his indefatigably elegant glass screen around Sloane Square and into King's Road with panache. Unlike Mendelsohn who performed the same trick with defiant bands of horizontal glass, Crabtree's glazing emphasizes the vertical and so walks around the building rather than rushing it as Mendelsohn does. Beyond this, the building is a simple frame containing triple-height galleries and a fine spiral stair. It is light and airy and impossible to get lost in. The top floor is set back, Mendelsohn-style, like an ocean liner.

What is remarkable here is that the shop was designed for the deeply conservative top end of the British middle class who, on the whole, preferred mock Tudor beams and Neo-Georgian pediments to the new streamlined Modern architecture arriving from the Continent. Crabtree was able to convince them that Modern architecture was not some dangerous foreign perversion, and that surely was a feat worth recording.

Museum of Modern Art

PHILIP GOODWIN AND

EDWARD STONE, 1939

NEW YORK CITY, USA

WIDELY USED in propaganda extolling the virtues of Modern design in the United States, the Museum of Modern Art was the first major International Style building on the east coast. As crisp as Gropius's Bauhaus (p.142), the Museum of Modern Art is, in effect, a very simple container with a cool, clinical façade. The six-storey building comprises a basement lecture theatre, a lobby and gallery at street level, two floors of exhibition space, a third-floor library, fourth-floor offices and a club room with terraces under the concrete "sunshade" at the top.

It is significant that in the USA, the Modern Movement arrived with the tag "International Style", a brand dreamed up by the architect Philip Johnson and historian Henry-Russell Hitchcock. It demonstrated that, for many US architects, Modern architecture was just one more style in the great panoply that led from Classical to Gothic, from Art Nouveau to Art Deco. To an extent this was true: in Europe, the Modern Movement was a part of a cultural and artistic revolution. It was often wrapped up in left-wing political gambits, which is why its progeny were banned by the Nazis. In the States, Modernism was freed of political and social undertones: all that really mattered was style, something Philip Goodwin and Edward Stone (1902–78) gave the Museum of Modern Art.

Rockefeller Center

REINHARD, HOFMEISTER,
ET AL, 1940
NEW YORK CITY, USA

ICE RINK. Christmas tree. Fairy
lights. Radio City. The Rockefeller
Center is a magnificent and generous
fusion of rampant capitalist enterprise
and civic delight. It is a huge complex
of ten giant buildings – some very
tall – grouped with bravura and
brilliance on a 12-acre site bounded
by New York's Fifth and Sixth Avenues
and by 48th and 51st Streets. The
buildings build up from the pavement
to a climactic peak, like a man-made
mountain range. Each steel-framed
behemoth is clad in expensive stone,
granite and marble, while finishes
throughout the complex are as good
to look at as they are to touch.
Passageways through the complex
connect the various buildings,
binding them to the whole.

It is rare that a complex given to
generating capital and maximizing
profit has been so generous and
civically minded. The Center was
started in 1930 and its Art Deco
styling dates from then. During its
decade of construction, the architects
stuck to this style – to have changed
it would have undermined the
coherence of the ambitious whole –
creating what looks like a giant
Mayan temple complex seen through
the distorting mirror of the mid-
twentieth century. The Rockefeller
Center broke no new technological
barriers but it was an inspired example
of grouping modern buildings
to create a twentieth-century
equivalent of the Roman forum.

Pampúlha Yacht Club

OSCAR NIEMEYER AND
LÚCIO COSTA, 1942

PAMPÚLHA, BRAZIL

OSCAR NIEMEYER is one of the century's greats, an architect who has made poetry from concrete, and who ranks with his mentor, Le Corbusier, as one of the most memorable form-givers of the Modern Movement. Born in Rio de Janiero and in love with its sensual setting and atmosphere – its mountains, beaches and beautiful people – Niemeyer's take on Modernism was quite unlike that of austere and angst-ridden intellectual Europeans. His architecture was a celebration of life and nature, an attempt to harmonize natural beauty with the possibilities of Modern design, technology and materials. On the whole he was to succeed triumphantly.

His first significant project, built at a time when Brazil was at war with Germany and Italy, was a pleasure village – Pampúlha – for the wealthy. Here, as Hitler challenged Europe and the Japanese practised unspeakable cruelties in the Far East, Niemeyer experimented with the form of bright new architecture in the guise of a glamorous yacht club and casino. The lightness and elegance of the yacht club, with its twin inverse-sloping roofs, was to influence many buildings of the 1950s in other towns and cities given over to hedonistic pleasure, notably Miami, Havana and Los Angeles. Although a frivolous project, the design of Pampúlha allowed the young Niemeyer a chance to experiment with the forms of Modernism and to adapt a European way of thinking to the sensuous nature of Brazil, which was the cradle of Modern architecture in Latin America.

Ministry of Education and Health

LÚCIO COSTA, OSCAR

NIEMEYER AND

LE CORBUSIER, 1943

RIO DE JANIERO, BRAZIL

LE CORBUSIER VISITED RIO in 1936 and was invited to draw up plans for this new ministry building; Lúcio Costa (1902–98) and Oscar Niemeyer joined him to see the sculptural building through to completion. The result was a quiet and distinguished triumph, Corbusier's concrete architecture reworked for Rio's dazzling climate. The most distinctive feature of the building, its permanent sun-louvres (*brises-soleil*), hide its internal life so that the ministry appears to be a beautifully controlled sculpture rather than a machine for working in. The building introduced Latin America to Modernism. There eems little doubt that Le Corbusier benefited from working on the Rio ministry: his postwar successes – notably the L'Unité d'Habitation in Marseilles (p.190) – owe a debt to the experience of working with the sun in Rio.

Until Le Corbusier's visit, Latin America was a Modern Movement free zone. The change that came in a decade was remarkable. Sadly, the standard of design set by Niemeyer and Le Corbusier was rarely matched and never excelled. The success of the ministry building was to lead Niemeyer on to the design of the centre of Brasilia in the mid-1950s, from when he dominated the architectural landscape of Brazil until exile after the military coup in 1964.

Kauffman House

RICHARD NEUTRA, 1947

PALM SPRINGS,

CALIFORNIA, USA

THE ALLURING Kauffman "Desert" House is undoubtedly a Modern masterpiece. It was yet another perfect home for Edgar Kauffman who had, a decade earlier, commissioned Frank Lloyd Wright to design Falling Water (p.176). Although a large house, complete with servants' quarters, it sits so low in its spectacular setting that it seems no more than a super-sophisticated shack. Until you get up close: then Neutra's genius and sheer finesse show at every turn. The house opens up into the landscape like some enormous yet unshowy flower: walls slide back to let the outside world into the interior and there are magical moments when inside and outside blur together seamlessly. This is a perfect summer retreat, well able to cope with heat and sun and to make the best of them.

The Kauffman House marked, perhaps, the zenith of Neutra's career, one that had taken him a very long way indeed from turn of the century Vienna. He believed that a house like this, designed to become a part of the landscape it adorned, was a "harbour for the soul". Despite the ultra-Modern appearance of the Kauffman House, Neutra condemned design that was merely fashionable: he wanted to create a "slice of eternity". In the design of the Kauffman House he got as close to achieving this goal as any twentieth-century architect ever did.

Equitable Savings and Loan Association Headquarters

PIETRO BELLUSCHI, 1948

PORTLAND, OREGON, USA

THIS CRISP, ELEGANT and supremely taut building might have been designed and built at any time in the 1980s or 1990s for a Western city centre. In fact it dates from 1948. Pietro Belluschi (1899–1994) created what was probably the first smooth-skinned office building, a type that has been repeated endlessly ever since. The skin of the building is almost flush, like the skin of a snake; or, perhaps, this is architecture created by a cheese wire. The specification of the building was very much up to date with double glazing, solar-tinted windows and air-conditioning, demonstrating clearly the technological advances made in the United States during four years of intense war production and an investment in research and development.

Belluschi was born in Ancona in Italy. He studied at Rome and then in the United States at Cornell University. In 1943 Belluschi founded his own office in Portland, which was taken over by the giant Skidmore, Owings and Merrill in 1950. From 1951 to 1965 he was Dean of the School of Architecture and Planning at the Massachusetts Institute of Technology, but set up in practice again in Portland in 1965. His later concerns were a continuation of the theme established by the Equitable Savings Building: how to make an architecture that was a smooth, polished and, it seems, anonymous container of contemporary functions.

Eames House

CHARLES AND RAY EAMES,

1949,

NO 8, PACIFIC PALISADES,

CALIFORNIA, USA

THIS BRILLIANT HOUSE by the
husband and wife team Charles
(1907–78) and Ray (1916–88)
Eames was one of the first to be
built entirely from off-the-peg
industrial components and to make
this form of construction glamorous.
The house was one of a number of
experimental houses commissioned
by John Entenza, publisher of *Arts
and Architecture*. Entenza wanted
to show a postwar public, hungry
for ideal new homes, that modern
architects could offer more for their
money than conventional house-
builders. His "Case Study" programme
was a success: the first six houses,
made of timber and completed by
1948, attracted 370,000 visitors.

The Eames House consisted of a
two-storey living space and studio
divided by a courtyard. The exterior
was a glamorous machine, echoing
the forms of a traditional Japanese
house, while the double-height
interiors were a revelation: light, airy,
open and still looking and feeling
Modern 50 years on from their
completion. The Eames had a gift
for creating a Modern look that was
easy on the eye, comfortable and
relaxed with none of the repressed
earnestness of contemporary
European design, nor the work ethic
aesthetic of Chicago and New York.
The Californian climate had brought
out the best in Rudolf Schindler
and Richard Neutra: it did the
same for Charles and Ray Eames.

Glass House

PHILIP JOHNSON, 1950

NEW CANAAN,

CONNECTICUT, USA

PHILIP CORTELYOU JOHNSON, born in 1906 into a wealthy New England family, was the most influential early protagonist of European Modern Movement ideas in the United States. Much later, he was to become champion of Postmodernism, Deconstructivism and just about every other "ism"

architects were to dream up in the last quarter of the century. The uncrowned king of US architecture, Johnson was able to make and break careers. A witty, urbane character, he studied philology at Harvard before becoming the first director of the Architecture Department of the Museum of Modern Art, New York, from 1930 to 1936. The hugely influential "International Style" exhibition he curated at MOMA with the historian Henry-Russell Hitchcock in 1932 brought the work of the European masters – principally Mies van der Rohe – to light in

the United States, although Johnson seemed unaware, or was simply dismissive, of the work of Schindler in California. Having visited Mies in Germany, from 1930, and flirted with Nazism, Johnson trained as an architect under Gropius and Breuer at Harvard (1940–43).

In 1949 Johnson built his Glass House retreat, clearly inspired by Mies, in the woods at New Canaan. An exquisite steel-section and sheet glass pavilion, it remains one of the most perfect and undiluted essays in Modern Movement design and propaganda.

Farnsworth House

LUDWIG MIES VAN DER
ROHE, 1951

PLANO, ILLINOIS, USA

LUDWIG MIES VAN DER ROHE
arrived in the United States in
1937. He had succeeded Gropius as
Director of the Bauhaus in 1930
but the school was closed by the
Nazis in 1933. Finding it impossible
to realize his form of Platonic
Modern architecture, Mies left to
teach at the Illinois Institute of
Technology, for which he built a
new campus from 1940.

Dr Edith Farnsworth
commissioned him to design a
weekend retreat in rural Illinois
in 1946. The result is one of the
most perfect expressions of the
Modern Movement dream, a
pavilion of light, transparency,
tautness and weightlessness. It is
one of those buildings that, first
seen, sends a shiver up the spine.
It is chaste: it is also sublime.
The living space – a single room
measuring 23 by 8.5 metres (77 ft
by 28 ft) and divided only by a
central kitchen and bathroom core
– is raised above the flood plain
of Fox River on eight white steel I-
section beams. These seem barely
to touch the glass box they

support, while the horizontal
planes of floor and roof seem to
float almost independently of the
I-beams. The whole assemble is
extraordinary: free-floating, yet
as taut as a drawn bow; ethereal,
yet as strong and substantial as
so few materials can be.

In moving to the States, Mies
encountered the wealth that
enabled him to realize some of the
most refined architecture of any
century. It was not one-way traffic,
however. Mies went on to design
offices and apartment blocks that
were hugely profitable for
developers; not for nothing did
American business executives say
"Mies means money".

Lake Shore Drive Apartments

LUDWIG MIES VAN DER ROHE, 1951

CHICAGO, ILLINOIS, USA

THE TWIN LAKE SHORE DRIVE apartment blocks were Mies's dictum "less is more" taken to a new extreme. Their utter simplicity – or what appears to be utter simplicity when first seen – is the result of immense thought and calculation. The blocks are supported by Mies's trademark I-beam steel sections that rise the height of the buildings. These give the 26-storey blocks a powerful vertical emphasis and an equally powerful abstract quality. This abstractedness is heightened by the way in which the two blocks are related: situated at right angles to one another, the broad front of one meeting the narrow side of the other. Walking around them, they appear to waltz slowly around one another in a configuration that seems to change with each step. Neither of these purist, Platonic blocks can be said to have a front or a back. They are designed as perfect shapes: nothing is allowed to upset this purity. This includes the blinds protecting the floor-to-ceiling windows of individual apartments from the glare of the sun. Originally, these were uniform, so that no one detail – a colourful blind, a florid curtain – was able to challenge the purity of the whole. The messiness of everyday living – laundry, storage, car parking – was swept beneath the twin blocks. The influence of the Lake Shore towers on twentieth-century architecture was incalculable.

Royal Festival Hall

LCC ARCHITECTS
DEPARTMENT, 1951
LONDON, ENGLAND

THE ONE LASTING LEGACY of the 1951 Festival of Britain on London's South Bank, the Royal Festival Hall was one of the first major Modern public buildings in Britain. Commissioned in 1948, it was designed by a team led by Leslie Martin (born 1908) and Peter Moro (born 1911) for the London County Council. The building took its aesthetic cue from Modern architecture in Scandinavia, but its form was determined by the need to find a way of constructing a sound-proof auditorium. Not only did the Bakerloo Line of the London Underground run beneath the building, but planes flew overhead, Waterloo mainline station was in whistling distance and trains from Charing Cross station rumbled across Hungerford Bridge. Martin's ingenious solution was what he described as an "egg in a box": the 2,740 seat auditorium would be lifted into the very centre of the structure. It was a solution that never fails to delight and baffle visitors to this building; the auditorium floats serenely and magically above lobbies, bars, cafés, shops and exhibition space.

The Royal Festival Hall was built in concrete at great speed, although to a high standard. The original river front was temporary. Martin left the LCC in 1956, but the front was redesigned very much the way he had intended in 1964.

Brynmawr
Rubber Factory

ARCHITECTS CO-
PARTNERSHIP, 1952
EBBW VALE, SOUTH WALES

UNEMPLOYMENT IN EBBW VALE, a coal-mining district of south Wales, reached 82 per cent shortly before the outbreak of World War Two. When a socialist government was voted overwhelmingly into power in Britain in 1945, it promised to help this downtrodden area. The government paid for this imposing new factory, designed for the manufacturer of rubber goods by the socialist practice Architects Co-Partnership with the idealistic and inventive engineer Ove Arup. It was an expensive gesture and ultimately an economic folly. The factory has long been closed – and the object of several failed attempts to save it from demolition – and Ebbw Vale remains poor.

At the time of its design and construction – stretched out over seven long years – the Brynmawr Rubber Factory was one of the finest buildings of its kind, as well as one of the most altruistic. Not only did workers and management use the same entrance and canteen (enlivened by contemporary artworks), but working conditions – because of the architecture – were among the best to be found anywhere in Britain, although that isn't saying much for a country that, even at the end of the twentieth century, relied heavily on some of the cheapest and most easily dispensable labour in Europe.

The design of the factory was based around a grid of nine spectacular concrete domed vaults, each measuring 26 by 19 metres (85 ft by 62 ft); it was light, airy, handsome and doomed from the start.

Unité
d'Habitation

LE CORBUSIER, 1952

MARSEILLES, FRANCE

THIS TITANIC BUILDING was
designed to house 1,600 working-
class Marseillaise. Well before the
end of the century it had become
one of the most fashionable
addresses in the great Mediterranean
seaport, populated almost entirely
by middle-class professionals. Who
could blame them for wanting to
live here? This was no cheapskate
local authority housing block, but
the representation, in thousands of
tons of weather-boarded and bush-
hammered concrete, of social and
architectural ideals Le Corbusier had
been struggling with for 30 years.
In effect, the 337 flats on 17
storeys above the streets of
Marseilles, are interlocked around
central streets within the building
and raised on massive concrete
supports above a beautifully
maintained park. The flats boast
double-height living rooms and
each, because of the concrete
construction, is quiet and well
insulated. On the fourth floor there
is a hotel (Hôtel Le Corbusier) and
a variety of shops including a
poodle parlour. The roof with its
surrealistic landscape of vents and
towers, swimming pool and spaces
to play has become an icon of
Modern design at its most
sculptural and challenging.

Le Corbusier designed five more
Unités (Nantes-Reze, 1957; Berlin,
1958; Meaux, 1959; Briey-en-Fôret,
1960 and Firminy-Vert, 1968), but
these were compromised and the
original remains unchallenged.

Säynätsalo Town Hall

ALVAR AALTO, 1952

SÄYNÄTSALO, FINLAND

AALTO DID MORE than almost any other Modern architect to connect his buildings to Nature. And, this is why his centenary in 1998 was so widely and enthusiastically celebrated. Perhaps his concern for Nature was natural enough for a Finn brought up in a largely unspoilt land of lakes, woods and wildlife; perhaps it was his time as a front-line soldier during World War Two that encouraged this great architect to see Nature as the balm for the machine-like quality of modern architecture and urbanism.

Shortly after the war he designed this romantic and much-loved town hall, or civic centre, in rural Finland. A huddle of elegant brick, timber and copper pavilions mounted on a capitol-like plinth and connected by stairs planted with grass and meadow flowers, the complex offers both intimacy, adventure and great spatial play. In short, it is a delight and a perfect answer to anyone foolish enough at the end of the twentieth century to say that Modern architecture is inhuman. Somewhere else, yes, but not here. The centre includes a council chamber as well as a public library, post office, bank and shops.

Sadly, the hand-crafted bricky style of Säynätsalo was to be much copied, without much inspiration, in Britain and elsewhere in Europe in the 1970s as an antidote to the unpopularity of concrete estates and "high rise horrors". The original is peerless.

Lever
Building

SKIDMORE, OWINGS AND
MERRILL, 1952

NEW YORK CITY, USA

THE LEVER BUILDING is one of the
most influential of all twentieth-
century buildings. From the
perspective of the end of the
century it might look like any other
office block, but that's the point:
countless thousand office blocks
look like the Lever Building.

Consisting of a two-storey slab
around a central courtyard and a
21-storey curtain-wall tower, the
design owes much to Mies van der
Rohe and the International Style
aesthetic that permeated the United
States from 1932. The fact that the
building was much copied is
largely, perhaps, because Skidmore,
Owings and Merrill (SOM) managed
to get under the skin of the newly
emerging postwar corporate
America and created a house style
for it. The firm was founded in
1936 by Louis Skidmore (1897–1962)
and Nathaniel Owings (1903–84),
who were joined three years later
by John Merrill (1896–1975). The
partners established a form of
architectural teamwork: anonymity
ruled the roost and there were to
be no prima donnas. Offices were
soon established in Chicago and
San Francisco as well as New York.
If SOM did have a star at the time,
it was Gordon Bunshaft (1909–90)
who was the creative talent behind
the design of the green-skinned
Lever Building. His later
masterpiece was the Ford
Foundation, New York (p.224).

Hunstanton School

ALISON AND PETER
SMITHSON, 1954
NORFOLK, ENGLAND

THE SMITHSONS, Alison (born 1928) and Peter (born 1923), were a fashionable and formidable duo who will be forever associated with the tag New Brutalism and remembered for the aggressive housing they built for the London poor (Robin Hood Gardens, 1972) and for the Mies-inspired school they built at Hunstanton on the north Norfolk coast. Normally portrayed in bright sunlight, photographs have never prepared visitors to this symbol of the New Brutalism for the bitingly cold winds that scythe across the North Sea here from Siberia and the Arctic; the school can be very cold, a condition not helped by the extensive glazing, which has tended to fall out as this exposed building expands and contracts. The school was proof, despite the propaganda, that Modern architects were not necessarily functionalists: "functionalism", like New Brutalism, was often just a fashionable, and for most architects, irritating tag.

Hunstanton School certainly looked the part and was widely published at the time of its completion. Formally, it is satisfying, a neat, logical plan realized in exposed industrial materials and free from any form of gratuitous expression, much less decoration. The Smithsons redeemed themselves a decade later with the Economist Building, London (p.215).

General Motors Technical Center

EERO AND ELIEL SAARINEN,
1955

WARREN, MICHIGAN, USA

THE SAARINENS, father (Eliel,
1873–1950) and son (Eero, 1910–61)
arrived in the United States in
1923. Eero studied sculpture in
Paris – which is evident in his work
– and architecture at Yale before
joining his father in practice in
Ann Arbor, Michigan in 1937. He
set up shop in his own right in
Birmingham, Michigan in 1950.

Before Eero soared into the realm
of sculptural fantasy, he was
commissioned to design and
masterplan General Motors'
ambitious 330-acre Technical
Center, which was to include 25
buildings gathered around a lake
on a revolutionary style of business
"campus". Working with his father,
Saarinen created a regimented
parade of handsome, Mies-inspired,
low-rise blocks in steel and glass.
Their cool geometric perfection was
set off by two baroque elements:
the domed lecture theatre, covered
with a reflective skin of aluminium,
and the water tower, a beautiful
aluminium ellipse mounted high

above the lake on three long legs.

The Technical Center was a way
of showing that corporate America
had come of age: grim, makeshift
factories and faceless counting
houses had given way to a form of
business that invaded the territory
of universities and monasteries
before them. Perhaps it was all a
bit of a sham – General Motors –
informal motto: "what's good for
General Motors is good for the
world" – was hardly the most
altruistic corporation, yet
Saarinen imbued it with a
Platonic perfection and a state
of what looked like grace, even
if was nothing of the sort.

Arvesu House

ALEJANDRO DE LA SOTA,
1955, MADRID, SPAIN

THIS SPECIAL HOUSE was
demolished in 1987. What a
waste. It was one of the quiet
masterpieces of Alejandro de la
Sota (born 1913) and was designed
as a retreat from the sheer busyness
of the world. The idea was for a
very private house screened by an
enigmatic brick wall that, in the
architect's original design, had no
windows. All daylight would come
from the south-facing garden front
and from skylights. In the event de
la Sota's client demanded windows
and a few apologetic specimens did
indeed peek through a wall that
looked as if it had been woven.

This curious use of brickwork
would have made sense if you
could have seen the house in
daylight: the sun played on its
weave creating an entrancing
dance of shadows. This imbued the
house with not only warmth and
life but a sense of age that few
Modern architects were able to
evoke – assuming they wanted
to. On its garden side, the house
featured extensive glazing, a
balcony running from one end to
the other and a garden that sloped
down to a circular pool. The
interior, a place of curves too,
flowed easily and elegantly and
featured one of the most satisfying
of all Modern stairs, a graceful
realization of a single curve sketched
with a pencil. A perfect example
of how less can indeed be more.

Capuchinas Chapel

LUIS BARRAGÁN, 1955

COLONIA TLALPLAN,

MEXICO CITY, MEXICO

A LYRICAL WORK by a great poet and colourist, the Capuchinas Chapel was also an expression of Luis Barragán's outgoing spirit. When asked to redesign the chapel on a small scale and on a very modest budget, Barragán offered to build something a little more ambitious and paid for the extra works himself. Perhaps this could be seen as "vanity architecture". Even if it were, the result was very moving and in the right light – most of the year – achingly beautiful. The chapel is designed with daylight filtering from a lattice and a tall, thin stained glass window at its west end. This finds its way to the altar which is crowned with a simple gold *reredos* (wall-hanging) by Mathias Goeritz that captures and diffuses the last of its abstracted beams.

The materials used throughout are simple – roughcast plasterwork, concrete, timber planks – but the colours and the fall of light here are truly sublime.

Barragán did not train as an architect: his introduction to the Modern Movement was gradual, and while he moved towards a romantic Modern aesthetic very much of his own, his passion for such buildings – and gardens, always gardens, such as those of the Alahambra in Grenada which he loved – shone through in all his light-filled, life-enhancing designs.

Crown Hall

LUDWIG MIES VAN DER
ROHE, 1956

CHICAGO, ILLINOIS, USA

HAVING FINALLY BROKEN with
Nazi Germany in 1937, Mies took
up a teaching post at the Armour
(later the Illinois) Institute of
Technology, Chicago a year later. In
1940 he was asked to mastermind
a new campus, which he designed
as a kind of minimalist Greek
Acropolis except that, unlike the
Greek model, Mies' ideal "city"
was all on the level and decoration
non-existent. Here, if anywhere, his
ascetic philosophy of "less is more"
is most clearly expressed.

The heart of the campus is the
Crown Hall, a large single space
building measuring 67 metres
(220 ft) by 36.5 metres (120 ft)
by 6 metres (20 ft) high. Like
other of Mies's finest buildings,
it appears to be floating off the
ground and seems to be little more
than a volume of air contained
within two long slabs of steel. This
illusion is helped by the approach
to the Hall, which is reached up
two flights of stairs that also look
as if they float in air. Except for
the fact that the hall stands on a
solid, yet all but invisible,
basement it really does have an
ethereal and otherworldly character,
saved by the life students bring
to it. Thrilled by the industrial
possibilities of US architecture,
Mies built the superstructure
of the Hall from four giant
prefabricated steel girders that
were driven to the site. In fact,
like all Mies's US buildings,
stringent fire regulations meant
that what appear to be exposed
structural steel beams are, in fact,
a bit of a fraud: they are effectively
a form of severe decorative
cladding over an internal structure
of steel and concrete designed so
that in a blaze the steel girders
would not buckle.

Maisons Jaoul

LE CORBUSIER, 1956

NEUILLY-SUR-SEINE, FRANCE

IN THE 1950s, Le Corbusier turned away from the machine-like aesthetic of his early years and developed a moody architecture that was highly individualistic and responsive to site and locale rather than to purely abstract ideas of what was rational, revolutionary and deterministically futuristic. His new trademarks were raw, board-shuttered concrete, vaulted roofs and tough and rugged forms. Despite their overt toughness – a muscularity that helped give rise to the very rough and tough Brutalist school of design in Britain – the Maisons Jaoul are delightful, womb-like houses to live in.

Built of brick and concrete, the pair are set at right angles to one another and dig deep into their shaded site. Gardens are at basement level, roofs are planted with grass. The house interiors are a revelation, with their vaulted ceilings; they are quite unlike the clever, white, urbane villas and apartments we associate with Corbusier in his first forays into Modernism. Instead they have a gently brooding quality: you feel like curling up like a cat or dog inside and dreaming long dreams.

Although romantic and superficially fortress-like, the Maisons Jaoul are rationally planned, their proportions rooted in Corbusier's "Modulor", a personal and possibly idiosyncratic reworking of the rules of Classical proportion. This pair of houses on the fringes of Paris was hugely influential, their design echoing as far afield as downtown Tokyo and the Sussex coast.

Peace Pavilion

KENZO TANGE, 1956

HIROSHIMA, JAPAN

THE ATOMIC BOMBS dropped by
US B-29 bombers on Hiroshima and
Nagasaki in April 1945 prompted
the Japanese surrender and the end
of World War Two. The bombs, said
Emperor Hirohito in an infamous
broadcast, meant that the "war was
not necessarily proceeding to Japan's
advantage". Where the centre of
Hiroshima once stood, Kenzo Tange
(born 1913) was commissioned to
design a Peace Pavilion that was
also to form the core of the
reconstructed city. The result is
a strong and simple cultural hall
aimed at reconciling the forms of
traditional Japanese temples with
Modern concrete architecture.

Tange, who was born in Osaka
and studied in Tokyo, had spent
the war years thinking about ways
in which Japanese architecture
might face the future. The goal he
set himself was to bring together
the two extremes of ancient
Japanese art, *Yayoi* (equivalent to
the Greek Apollonian, rational,
world view) and *Jomon* (equivalent
to the Greek Dionysian, or
irrational force). Tange was to
work through this conundrum
with increasing rigour in the
1960s; the Peace Pavilion was only
a beginning. The young Tange had
worked in the office of Kunio
Mayekawa in Tokyo. Mayekawa
had trained with Le Corbusier; like
Tange, it was the poetic quality of
Corbusier's architecture that caught
his imagination and which was to
have a profound effect on
Japanese design after the war.

Shodhan House

LE CORBUSIER, 1956

AHMEDABAD, INDIA

THIS SUPERB INDIAN HOUSE has the appearance of some sort of three-dimensional mathematical puzzle. In fact its complex concrete façade – more of a screen, perhaps, than a façade – is a floor-to-roof sunshade, and a very effective one too. The villa itself is hidden on no fewer than seven floors behind the deep concrete *brise-soleil*, the floors connected, as in Corbusier's Villa Savoye (p.161) of nearly 30 years before, by ramp. The principal rooms are on the first floor; above this large villa are three self-contained but interconnecting apartments. Under what looks to be a free-floating concrete parasol at the top of the building, there is a hanging garden. There are also plenty of spaces to sit outside, protected from the 40°C (104°F) midday sun, and to look over the gardens and swimming pool.

Here, in Ahmedabad, Corbusier pointed the way to a new type of house for blazingly hot climates without the need for wasteful air-conditioning and complex building services. However, the fact that the Shodhan House remains a one-off lies partly in the fact that it is so "primitive": in 1950s' India, the wealthy often wanted to show that they could afford luxuries like air-conditioning and to prove that anything the Americans could do, they could do too. At the end of the century, any sane person – or aesthete – having the choice between a hermetically sealed air-conditioned box and this intriguing, multi-layered house, so very aware of the changing elements, would know which one to move into.

Courts of Justice

LE CORBUSIER, 1956
CHANDIGARH, INDIA

PUNJAB WAS ONE of the new states formed in the newly independent Republic of India in 1947. It needed a capital. And remarkably it got one that in its curious and iconoclastic way is one of the wonders of the urban world. The new city, Chandigarh, was masterminded by a team of Indian architects and planners working under the direction of Le Corbusier who had been persuaded to work in India by the British architects

Jane Drew and Maxwell Fry. Le Corbusier designed the core of the city and its principal official buildings – the Courts of Justice, the Palace of Assembly, the Governor's Residence and the (later) Court of the Open Hand. What Le Corbusier created here was magnificent sculpture – a sculpture that works as architecture – brought together under the dazzling Punjabi sky. The prime consideration was water and shelter from a sun that is merciless in summer. So, the Courts of Justice stands on the edge of a man-made lake. By night the lake brims with starlight. The façade of the Courts forms a complex sunscreen that

really does keep the sequence of courtrooms and waiting rooms inside cool. The dense mass of the concrete walls helps to keep heat out, too.

As with Le Corbusier's other buildings here, the Courts of Justice is a flamboyant sculptural gesture, alien to the historic artistic landscape of India and yet a part of it. Perhaps the happy thing here is that Le Corbusier and his European colleagues were able to build only so far and no more: the result is a city which brings the most sophisticated and romantic architectural sculpture together with the miasmic world of the modern Indian city.

Case Study House No 21

PIERRE KOENIG, 1958

LOS ANGELES, CALIFORNIA, USA

THE CASE STUDY HOUSES always seem so perfect. This is partly because they nearly all share a purity of line and because they have been so memorably photographed by Julius Shulman, a craftsman behind the lens, who has handed down to us images of what a perfect mid-twentieth-century West Coast way of life was meant to have been. When faced with the clutter of our own homes and the density of the fabric of most world cities, houses like Case Study No 21 designed by Pierre Koening (born 1925) are hugely enticing. They were meant to be dreams made real, or as the architect Richard Neutra put it, a "harbour for the soul" and a "slice of eternity".

Koenig's house was a showcase of contemporary building technology, domestic design, furniture and fittings. It was meant to show just how relaxed and easy Modern living was; the entire house is premised on the idea of easiness and accessibility. Roll your jeep up under the steel-framed *porte-cochère* (not that you would have called it that in Fifties' California), ease out and in to the fully glazed kitchen, fix yourself a drink and out onto the sun lounge for a laid-back evening watching the sun set over LA. Bring together the latest in refrigerator design with a Zen-inspired pool and rock garden, the chasteness of Mies van der Rohe with the voluptuousness of the latest plastic and steel-framed furniture and you have a home that's as stylish, as sophisticated and as relaxed as the conceit of California itself.

Seagram Building

LUDWIG MIES VAN DER
ROHE, 1958
NEW YORK CITY, USA

"MIES MEANS MONEY", said US property developers, watching in awe as this inspired Modern Movement giant raised towers of steel and glass in Chicago and paved the way for the global office block that in lesser hands was to prove a large part of the undoing of the Modern Movement in the public eye. When Mies came to New York the meaning of the developers' phrase was turned on its head with the Seagram Building. Here, Mies certainly meant money: this sheer, 38-storey headquarters for the Canadian distillers, was clad in bronze and cost a mint. It was, and remains, one of the greatest achievements of the Modern Movement, a purist building standing in its own exclusive plaza and not only owing nothing to the world around, but looking with a kind of silent disdain on the busy streets and even busier architecture it surveys.

The Seagram headquarters was to have been a much lesser building; it was the president of Seagram's daughter, Phyllis, who brought Mies into the picture. The result is breath-taking. Designed with help from Philip Johnson, the building soars effortlessly from its plaza set back from Park Avenue into the Manhattan skyline. The vertical emphasis of the building is as emphatic as it is relentless. This is the building that launched far more than a thousand corporate headquarters. It is by far the best of them.

Pirelli Tower

GIO PONTI, 1959

MILAN, ITALY

THE PIRELLI TOWER is the first monument in a profoundly monumental city to greet the traveller who comes to Milan by train. The 34-storey tower is very unlike the steel and glass towers pioneered by Mies and Skidmore, Owings and Merrill in New York and Chicago. In this case a team of architects and engineers, including Pier Luigi Nervi and led by Gio Ponti (1891–1979), developed a sophisticated concrete skeleton that allowed the building to rise high while maintaining a delicate, streamlined profile. The result is a distinctive building that represents an alternative to the steel and glass shoeboxes that have littered the skyscapes of so many cities across the world. It also marked a high point in the long career of Ponti, an eclectic designer who had founded the art, architecture and design journal *Domus* in 1928, and edited it until his death.

Ponti, who was born, educated, lived and died in Milan, spent his first years as an architect working in a stripped Neoclassical style – one of the hallmarks of Italian Fascist design – yet lacing his buildings with gorgeous and even Surrealist interiors. His change of heart appeared to come with the design of a Modern pavilion for the Catholic Press Exhibition held in the Vatican City in 1936. His two Modern masterpieces were chaste and simple, although impressive: the Superleggera chair of 1957 and the Pirelli Tower.

Alton West Estate

LCC ARCHITECTS
DEPARTMENT, 1959
ROEHAMPTON, SURREY,
ENGLAND

ARCHITECTURALLY, if not socially, this was one of the more successful attempts made at exporting Le Corbusier's L'Unité d'Habitation from warm and sunny Marseilles. This vast aggregation of local authority flats sits together in carefully considered concrete blocks that stand on *piloti* and overlook the dreamy landscape of Richmond Park, a vast acreage of plantations, herds of deer, exquisite eighteenth-century buildings and a famous escape for Londoners in need of fresh air and a Sunday afternoon walk with the dogs.

Sadly, few of the middle-class dog walkers who stroll across Richmond Park have much good to say about Alton West Estate, which steals a significant part of a once famous view from here of central London and St Paul's Cathedral. Rusting cars, litter and louts do not help make an English L'Unité out of Alton West, nor Marseilles from Roehampton. Nevertheless, the six- and twelve-storey blocks of flats are nicely arranged and thoughtfully designed. They occupy a kind of annexe to Richmond Park and the tall blocks are interwoven by staggered rows of single-storey houses for the elderly.

It is significant, however, that although the standard of design here and the setting is considerably higher than those of council estates almost anywhere else in British cities, Alton West is not much fun. Perhaps the British do find it genuinely hard to live in blocks of flats or perhaps they are simply too poor to enjoy the life lived by the professional classes who occupy L'Unité d'Habitation so successfully. Still, at Alton West, they do have the park.

Monastery of Sainte-Marie de-la-Tourette

LE CORBUSIER, 1960
EVEUX-SUR-L'ARBRESLE,
FRANCE

THIS IS A BUILDING you need to experience at length for it to make sense. To many it seems confusing and ugly, but it grows on you and you come to understand why so many believe it to be one of the greatest buildings of any era. It is the home of an Order who live to work and pray. Although the roughcast architecture is stripped to material basics, it is profoundly rich in terms of the way Le Corbusier handled space and brought light to play on walls and interior surfaces. The monastery is gathered around a cloistered garden. The public rooms are at ground level with two floors of narrow cells above. The monastery is full of sculptural invention: each pyramid, tower or protuberance serves a distinct purpose, bringing light into the recesses of a mind-game of a building that serves to inspire as much as it does to strip away the Modern world it owes its architecture to.

Plaza of the Three Powers

OSCAR NIEMEYER AND
LÚCIO COSTA, 1960

BRASÍLIA, BRAZIL

THE PLAZA at the core of the new Brazilian capital is reached by a 9.6-kilometre (6-mile) long avenue planned by Lúcio Costa. Do not try walking it on a steamy day. Brasília was, and remains, a heroic political and urbanistic statement. This is a great new city and, boy, can you feel the weight of that intent. The problem here is a simple one. The climate threatens the monuments designed by the brilliantly facile Niemeyer, while the heart of the city stands remote, physically and symbolically, from the shanty towns that surround it. The idea of Brasília though impresses in much the same way as the building of the Opera House on the Amazon at Manaus does. It was always a brave and vainglorious concept. At the end of Costa's avenue stand the thrilling shapes of Niemeyer's Congress building and its attendant administration block. This sculptural group rises effortlessly from the Plaza of the Three Powers. Since it was first built, it has retained the power of surprise and dramatic composition. The difficulty in coming to terms with these buildings is that they really do seem pretty inhumane: designs that belong to the drawing board and the grand architectural model.

Niemeyer continued to work on and off on the design of Brasília until 1979. By then, nature had already got to work on his monuments: Brasília will only ever be perfect in the architect's imagination.

Children's Home

ALDO VAN EYCK, 1960

AMSTERDAM, THE

NETHERLANDS

A HOME AT the end of the century to the Berlage Institute (an architecture centre), this former orphanage was an ambitious and highly influential attempt by Aldo van Eyck (born 1918) to reinvent officious civic buildings. It was conceived as a small city made of single-storey pavilions that were linked by a pattern of courtyards. As such it would be an enjoyable experience to wander through, and full of daylight. In practice it was never so attractive; the concrete panel and glass brick construction soon tired and the building lost its lustre. The ideas behind it, however, remain valid as they show an alternative to the banal, hermetically sealed, box-like buildings that dominate city centres worldwide and which make no one particularly happy save the boss with the wood-panelled office and cocktail cabinet in the corners with the best views.

Perhaps the difficulty with van Eyck's architecture is that it posits a humane world, yet realizes it in materials that are often too tough for comfort. As a result, they appear to be unyielding.

Van Eyck was born in Driebergen, The Netherlands and educated in Zürich, Switzerland. An influential and garrulous teacher, he was also editor of the architecture magazine *Forum*. Van Eyck has had a major influence on the work of many European architects in search of a form and organization of Modern architecture that creates spaces for people to interact rather than impressive, yet isolated monuments.

Kurashiki City Hall

KENZO TANGE, 1960

KURASHIKI, JAPAN

TANGE WAS PERHAPS the architect most influenced by the forms of Le Corbusier: he took them home to Japan and made something new and convincing with them. This was far from easy. Le Corbusier's forms were extremely powerful and highly personal, and it was only too simple to ape the master's designs rather than to reinterpret them or else to adapt them to new locations and climates.

In the design of the City Hall at Kurashiki, Tange can be seen to be moving towards a personal view of Le Corbusier, working hard with the idea that traditional Japanese architecture could be translated through Brutalist concrete structures into something new, yet with a soul rooted in the distant past. In the immediate postwar period and as the Japanese economy made its spectacular recovery, Tange's approach appeared to make good sense. Japan might have been ready and willing to move forward rapidly into a new machine age, yet its culture and sense of pride had been badly damaged by the experience of misguided imperial conquest and a notably savage war. What Tange offered in buildings such as the City Hall at Kurashiki was Modernism and certainty at one and the same time. With its narrow, slitted window openings and beetling concrete cornice, the building has a fortified manner that was to be echoed in Tange's later projects culminating in the Yamanashi Press and Broadcasting Centre (p.350).

Keeling House

DENYS LASDUN, 1960

BETHNAL GREEN,

LONDON, ENGLAND

BORN IN LONDON IN 1914, Denys Lasdun trained at the Architectural Association, London, and designed most of his buildings there. He first worked for Wells Coates, before joining Berthold Lubetkin at Tecton. During World War Two Lasdun served as a Major in the Royal Engineers, building airfields for Allied fighter squadrons at the beginning of the invasion of Nazi-occupied Europe in summer 1944. After the war, his attention was turned to rehousing Londoners bombed by the Luftwaffe and V1 and V2 rockets. There were various plans at the time to rebuild damaged housing in London's East End. Lasdun built two unusual "cluster" blocks in Bethnal Green, one of eight, the other of fifteen storeys. The idea was to offer families spacious flats leading off from a central service core. Each flat would be surrounded by daylight and enjoy a variety of views. In practice, the flats needed a degree of maintenance local authorities were either hard-pressed or unwilling to fund, which led to the slow and sad decline of Keeling House despite its popularity with residents. Rightly, they felt that if moved elsewhere they would never find such generous amounts of space and light again. The fate of Keeling House became a *cause-célèbre* in conservation circles in the 1990s as the Modern Movement itself seemed more and more like a distant historical episode.

Pan-Am Building

WALTER GROPIUS AND
PIETRO BELLUSCHI, 1963
NEW YORK CITY, USA

HOW THE MIGHTY FELL. It is hard to connect Gropius, founder of the Bauhaus and one of the most important pioneers of the Modern Movement, with this bulky skyscraper looming over Grand Central Station. It's enough to make one sit down and weep. Gio Ponti and Pier Luigi Nervi had only recently shown how well a building of this scale could be made to work (p.204). Gropius's design was bombastic, although there are signs that he was hoping to mitigate its bulk. The building's ten-storey base respects the cornice line of Grand Central Station, before the 49-storey tower shoots up above it. The tower itself is designed to appear to be cast in sections, but even then it has a weighty look that Mies van der Rohe avoided with flair in the design of the Seagram Building (p.203).

For several years this lozenge-shaped tower was used as a helicopter landing pad. No one who has arrived in Manhattan by Pan-Am helicopter will ever forget the experience. Tragically, a helicopter slipped off the top of the building in bad weather and this *Bladerunner* experience has since been denied future generations. Gropius designed some more subtle buildings in Berlin in the years left to him, although he continued to live in the USA. The Pan-Am Building is perhaps the physical zenith and cultural nadir of his career at one and the same time.

Apartment Block

ALEJANDRO DE LA SOTA,
1963, SALAMANCA, SPAIN

IT WOULD BE EASY to walk past
this apartment block. It stands six
storeys high in a narrow street in
the centre of Salamanca. The ground
floor is home to a variety of dusty
and shabby shops. At least one or
two are usually boarded up or for
let. But if you bother to look up,
you will soon see why it deserves

recognition. Instead of scruffy
concrete or cheap render, the walls
are faced in handsome and well-
dressed local Salamanca stone. This
simple fact imbues the block with a
certain grandeur. This might be the
home of ordinary people, but the
materials employed are aristocratic.
And then there is the key detail
that makes a simple block of flats
humane and likeable: the projecting
windows or *miradores* designed so
that those inside can peep up and
down the street as people always
have done in the traditional houses

of this part of the world. Because
the street is narrow, the *miradores*
cannot project very far, yet the fact
that de la Sota insisted on them
is an encouraging sign: a Modern
architect knew when to pay heed to
local tradition and to incorporate
it convincingly into an otherwise
rational, shoe-box construction.

The detailing of the *miradores*
is particularly satisfying, the glass
is supported by clearly expressed
steel brackets that seem to cling
to the warm stone walls with a
limpet-like certainty.

Castelvecchio Museum

CARLO SCARPA, 1964

VERONA, ITALY

THIS WAS AN IMPORTANT project in the history, not so much of conservation, but of the reuse of historic buildings. This issue became increasingly important in the years following World War Two. Not only had the war itself witnessed the destruction of very many historic buildings, but rapid new development in the 1950s – notably in Germany and Italy –

meant the destruction or usurping of even more. Increasingly, too, old buildings, notably churches, lost their purpose. If they were not to be demolished or a burden on those charged with their upkeep, what useful role could they serve? And if they were to be converted, how could this be done without undermining their structural and aesthetic integrity? At Castelvecchio in Verona, Carlo Scarpa (1906–78) showed the way forward. The Venetian architect transformed the medieval castle into a museum and art gallery with the lightest of touches.

The project began in 1956 and was carried out over the period of a decade. Scarpa's genius was to make the lightest, smallest and most delicate interventions into the fabric of the old building and yet each of these spoke of an intelligent and highly tuned modern sensibility. Here was proof that the work of ancient and modern architects could sit happily together, one enhancing the aesthetic and logic of the other. Scarpa's ability to surprise and delight with the simplest architectural gesture has helped make this museum a model of its kind.

Faculty of Mechanical Engineering

ALFRED NEUMANN AND
ZVI HECKER, 1964
HAIFA, ISRAEL

IT TOOK SOME WHILE before
Israeli architects began to find a
recognizable voice. When it came,
it was hard and clear and one that
had been learned in the heat of
the desert and, perhaps, in the
mentality of defence. Many of the
most impressive Israeli buildings
have the look of modern fortresses.
This makes sense in a country

continually threatened with
invasion. Yet, such buildings are
also defences against a climate
that can be a hard enemy too.

Neumann (born 1924) and
Hecker (born 1931) designed the
Faculty of Mechanical Engineering
at Haifa – only one of several
planned pavilions was built – as
a shelter from the sun that did
away with the complications of the
brise-soleil that had been devised
by Le Corbusier and developed by
many architects, not least Corbu
himself, ever since. The solution
at Haifa was to design the whole
structure of the building as a
concrete sunshade – thus its

dramatic façades in which the
windows, invisible from almost any
oblique angle, slope steeply down
and backwards into the depth of
the reveals to keep the sun at bay.
This represented an important,
energy-saving move away from
flat-fronted buildings that required
too much in the way of ingenuity,
inconvenience and electricity to
keep them cool and their interiors
free from glare.

To an extent, the Faculty of
Engineering was also a way of
connecting contemporary Israeli
architecture with ancient
precursors such as temples in
the guise of ziggurats.

Economist Buildings

ALISON AND PETER
SMITHSON, 1964
ST JAMES'S, LONDON,
ENGLAND

THE SMITHSONS redeemed themselves after the strictures of Hunstanton, (p.193) with the Economist Buildings, a handsome trio of small towers – publishing offices, bank and club – grouped informally on a tiny, stepped and ramped piazza off one of central London's finest eighteenth century streets. That the new buildings and their Georgian predecessors sit so well together is as surprising as it is pleasing. Packing a group of smallish blocks together in a new city piazza made much sense in this sensitive area. At the time of their construction, the centre of London was being ruined by a rash of vile and foolish office blocks designed to make as much money for developers as quickly as possible before someone noticed that something was going horribly wrong. London's powerful conservation lobby gained its teeth at this time; it is significant that it has never had a problem with the Economist Buildings. Thoughtful and well constructed, they are also well mannered and do not try to "fit in" stylistically with their Georgian neighbours. There is no need, as the Smithsons proved, for them to do so.

When Peter Smithson, in later years, went on to berate errors made in British urban architecture in the 1960s, it was easy enough to listen to him. Whatever else, he had the Economist Buildings behind him.

Fondation Maeght

JOSEP LLUÍS SERT, 1964
ST-PAUL-DE-VENCE, FRANCE

ONE OF THE MOST MAGICAL of all
art spaces, the Fondation Maeght
shows some of the twentieth
century's greatest art in galleries
and courtyards designed by the
Catalan architect Josep Lluís Sert
(1902–83). In the blissful climate
of St-Paul-de-Vence, Sert shaped
an architecture from brick and
concrete that was remarkably open

and free. This is the antithesis of
the work of Mies van der Rohe:
at once sculptural, playful and as
open as possible to the elements.
Even on a rainy day, doors can be
kept open. There is a refreshing
lack of preciousness in evidence
here which adds to the pleasure
of Sert's sensual design. If the
building picks up a sculptural trick
or three from Miró and Braque,
this is clearly intentional; there is
no Postmodern irony involved,
just a knowing and rather gentle
whimsy that suits the location
well. Appropriately, Sert went on

to develop the ideas guiding the
Fondation Maeght further with
the Fundación Joan Miró (1975) in
Barcelona. The architect was born
and educated in Barcelona. He
worked for Le Corbusier and Pierre
Jeanneret in Paris between 1929
and 1931 before setting up on his
own back in Barcelona in 1931.
When Franco took the city, he left
for the USA where, in 1953, he
became Dean of the Graduate
School of Design at Harvard. He
returned to his native city, and it
is nice to be able to say that his
last buildings were his best.

Park Hill and
Hyde Park Estates

J. L. WOMERSLEY, ET AL,
1965, SHEFFIELD, ENGLAND

THESE VAST local authority estates were in no way cynical attempts to rehouse Sheffield's working classes in modern slums, although today they might seem that way, and much here has either been demolished or rebuilt. The idea, based in part on Le Corbusier's hugely influential L'Unité d'Habitation in Marseilles, was to build a modern version of traditional streets of terraced houses but in the sky rather than on the ground. The "houses", or duplex apartments, were entered by individual front doors leading off "access decks" (or streets in the air) and gathered together in Brutalist concrete blocks connected by concrete bridges. The "access decks" and bridges proved to be a perfect way for muggers and burglars to race through the estates, and have since been demolished. Clearly these monumental and relentless housing blocks were designed, despite their formidable appearance, for a more innocent age.

The designers from Sheffield City Architects Department who were involved in the project were much influenced by Le Corbusier and the Smithsons (p.215). The forms they created – tough, stark, gridded – were meant, in part, to reflect the tough, stark and gritty world of poor, working-class life in the northern England of the 1950s; but what hope they were meant to give people is unclear. Sheffield was not Marseilles, lacking the sun, warmth and vibrant street and café culture that might have redeemed these craggy and daunting housing estates.

Centre Point

RICHARD SEIFERT, 1966

LONDON, ENGLAND

THE BEEHIVE concrete sections, slim profile and catwalk stance of this 34-storey Pop-era office block have all helped turn what was once the most unpopular building in London, built by the highly litigious developer, Harry Hyams, into a much-liked and even respected monument to Mammon. Although completed in 1966, the tower stood empty for many years. Quite why remains a mystery, but be careful how you tell the story if you do: Mr Hyams' lawyers will be waiting like vultures for you to slip up. The tower dominates many views of central London and it is unfortunate, given its latter-day popularity, that its top floor cannot be opened as a bar, restaurant and public viewing gallery.

The tower is part of a bigger development that includes flats and shops and connects directly to Tottenham Court Road tube station. The architect was Colonel Richard Seifert (born 1910) who became a household name in the 1960s and '70s: his buildings were said at the time to have had as much, if not more, impact on central London than any architect since Christopher Wren. True or not, Seifert's highly distinctive towers – beehives, drums, strutting boxes – have ridden out the ridicule. The pipe-smoking Colonel (he served with the Royal Engineers during World War Two) designed, it now seems agreed, some of the sassiest commercial buildings of the 1960s.

St Peter's College

GILLESPIE, KIDD
AND COIA, 1966

CARDROSS, SCOTLAND

THE ARCHITECTURE OF Le Corbusier translated well into Scotland in the 1960s. Although the climate of the south of France and the west of Scotland could hardly be more different, Corbu's roughcast concrete style could, in the right hands, be seen as a natural successor or complement to traditional Scottish tower houses with their rugged forms and tough materials. Those hands belonged to the Glasgow firm Gillespie, Kidd and Coia.

St Peter's College is a Roman Catholic seminary inhabiting a severe Victorian building that was very successfully added to by Jack Coia (1898-1981) and his team. The low-set and rhythmic four-storey addition was in part derived from the forms of Corbusier's Maisons Jaoul (p.198) and in part by the plan of the monastery at La Tourette (p.206): the refectory and public rooms were at ground level, the seminarists' rooms stacked in tiers on the three storeys above. The ground floor led into an imposing and brooding chapel that adopted the organic plan of Ronchamp (p.101). Although the debt to Corbusier was strong, and obvious, St Peter's had a character and spirit very much of its own, a muscular architecture for those studying for the demanding life of the Catholic priesthood. It has since been abandoned and left to rot.

Habitat Housing

MOSHE SAFDIE, 1967

MONTREAL, CANADA

ONE OF THE BIG SURPRISES of the Expo '67 Montreal World Fair were the 158 beehive apartments designed by the Israeli-born architect Moshe Safdie (born 1938). Known as Habitat, this experiment in Pop-age living was to become one of the most fashionable addresses in Montreal. Habitat was Safdie's first major work. He was 29. After graduation from Montreal's McGill University, he worked with Louis Kahn in Philadelphia before going on to run his own studio.

Habitat might have seemed a surprise success with professional families, yet they were clearly able to see well beyond its prefabricated concrete panel construction to its intriguing and even poetic disposition. There were no fewer than 15 different layouts among the apartments, each with its own roof terrace and particular view. At one point it was suggested that Habitat be expanded to a total of 900 apartments, but this fell through and the houses remain an intriguing one-off in North America, although Safdie developed the idea in Israel.

After Habitat, Safdie went on to teach at the Ben Gurion University at Beersheva, Israel, before taking a post at Harvard. Subsequently, he returned to Israel where he developed a new monumental architecture based on the severe grids and geometry adopted from his experience both with Kahn and with Expo '67.

Cathedral of Christ the King

FREDERICK GIBBERD, 1967

LIVERPOOL, ENGLAND

KNOWN BOTH AFFECTIONATELY and condescendingly as "Paddy's Wigwam" – Liverpool is a city of Irish immigrants: the cathedral looks like a Red Indian tent to Liverpudlians – the Roman Catholic Cathedral is more likely to have been based on the design of Oscar Niemeyer's "Crown of Thorns" cathedral at Brasília, and even perhaps on the Gemini space capsules of the early NASA orbital launches. The cathedral, by Frederick Gibberd (1908–84), stands on a prominent site at one end of Liverpool's Hope Street: at the other end broods the almighty Gothic Anglican cathedral by Giles Gilbert Scott (p.114). Gibberd's church, although a striking design, occupies just a fraction of the terrace that was to have been one of the most imposing and brilliant ecclesiastical buildings of all times – Edwin Lutyen's vast domed Catholic cathedral. In the event, only the crypt was built. Gibberd's slighter design, built at great speed and rather cheaply, in just a few years, consists of a skeletal cone made up of slim concrete buttresses and topped with a lofty lantern filled with stained glass by John Piper and Patrick Reyntiens. Between the buttresses at ground level is a circle of chapels, each different. The congregation sits in the round bathed in coloured lights: the altar is central following the precepts of Vatican II. Restoration began on the cathedral in the 1990s.

Hayward Gallery

LCC ARCHITECTS
DEPARTMENT, 1967
LONDON, ENGLAND

THREATENED WITH DEMOLITION at various times in the 1980s and 1990s, the Hayward Gallery – a Brutalist concrete culture bunker on London's South Bank – has survived to become admired by younger generations for whom its bizarre, defensive architecture is an adventure rather than a threat. The gallery had a long gestation and was finally built, after long delays, during the 1960s. It was designed by a team of young "Turks" led by Norman Engleback (born 1930) under the direction of Hubert Bennett (born 1909). The heavy-duty concrete construction, although heavily influenced by Le Corbusier and the Brutalists, was considered necessary because at the time of its design there were plans to build a helicopter terminal near the gallery. Despite its menacing, military style, the Hayward is a well-finished building and was expensive to construct. Originally, and again to prevent noise from overflying helicopters seeping in, the galleries were to have been enclosed and artificially lit. In the event, the committees involved in its progress demanded daylight ("God's own daylight", said the sculptor Henry Moore) and insisted on top-lighting in the upper galleries, giving the building its distinctive roof profile.

A number of exhibitions in the 1990s – most of all Richard Long's "Walking in Circles" – gave the building the profile it needed to make it popular with a newly receptive audience. It remains a difficult building, yet as endearing as a boxer with a "cauliflower" ear.

Marina City

BERTRAND GOLDBERG, 1967

CHICAGO, ILLINOIS, USA

BY NIGHT, car headlamps swoop around the spiralling ramps of the car parks that occupy the lower heights of these characterful circular downtown apartment blocks: the effect is dizzying, dazzling and utterly compelling. Like two giant corn cobs, the twin towers of Marina City rise high into the Chicago skyline. Each supports 40 floors of balconied apartments over spiralling elevated car parks. If it seems odd to live so high off the ground, it seems stranger to see automobiles parked so very high off the streets they are designed to roar along.

Marina City was the finest work of Bertrand Goldberg (1913–97) and one of the most imaginative and convincing examples of how to live high in the city sky. Goldberg's genius was to take advantage of a river setting and to adopt an architectural form that allowed for so very many balconies – and thus life outside – without undermining the formal strength of his highly sculpted towers. These were the antithesis of, for example, Mies van der Rohe's sleek-skinned Lake Shore Drive apartments nearby (p.187) and were considered by many critics to be kitsch. This is unfair. Once seen in real life, Marina City has much of the verve promised in the paper architecture of the Futurists and seems an ideal answer in some ways to the question of what to do with the cars we say we despise yet can't seem to do without even if we live in city centres.

Ford
Foundation

NOT FOR THOSE who suffer from vertigo or agoraphobia, the Ford Foundation is, for the brave hearted, an almost unparalleled and hugely impressive achievement. The offices of the Foundation are planted on two sides of a 12-storey greenhouse or atrium. Windows open into this world of lush planting, vertiginous columns and vast sheets of plate glass; so office workers look out to the city beyond through a layer of greenery and glazing. The views can be quite surreal. Even more so, the executive suites and dining rooms occupy what seems like a perilous two-storey gallery, running along the street front on top of the gallery with nothing below but the depths of the giant atrium. Doubtless, it was the Ford Foundation that made the atrium popular, and something of a cliché, in office buildings 20 years later. Here, though, the concept is as impressive as it was original. Also impressive, from an urban point of view, was the fact that this radical building sat flush and neatly with the line of the street.

The building was designed by Kevin Roche (born 1922), an Irish architect who worked for Michael Scott in Dublin, and Maxwell Fry and Jane Drew in London before emigrating to the USA in 1948, where he became head of design with Eero Saarinen's office in 1954. Here he met John Dinkeloo (1918–81), an architect and inventor of great distinction.

Centre
Le Corbusier

LE CORBUSIER, 1967
ZÜRICH, SWITZERLAND

ORIGINALLY DESIGNED as a private
house, the Centre Le Corbusier,
completed two years after his
death, shows a further turn in
direction at the end of a long
journey of a great artist who chose
building as his most convincing
medium. Here, the house is
conceived as what is potentially an
infinite sequence of prefabricated
geometric panels that can be
arranged in chess-board moves
or simply a straight line. In fact,
their arrangement and number is
governed and determined by the
umbrella roof suspended above
them by a variety of steel poles
and columns. The effect is rather
like seeing a Greek temple with a
modern building inserted beneath
its pediments and between its
columns. On another level, it is
like looking at a sequence of
abstract canvases displayed beneath
a giant frame. What we can be
sure of is that at the end of a long
and remarkably fruitful life, Le
Corbusier's capacity for invention
and reinvention was far from
exhausted. The man himself,
however, felt he had accomplished
enough, and when he swam to
his death in 1965, a number of
friends and observers believed
that he had intended to die
swimming into the sun he
worshipped rather than to
wait while his enormous and
unprecedented talent expired.

Neue Nationalgalerie

LUDWIG MIES VAN DER
ROHE, 1968
BERLIN, GERMANY

IT MIGHT BE UNWISE to call the
Neue Nationalgalerie a *reductio ad
absurdum*, yet there is an unsettling
feeling in this vast and empty
building that Mies had gone too
far and even lost his own
exquisitely refined plot. Most of
the artworks on show here line
the relentless walls of basement
galleries lit from one side by a wall
of glass, or else occupy rather
breathless sub-surface rooms. The
upper gallery, housed under the
great coffered canopy, supported by
just eight deeply recessed cruciform
steel columns and encased in walls
of floor to ceiling glass, seems
formless. On days of low sun – of
which there are plenty in Berlin –
fusty curtains are drawn across the
giant windows, making the space
sombre and rather like a giant
funeral parlour.

As a monument, the gallery
is memorable; as an art gallery it
seems deeply unsatisfying and even
wrong-headed. It would almost
be better left empty, a mid-
twentieth-century reinterpretation
of a Greek temple, as cold and
passionate as a winter dawn rising
over the lakes of the nearby
Tiergarten. This was the last of
Mies's major buildings and the last
in a long line of purist pavilions
or secular temples he had been
occupied with since at least the
Barcelona Pavilion of 1929 (p.152).
It is comforting to know that the
hard-drinking, fine-living architect's
own Chicago apartment was
comfortable, bourgeois and even
a little old-fashioned.

Student Housing

DENYS LASDUN, 1968
UNIVERSITY OF EAST
ANGLIA, NORWICH,
NORFOLK, ENGLAND

LOOKING MUCH LIKE twentieth-century Aztec or Mayan stepped temples, this university housing was opened the year that students across Europe and the United States took to the streets and hoped for the Revolution to come before their grants ran out and they had to get jobs, get married

and settle down. The Revolution might have been a serious proposition in France or Germany, and even to an extent in the USA where the student uprisings were part of a general reaction against Washington's futile war in Vietnam. In Britain, life was cosier: there wasn't that much to rebel against. There were grants aplenty, jobs galore, great music, more freedom than many knew what to do with, and lavish university expansion schemes that meant cheap accommodation in buildings designed by some of the country's finest architects.

At UEA, a new university set

outside Norwich, Lasdun designed this cluster of distinctive pyramid blocks offering generous rooms and plenty of spaces to sit outside. Within a few years, the interiors were squalid – nothing to do with the architect – and the ziggurats, it was said, were gradually slipping down towards the lake below them. They still stand, however, a loose-fit monument to the heroic age of tertiary education in Britain when a university degree – even in the arts in which UEA specialized – was a passport to a groovy and well-paid job. As a formal composition, Lasdun's concrete pyramids stand up well.

Lake Point Tower

SCHIPPOREIT–HEINRICH
ASSOCIATES, 1968
CHICAGO, ILLINOIS, USA

THIS SHIMMERING 196-metre
(645-ft) apartment block standing
in solitary splendour over Lake
Michigan was designed by former
students of Mies van der Rohe.
It is, in effect, the realization –
with Chicago money, muscle and
can-do know-how – of Mies's 1921
project for a curved glass office
tower, which was never built due
to lack of funds and the necessary
structural and glass technology.
So, while it is a home for those
lucky enough to be able to afford
one of its 900 apartments, it is
also a homage to one of the
century's greatest architects built
at the end of his life. And, of
course, a show-off exercise in US
building skills.

The tower is clover-shaped in
plan and clad in a pretty much
skin-tight glass cat-suit. Even
Spider Man would find it hard to
climb. The plan and flush glazing
conspire to catch the sunlight at
all times of day, although it is at
sunset, as Lake Michigan appears

to catch fire, that Lake Point Tower
comes into its own. The sense of
detachment that comes from living
here – high up and away from
the city centre – is a Modern
Movement dream come true. From
any one of the tower's apartments,
residents have the feeling of
looking down on the restless city
beyond and below as if it were
little more than a movie shown in
Cinemascope. They enjoy the view
of the world shared by Mies van
der Rohe and Le Corbusier in the
1920s as they sought to create
cities in which professional people
would live in serviced flats above
parkland and lakes.

San Cristobal
Stud Farm

LUIS BARRAGÁN, 1968

MEXICO CITY, MEXICO

THE FLAMBOYANT Luis Barragán (1902–87) had a magnificent eye for colour, and for many people who find the strictures of, say, Mies van der Rohe too clinical and monochrome to bear, this Mexican architect offered a palette of exquisite natural pigments that made Modernism sensual, warm and, quite simply, delightful. This stud farm – house, stables, lake,

gardens – outside Mexico City is perhaps the closest Barragán got to shaping an architecture, and a landscape, in which the formalism of Modern architecture was reconciled with nature, colour, animals and the good life under the sun. Here, he employed an abstract constructional geometry brought to rippling, ever-shifting life by the play of bright sunlight and shadows on water and lush, perfumed plants and trees. The smell of horses and saddle leather is an added bonus.

Significantly, and like many of the century's most sensual and

least fettered architects, Barragán was self-taught. He had trained as an engineer, but as an architect he invented himself. His earliest designs were much influenced by Moroccan and Islamic architecture in general; it was only when he moved from Guadalajara to Mexico City in 1936 that he became aware of the Modern Movement. From then on he developed his highly individual and very beautiful approach to architecture: if anyone thinks Modern architecture is cold, they have never experienced anything like this superb built landscape in Mexico.

Expo '70

THIS WAS THE FIRST of the world fairs to be held in Asia and it was easily one of the best, at least from an architectural perspective. The site was laid out by Kenzo Tange but architects from all around the world contributed a zoo of gloriously inventive, daring, perverse and even funny structures.

Expo '70 marked, in fact, the zenith of architects' first-time around fascination with inflatable structures, fabric construction and new ways of defying the downwards pull of gravity, a force that architects have wrestled to overcome since Daedalus, the "first" (and mythologized) architect built wings to fly with his ill-fated son, Icarus, from Crete to Greece.

The zany structures that animated Expo '70 were not wasted. Many of the ideas and the aesthetics that inspired them, were

to emerge in mature expressions of tented and soft, fabric-based, architecture in the last two decades of the century. They also set the tone for transportable and inflatable sets for rock concerts, for the bouncy castles of childrens' fairgrounds and the settings for art events and political galas. The idea that the Modern world could invent, use and enjoy a soft, transient architecture, as nomads around the world had done for millennia, was as surprising as it was enjoyable.

Weinstein House

RICHARD MEIER, 1971

OLD WESTBURY,

NEW YORK STATE, USA

WHITER THAN WHITE, the single-minded architecture of Richard Meier (born 1934) is as unmistakable as it is satisfying or numbing, depending upon your point of view. Meier, the white knight of Modern architecture, saddled up his white charger in the mid-1960s, having graduated from Cornell University and worked for Skidmore, Owings and Merrill and Marcel Breuer. Over the next decade, he received several commissions to design the white houses that he has been associated with ever since. Each is a play or variation on its siblings and these houses do indeed form a close-knit architectural family. Nevertheless, they are also highly responsive to their individual sites and are thus different from the starship villas of the early Modern Movement that appeared to have landed in green fields with no thought of what the local terrain might look or feel like.

Meier worked in loose collaboration with other "whites" who became known as the New York Five. Their theorist was the erudite Peter Eisenman (born 1932), but Meier was the one who built quietly and prolifically. The Weinstein House in New York State is a deeply satisfying Meier design, showing how many ways a cube can be cut through, rearranged, its geometric possibilities exposed. The various elements of the house appear to lock together even as they are pulling apart – a sense of being together wisely divided by an equal and opposite sense of privacy. Truly brilliant.

Florey Building

JAMES STIRLING AND
JAMES GOWAN, 1972
OXFORD, ENGLAND

MISTAKEN ENDLESSLY for a multi-storey car park – there is a public car park alongside it – the ugly backside of the Florey Building belies its river frontage. This is hidden because the bright orange back of this students' hostel wraps around it, keeping prying eyes at bay and holding the hoi-polloi back from the precious world of the Oxford undergraduate. The several tiers of student rooms here are held up on concrete stilts and gathered around an internal courtyard, opening on one side to the lugubrious River Cherwell below. The difficulty here is that residents are completely exposed to view and the shy or modest feel the need to keep the blinds of their floor-to-ceiling windows drawn for much of the day.

If this is perverse, then the arrangement of the rooms is even more so, particularly if you happen to be one of the unfortunates through whose room the concrete buttresses that support the building passes through at an oblique angle. And then there is the small question of how, after a few drinks in the student union bar, to negotiate a bed that is mounted at the top of ladder-like stairs.

Was big, braw Jim Stirling having a joke at the expense of fey intellectual students? It certainly seems that way, although as a work of sculpture, the Florey Building is nothing if not impressive.

Lethbridge University

ARTHUR ERICKSON, 1972

ALBERTA, CANADA

AN OCEAN LINER or spaceship of a building berthed or come to land in the rural vastness of Alberta. This is Lethbridge University by Arthur Erickson (born 1924), perhaps the most important Canadian architect of the century. Here, every function and activity has been housed under one enormous roof, even student accommodation. No messy extrusions. No outbuildings of any sort. This is a powerful, and even overbearing concrete megastructure, and yet it makes some sense in a vast landscape in which a gentler touch would make little impact. Assuming the University did want to make its mark on a boundless landscape, it chose the right architect.

Erickson studied in Vancouver and Montreal. A dynamic architect, by the 1980s he had offices across the world. His buildings have, for the most part, been as ambitious in scale as his world view. They are often in spectacular locations and do their muscular best to make their presence felt in no uncertain terms. The most impressive of the earlier buildings are the Simon Fraser University, Burnaby, Vancouver (from 1963) and the Justice Building (1980), which occupies a whole city block in Vancouver. The scale and bombast of Erickson's architecture, although he has built some small wooden houses influenced by Mies van der Rohe, may be a natural reaction to the scale and power of the Canadian landscape and climate. It is hard to imagine Lethbridge University sitting well in the exquisite confines of Europe.

Centraal Beheer

HERMAN HERTZBERGER,
1972
APELDOORN, NETHERLANDS

A BIG YET MODEST BUILDING,
Centraal Beheer was designed as an
office for over a thousand insurance
clerks. To make their day more of a
grind than it needs be, such white-
collar workers have all too often
been filed into bland, sub-Miesian
office blocks. Hertzberger (born
1932) came up with an idea that
had been discussed during the
1960s, yet rarely realized: the office
as interior landscape. Inside what
is a fairly dreary, low-lying grey
concrete structure composed of a
large number of interlocking
pavilions is a complex office
divided and subdivided into spaces
that give each clerk or group of
clerks a home of their own. The
apparently informal layout and the
relaxed attitude of management
here meant that workers were
encouraged to customize their
workspaces to the point where the
office began to take on the look of
a bureaucratic Hanging Gardens of
Babylon. This was very much in
keeping with Hertzberger's belief
that the architect's role was not to
try and determine the way people
occupied a building, but to design
buildings that allowed people to
use them as they wanted to. Like
many Dutch architects of his
generation, Hertzberger appeared
to see no contradiction between a
deep-rooted humanity and architecture that relied almost unduly
on dull concrete and breeze-blocks.

Bianchi
House

MARIO BOTTA, 1972

TICINO, SWITZERLAND

A HOUSE FOR a Swiss schoolteacher, this simple, geometric tower rises three storeys from a field overlooking beautiful Lake Lugano. It is made from lightweight concrete blocks and would be unremarkable save for three things: its marvellous setting against the lake and the snow-capped mountains beyond, the rigour of its geometry and the enclosed, steel-mesh bridge that connects its top floor to the otherwise unreachable road alongside. The result is as simple as it is satisfying.

Mario Botta (born 1943) trained as an architectural draughtsman from the age of 15. Later, in Venice, he got to work on Le Corbusier's very last, unrealized project, a hospital for the city on water. He also worked briefly with Louis Kahn. Botta had built his first house at the age of 18 but his precociousness did not lead to preciousness. Far from it, his concerns were always with the elemental building blocks of architecture – the cube, sphere and cylinder – and in setting these in subtle juxtaposition with the Swiss landscape. In a sense, he was going back to the very beginnings of Western architecture, to the archetypal forms described by Plato. His interest in these forms, however, was far from being wholly intellectual: Botta was and is concerned very much with the craft of building and, in this sense, he is a rare talent, for many of those who think boldly in the abstract are often at odds or removed from the process of construction. It is the two things combined that makes great and desirable architecture.

Trellick Tower

ERNO GOLDFINGER, 1972

LONDON, ENGLAND

A WEST LONDON LANDMARK, Trellick Tower is the most visible component of a large local authority estate designed in a heroic and Brutalist manner by Erno Goldfinger (1902–87). And, yes, before you ask, Goldfinger was a friend of Ian Fleming, author of the James Bond thrillers. Although bombastic, Trellick Tower was to become a highly coveted address by fashionable young things living around the glamorous Portobello Road market in the 1990s. For several years until then it had been used as a prison in the sky for some of the area's poorest and most problematic families. What the tower offered, aside from memorable architecture and stunning views all around London, were duplex flats, modelled on those of Le Corbusier's L'Unité d'Habitation (p.190), which were spacious, light and airy and with windows on both sides of the tower.

Goldfinger's monumental works have been described as the product of "structural rationalism", which makes a certain amount of sense, and yet the force and brute nature of Trellick Tower seem fairly irrational. If Trellick hadn't become so fashionable in the last decade of the century, one might be tempted to say that this is the sort of architecture one wouldn't want to bump into on a dark night. A sibling estate, without the full-on drama of Trellick was built in London's East End and, famously, Goldfinger lived in the tower (although for not that long).

Thau School

MARTORELL–BOHIGAS–
MACKAY, 1972
BARCELONA, SPAIN

THIS MODERN SCHOOL divided into infant, junior and senior blocks does that clever thing: without recourse to pastiche and as if with a nod over the architects' shoulders, it recreates the urban landscape of the ancient Greek *agora* or market place. The school is a city centre in miniature with squares, terraces and stairs connecting the various parts. The symbolism is simple and satisfying: as the children progress up through the years, so they climb higher up the stairs, modelled on the tiers of a Greek theatre, with the peak of the hills that form the backdrop to the school signifying the heights yet to be attained.

The buildings themselves form a strict geometrical composition, but the severity of the plan and its cool, rational architecture is continually mollified by views out to other parts of the school, to the *agora*, its steps and the rising landscape beyond. Not surprisingly, Oriol Bohigas (born 1925) is a highly gifted urban planner who was responsible for a significant part of Barcelona's physical and cultural revival after the death of the dictator, General Franco, in 1974. His colleagues in on the Thau School project were Josep Martorell (born 1925) and the Scottish-born David Mackay (born 1933). Bohigas has been an advisor to the city of Barcelona since 1981.

Kimbell
Art Gallery

LOUIS KAHN, 1972

FORT WORTH, TEXAS, USA

"THE FIRST THING you want in most museums is a cup of coffee. You feel so tired immediately". Louis Kahn (1901–74) felt the way most of us do when faced by a big museum full of very important art. The aching shoulders, the exhaustion, the feeling of guilt as you fail to take in the subtleties of all that Art that is meant to be good for you. And all you want is to sit down and drink a coffee. The café in this superb museum is one of the best in the world. Kahn has given it equal ranking with the galleries, and that is the work of a very civilized and intelligent man, which this Estonian architect, whose poor Jewish parents settled in the USA in 1904, most certainly was. Kahn came from nothing and gave everything back: he was a genius, up there with Mies and Le Corbusier, but his buildings were somehow warmer and, even when designed on a heroic scale, engaging.

The Kimbell is designed on a small scale. A group of barrel-vaulted pavilions are linked, interspersed with courtyards and gardens and bathed inside with the most subtle and delicate wash of daylight. The materials used throughout are the very best. This, of course, is often possible in the USA where wealthy patrons (in this case Kay and Velma Kimbell) can indulge their architects to degrees their European counterparts can only dream of. This was Kahn's favourite of his own buildings. He was right to be proud of it.

Willis Faber
and Dumas

FOSTER ASSOCIATES, 1975

IPSWICH, SUFFOLK, ENGLAND

THIS SLEEK OFFICE BLOCK still comes as a surprise, for it sits in the heart of Ipswich, a country town that is about as sleepy as they come in southern England. By day, the jet black glass gives away nothing of the interior and the building is Sphinx-like in its silence. As the sun sets, the interior begins to emerge and the reflections of the town in the all but seamless glass walls vanish. This daily spectacle makes the Willis Faber building (the Dumas got dropped along the way at some point in the insurance company's more recent history) as exciting a part of the townscape as it was when it opened 25 years ago. Since then, the building has been listed as being of historical and architectural importance even though it was less than the statutory minimum of 30 years old at the time. Such is Norman Foster's reputation.

The building's skin, like an Alaïa frock, is the most fascinating part of a building that, once through its triple-height lobby and up its smooth-running escalators (in place of lifts), is really a rather conventional open-plan office for insurance clerks. Many of these work facing inwards, unable to enjoy the views out of Foster's impeccable glass screen, which reaches right down to kiss the pavement. Staff did, however, in the early days at least, benefit from a swimming pool in the basement and an immaculately maintained lawn on the roof.

National Theatre

DENYS LASDUN, 1975

LONDON, ENGLAND

LASDUN HAS ALWAYS DESCRIBED this building as a series of terraces or architectural strata, and one sees what he means. From the outside this mountainous concrete building feels more like some strangely refined archeological outcrop than a place of public entertainment. And, from its tiered terraces, to be climbed over as if mountaineering in the city centre, there are superb views of other urban peaks, notably that of St Paul's Cathedral and Lloyds of London (p.363). Perhaps this curious way of looking at the National Theatre has helped endear it to the public since its completion, after a long gestation, in 1975. The interior has always been popular. The three theatres are superb and the lobbies enjoyable, save for the horrid carpets – quite why the British are so obsessed with carpet in public buildings remains a mystery.

The theatre sits alongside Waterloo Bridge and dominates a particularly fine bend on the River Thames. For the most part it is finished in weather-boarded concrete and is saved from seeming brutal by the quality of the materials used and by the intriguing play of horizontal and vertical planes on which the sun plays very effectively, as does electric light at night. The back side of the building is uninspired and merely functional as if Lasdun suddenly forgot what to do without the drama of the river to prompt him.

Student Housing

LUCIEN KROLL, 1975
CATHOLIC UNIVERSITY
OF LOUVAIN, BELGIUM

THIS WAS THE YEAR that Punk hit the headlines. It seems very unlikely that Lucien Kroll (born 1927) was ever a fan of the Sex Pistols, yet the university campus at Louvain he completed that year was about as punky as mainstream architecture gets.

Kroll, born and trained in Brussels, was a devout believer in the much talked about, yet little practised, notion of public participation in architecture. He genuinely believed that the users of a building should shape it with the architect acting as sounding board and guiding hand. The medical faculty and student residences attached to it have been a remarkable and perhaps unexpected success.

The buildings have grown in a rather shaggy, punk manner, but are entirely free of the bogus "community" architecture look that emerged in Britain at the same

time, whereby the architect patronized users by interpreting their wishes in Toy Town, comic book forms and details.

What Kroll allowed was for students and teachers to say what they needed and wanted and then to knit together the various strands into a loose-fit architecture. So, there were odd bits of gardens here, stairs there, jutting roofs and roof terraces galore: all these things are expression of what people say they want and they are not always quite where architects, with their tidy minds, want them to be.

Kalman
House

LUIGI SNOZZI, 1976

TICINO, SWITZERLAND

LUIGI SNOZZI (BORN 1932) is one of a loosely related group of architects from Ticino who has worked on developing a rational yet romantic architecture that owes as much to Cubism and Le Corbusier as it does to landscape and site. Perhaps this is because the locale – a beautiful setting of lakes and mountains – encourages the building of houses on sites that in lesser hands would be problematic, but for the Ticino architects are a natural challenge.

The Kalman House – on one level a simple concrete box sliced and sectioned – climbs dramatically up from its hillside setting. It may be an essay in strict geometry and in the use of a minimal palette of materials and colours, yet this is the point: the theatre of the enfolding landscape provides all the colour and decoration the house and its owners ever really need. This special relationship between house and landscape is emphasized by the bridge that juts out from the house and leads out to a pavilion from which the Kalmans can sit and look out across the mountains and watch the sun set across lake and valley.

In another less dramatic location the house would seem quite cold, if logical, intelligent and thoughtfully planned; here, the architect has played a knowing and gentle game, contrasting the mathematical construct of the building against nature's own rococo.

Byker
Wall

RALPH ERSKINE, 1979
NEWCASTLE-UPON-TYNE,
ENGLAND

THE BYKER WALL was premised on
a lie, which was not the fault of
Ralph Erskine (born 1914), its
popular Anglo-Swedish architect.
Originally, an urban motorway was
to have sliced through Byker, a
working-class district of Newcastle,
and the new housing, proposed to
raise the spirit of this depressed
area, was to be built in a way that
denied the roar of speeding traffic.
In the end, Newcastle's famously
corrupt local councillors were either
chucked out or imprisoned and
Erskine need not have designed
the "Wall" the way he did.
Nevertheless, this local authority
housing was instantly popular
and has rightly become famous.

The outlying wall of informal
flats and houses puts a big and
friendly, if rather shaggy, arm
around smaller blocks and
individual houses. It is one

kilometre (two-thirds of a mile)
long and rises up to a maximum of
eight storeys. The result is a cosy
and well-protected urban village.
Residents had a lot of say in its
design and layout. Erskine is a
good listener and able to produce
populist architecture that never
resorts to pastiche or whimsy.
He was born and brought up as
a Quaker in Saffron Walden and
moved to Sweden in 1939. In 1998
he was appointed architect of the
Millennium Village, an ecologically
correct new town on the
Greenwich peninsula in London.

Atheneum Visitor Center

RICHARD MEIER, 1979

HARMONY, INDIANA, USA

HAVING DESIGNED a number of chaste and beautiful white villas for well-heeled New Englanders throughout the 1970s, Meier was set to take off on a global trip in the next decade during which time he was to produce one memorable museum after the other. His crisp, white, impeccable style proved to be truly international. The missing link between the villas and the museums is this shining visitor centre for the community of Harmony, Indiana.

This was Meier's first public building and is without doubt harmonious. It stands on a pristine lawn and hints at a perfect social order. Meier's buildings have the disconcerting quality of looking exactly as they do in photographs: the grass is always green, the buildings fresh back from the dry-cleaners. It consists of three storeys of rooms gathered around a lecture theatre, linked by a highly articulated web of ramps, external stairs and bridges. What Meier has done is to take a classically white box and break it apart, reassembling some of what might have gone inside – such as the stairs – outside. This accessibility is reinforced by the feeling that some of the walls have been slid away from the box and projected as screens onto the lawn. With a push here and there, you feel that you would be able to straighten the whole thing up again. It is a nice conceit: a building that expresses democracy and order at one and the same time.

Barbican Centre

CHAMBERLIN, POWELL
AND BON, 1979
CITY OF LONDON, ENGLAND

THIS HEROIC HOUSING development
was in the making for something
like a quarter of a century. Despite
its formidable appearance – a huge
castle of solid concrete topped with
high and highly sculpted towers –
the Barbican is not a low-rent
council estate but an aggressive
aggregation of flats for City of
London professionals. In fact,

nearly the entire resident
population of the City of London
lives here.

The Barbican was built to an
extremely high standard and those
who live here will have nothing,
or not very much, to say against
it. Don't even think of entering
without a guide and compass.
Once inside its walls, the
uninitiated are faced by dark,
labyrinthine walkways that appear
to lead nowhere, but in fact link
together a complex arrangement of
internal squares, courtyards and
gardens. These are surprisingly lush
and attractive when you find them,
and the complex turns out to be a

bit of a softie at heart, with water
gardens and a waterfall, a medieval
parish church, sections of the
Roman wall that once bounded
what was Londinium, a smart
girls' school and an arts centre
within its formidable boundaries.

Shortly before they were
commissioned to design it, the
same architects had built the
comparatively bright and breezy
Golden Lane estate that is situated
alongside the Barbican. The
contrast between the two is
marked: where Golden Lane seems
open and willing to engage in
conversation, the Barbican is
aloof and silent.

Alexandra Road Housing

CAMDEN ARCHITECTS
DEPARTMENT, 1979
LONDON, ENGLAND

A DEFIANT LAST FLING, Alexandra Road marked the end of the giant concrete local authority housing projects in London that had been such a controversial part of the British architectural scene since the 1950s. It comprises two new carless streets, one a kilometre (two-thirds of a mile) long, running parallel to the busy electrified train line from London to Scotland. The result is an extraordinarily powerful, if utterly terrifying, experience. The ideas behind the project seem rational, yet it all seems so inhumane. If you happen to live half way down that one-kilometre street, you may well experience a sense of being quite lost to the world beyond the regimented, concrete confines of the estate. The density of occupation here (200 to the acre) is great by British or US standards, although typical of many continental European cities. While this is fine in principle, in practice it isn't because of the way in which Alexandra Road turns in on itself, partly as a defence against the noise of trains. Car parking is provided in a grim labyrinth below the streets.

The Camden Architects department was one of the last bastions of such designs, and though architects tend to defend its last ditch attempt at grand Modernism, people breathed a sigh of relief when this bombast came to an end.

Humbertus House

ALDO VAN EYCK, 1980

AMSTERDAM, THE
NETHERLANDS

THIS MULTICOLOURED city building is a home for single parents and their children. If this sounds like a little institutional, then it is, for the building represents the powerfully cossetting operations of the Dutch welfare state in the latter part of the century. When it was built, European societies were only just beginning to come to terms with the fact that the "nuclear" family (Mum, Dad, 2.4 kids) was breaking down and that many children would be brought up by one parent. As this realization dawned, so there appeared to be a need for local authorities and city governments to cope with what was perceived as a problem, rather than as a natural change in the Western social set up that had been brewing for many years.

The six-storey Humbertus House is a brightly painted creature composed of many different materials, of a complex arrangement of interlocking, intersecting blocks, of courtyards and roof gardens, big airy windows drawing quietly from historic precedent, of pergolas and walkways. Its informality was drawn together by a rigorous plan, as one expects from an architect who was very much a Modernist. Its complexity is rooted in van Eyck's fascination with the idea of such civic buildings being towns in themselves, with their own internal streets and squares.

Xerox Center

HELMUT JAHN, 1980

CHICAGO, ILLINOIS, USA

SUPER SLEEK, the Xerox Center
was very close in spirit to Mies van
der Rohe's glass tower project of
1921. It rises in 45 seamless storeys
above Chicago and is as poised and
polished as it is silent and apparently
impenetrable. Its aluminium and
glass skin, as tight as tight can be,
creams round the junction of South
Dearborn and West Monroe Streets.
This was about as far as this kind
of building – 60 years in the
conceptual making – could go before
running out of ideas or slipping
into the realm of sheer banality.
The Xerox Center comes close, but
Jahn (born 1940) is good enough
to have something left to say.

Like Mies van der Rohe, Jahn
was born and educated in Germany
before moving to Chicago to study
at the Illinois Institute of
Technology between 1965 and
1966 where, of course, Mies had
designed the campus and taught.
In 1967 he joined the Chicago firm
of C. F. Murphy, which he took
over as principal architect in 1983.

Jahn teaches at Harvard. His
buildings are characterized by the
use of simple geometric shapes
drawn out on a massive scale, as in
the State of Illinois Center, Chicago,
for example, in which the great
rectangular box of the structure is
cut through with a sloping glass
cylinder. It is all very impressive in
a controlled and slick way, but
you cannot help thinking that this
approach to architecture has to
lead to a dead end soon.

Koshino House

TADAO ANDO, 1981

ASHIYA, HYOGO, JAPAN

TO WESTERN EYES, the Koshino
House is rather like a monastery.
It consists of two wings separated
by a courtyard and connected by
an underground corridor. One
wing contains no fewer than six
children's bedrooms lined up in
a row like monks' cells. The other
comprises the parents' bedroom,
living room and kitchen. Both

are austere concrete structures,
but superbly finished and lit in
ways that are as haunting as
they are magical.

Tadao Ando is one of the finest
architects of the late twentieth
century. His houses are
extraordinarily beautiful, yet utterly
simple and built, for the most part,
from concrete blocks and slabs.
There is, however, concrete and
concrete, and in Ando's hands it
is a beautiful material. Most of
all, Ando understands, like Le
Corbusier before him, how best to
let daylight play on the depths of

this often misunderstood material.
The light effects that play across
the walls of the Koshino House
belie the need for decoration of
any sort – no pictures and certainly
no wallpaper.

Ando's particular sense of beauty
must be innate. Born into a working
class family of "untouchables", he
trained first as a boxer before
learning to build. He had no
formal training as an architect and
the Japanese profession was long
dismissive of his talent. However,
he has become one of his country's
most precious talents.

Medici House

MARIO BOTTA, 1982
TICINO, SWITZERLAND

APPROACH BOTTA'S *casa rotonda* one way and it can seem like a giant medieval knight's helmet; approach it from another direction and it resembles a pill box. It has a mysterious quality, as perhaps do all circular buildings, but is a fine family house as well as a rigorous expression of very elemental architecture. Here Botta has chosen the cylinder and, in his characteristic way, has cut it through with slits and other openings, not enough to reveal the interior but more than enough to create a play of deep shadows that animate a simple shape and one of the primary building blocks of architecture. You can walk right through the cylinder at ground level without entering the house. An arcade sliced through the building brings daylight into its core.

Up to this point in his career, Botta had built exclusively in the countryside and on the fringe of villages and small towns. His first urban building, an extension of the Staatsbank in Fribourg, Switzerland, was completed the same year as the Medici House. It seemed somehow overwrought as did many of Botta's later city projects. Undoubtedly, his finest work up until the end of the century remained the sequence of elemental brick houses built in his native Ticino.

Artist's House and Studio

GLEN MURCUTT, 1983

SYDNEY, AUSTRALIA

GLEN MURCUTT (BORN 1936) brought the Outback back to Sydney with this delightful super-sophisticated corrugated steel house. On any level it makes good sense. Raised off the ground on steel beams, it has some of the feel of the Farnsworth House by Mies van der Rohe (p.186). However, it is equipped for a life dogged by worrying insects, life-threatening spiders, unexpected snakes and bush fires. Raised above ground, it also stays as cool as an intelligently thought-through house without air-conditioning can. The reflective property of the corrugated steel and extensive use of wooden blinds keeps the worst of the heat at bay.

The plan is simple: one end forms a well-sheltered balcony and the rooms follow a simple logic. When Murcutt built this house, the area on the edge of Sydney really did feel as if it were in the Outback, or close enough; in later years, as more and more Australians were able to build second homes away from the city, it became less isolated. The idea, though, remains an interesting one, combining a nostalgia for Australia's settler past, its tin-shack architecture and Modernism. Quite an achievement. Not surprisingly. Murcutt became a popular architect and was to develop the theme of this house many times.

High Museum

RICHARD MEIER, 1983

ATLANTA, GEORGIA, USA

IN THE 1980s, cities across the world began to invest heavily in museums. There was a widespread belief that investment went where the quality of life was high and one of the measures of quality was the level of cultural life. Museums were popular in this sense not least because business corporations could make a soft impact on host cities by sponsoring the construction of museums and the exhibitions they mounted. In other words, there was an unspoken and reciprocal relationship between art and commerce, between businesses thrusting into the future and museums nurturing the past.

Richard Meier became the shining star of the new museum movement and has built several across the world. Perhaps none, though, has the sheer, brilliant impact of the High Museum. In a flippant mood, one could say that it is rather like a giant washing machine designed to make the past – the artefacts on show – cleaner, brighter and thus more appealing than they ever really were in daily use. Certainly, US museums have a habit of making exhibits of whatever age look brand new. Based on three cubes and a cylinder, this purist building boasts light, generous and ennobling circulation spaces and a cool dignity that is certainly very impressive.

Ministry of Foreign Affairs

HENNING LARSEN, 1984

RIYADH, SAUDI ARABIA

RICHARD BRYANT, the renowned architectural photographer was seized by guards in this vast and gleaming building. His crime was that his assistant had scratched a tiny patch of marble flooring with his camera tripod. It was a small diplomatic incident, and the editors of the *Architectural Review* in London were able to diffuse the situation. Still, it showed the esteem in which those employed to care for this impressive building held it. The building was a significant step forwards in terms of Western architects making an effort to find a form of design that was modern yet reflected Islamic and Arabic values. So many of the buildings designed for Saudi Arabia and the Middle East were as cynical as they were trashy. Henning Larsen (born 1925) took a polar opposite approach.

Designed in the guise of a fort, the building opens up, delightfully, into an internal street based on a traditional bazaar that runs right around its core. At the heart is a soaring triangular atrium off which lie the ministry offices which are grouped around nine courtyards. So, behind its foreboding walls, the ministry unfolds like a flower; this comes as a complete surprise and was proof, at long last, that Western architects had more in mind in the Middle East than flogging off designs that had been rejected in their home countries.

Saatchi Collection

MAX GORDON, 1985

ST JOHN'S WOOD,

LONDON, ENGLAND

CHARLES SAATCHI is an ad man who has enjoyed playing cards, racing go-karts and collecting contemporary art inspired by the world of advertising, or art that might be turned into advertising one day in the future. The art he liked, bought and championed came in a rush from 1988 when a new wave of young artists, spearheaded by the canny, media-friendly Damien Hirst, exploded out of Goldsmith's College in south London. Hirst showed what could be done in the name of art with pickling fluids, blood, semen and any other dangerous or provocative substance.

Saatchi's genius has been to show his conquests (he would buy up a fresh young artist's entire show in one unrefusable transaction) in a gallery that is as clean, as pure, as white and as light as the art was brutal and, to some, disgusting. He bought a former garage in a genteel stuccoed street in one of London's wealthiest suburbs and commissioned Max Gordon (1931-90), a Scottish-born architect settled in New York, to convert it. Gordon's genius was to make it look as if he had done nothing at all except to paint the walls white. In this sense, he was partly in league with a loosely connected group of architects, including John Pawson and Claudio Silvestrin (p.264) who made their names in London from the mid-1980s with an ascetic, minimalist architecture that all began with the design of chic art galleries.

Hong Kong and Shanghai Bank

FOSTER ASSOCIATES, 1986
CENTRAL DISTRICT, HONG
KONG

THE HIGH POINT and even the apotheosis of British Hi-Tech, Norman Foster's hugely impressive banking headquarters in the former British crown colony is best remembered for its enormous cost. As far as anyone can remember or tell it was the most expensive building of all time. Perhaps, perhaps not. Since then this questionable mantle has passed on to later buildings and Foster's mid-period masterpiece can be looked at without a thick veil of Hong Kong dollars blocking the view.

The bank was an important symbol of confidence and permanence in a city that had a possibly healthy habit of demolishing even its grandest buildings every so many years to make way for more lucrative successors and which was to be handed back to Communist China within just 11 years of the bank's completion. This steely machine for making money in is supported by eight ladder-like masts, cross-braced with struts that, in turn, hold up the floors. Floor space is as clear as possible. Lifts, stairs, lavatories and other services are pushed right to the edge of the tower. An imposing lobby, cleverly lit by daylight scooped from the sky, rushes up into the core of the building, adding a dimension of drama and life that the building's enigmatic, machine-like exterior belies. Nearly everything here has been custom-designed and made: very cool, very impressive.

De Menil Collection

RENZO PIANO,

BUILDING WORKSHOP, 1986

HOUSTON, TEXAS, USA

ONE OF THE BEST of new museums and galleries of the 1980s, the De Menil Collection was also one of the least pretentious. Its form and structure derive entirely from one detail, the finely profiled concrete "leaves" that span the entire building and act as light baffles. In the frazzling heat of Houston these allow the museum to be top-lit and naturally lit all day long. The "leaves", suspended by a simple steel frame, are angled so as to make the most of available daylight without allowing direct sunlight to sear into the galleries. Dominique de Menil, Piano's patron, was insistent that her choice collection of tribal art should be viewed in daylight. Where extra light is needed, this shines from spotlights incorporated into the leaves.

The rest of the structure was easy. Walls of weather-board are set back within the structural frame which thus acts as a sunshade around the museum. Inside, lushly planted courtyards are the only interruption in the flow of a simple and elegant plan. The galleries are not air-conditioned: this luxury is confined solely to the "treasury" (the store for the collection) located above the roof. In a city in which architectural bombast is the rule, the De Menil Collection is delightful. It is one of the softest of Piano's inspired "soft machines".

Musée
d'Orsay

GAE AULENTI, 1987
PARIS, FRANCE

THE GARE D'ORSAY, gracing the banks of the Seine, was always a pretty railway station but little used. Designed by Victor Laloux, it dates from 1900. Just 75 years later, President Georges Pompidou decided that it should be converted into a museum, and so it was. ACT, the team who won the competition for its redevelopment, were left largely to sort out the essentials, while the second prize winner, the Milanese architect Gae Aulenti (born 1927) was commissioned to design what was to become the eye-catching interior.

The exterior remains, thankfully, pretty much as Laloux shaped and decorated it. Aulenti's interior is simple, axial and very impressive. As if wanting visitors to make sure they knew that she planned to touch this grand old countess of a building as lightly as possible, Aulenti designed an interior that looks like a substantial and elegant exhibition installation and no more. It works extremely well. At no point is the station's superb interior denied or spoilt. Visitors stroll along what was once the trackbed and are diverted into simple, temple-like pavilions to gawp at the paintings or *objets d'art* of various periods. The interior works at its best, though, when you come across vast, pretentious canvases depicting stirring events in France's faultless history, mounted on modern walls and set against the further backdrop of Laloux's wonderful vault.

Hysolar Research Institute

BEHNISCH AND PARTNERS,
1987 STUTTGART,
GERMANY

GÜNTHER BEHNISCH (BORN 1922)
designed the breathtaking tents for
the 1972 Olympic Games at
Munich with the engineer Frei Otto.
Fifteen years later, he produced this
equally daring, if smaller and much
less well known, structure. A part
of the University of Stuttgart, the
Hysolar Research Institute was set

up to investigate the possibilities
of generating hydrogen through
solar energy. The complex and
inscrutable processes by which this
might be achieved is reflected in
Behnisch's good-humoured
building. Here is architecture as
experiment. It works well and hard
for its living, yet the playful aspect
is carried throughout the structure,
which includes funny angles, crazy
glazing and bits of building
shooting out at odd angles.
Undoubtedly, it evokes well a
world of nutty professors beavering
away in white coats and steel-
framed glasses on top-secret

experiments, and this is a large
part of its appeal.

The building was completed
the year before Philip Johnson
organized the "Deconstructivist
Architecture" show at the Museum
of Modern Art, and was, whether
Behnisch would have agreed or
not, part of a move that had
been gathering steam (or hydrogen)
as many architects tired of the
cheesy feyness of Postmodernism
and, bored by the skin-tight
school of super-smooth façades,
appeared to want to take the
whole subject to pieces and
to start again.

Mound Stand

MICHAEL HOPKINS, 1987
LORD'S CRICKET GROUND,
LONDON, ENGLAND

THE MCC (Marylebone Cricket Club) has for aeons been one of the last bastions of a very peculiar English male chauvinism. Florid-faced dutters, half cut on Pimms and champagne, were still snoring away summer afternoons in the famous Lord's Pavilion as willow struck leather and Michael Hopkins set to work on this impressive and festive stand for spectators and sleepers. The fact that the MCC commissioned one of the best and most popular new buildings of its time was simply extraordinary. In fact, the age-old club, far from being repentant, commissioned Hopkins a second time and then went a step further down the Modern line and roped in Nicholas Grimshaw (p.376) and Future Systems. Ever since, half-cut, florid duffers have been able to snooze through Test matches shaded by the white fabric tents of Hopkins' Mound Stand.

The building rests on an existing brick arcade and is held up by just six masts on the side of the pitch. These are entirely absent, or hidden from view, as far as spectators are concerned, and they enjoy a completely clear view of the action (or lack of it). The stand is ringed around with swish, fully glazed "hospitality suites" in which men in suits, as opposed to Panamas and blazers, drink large quantities of beer and ignore the cricket.

L'Institut du Monde Arabe

JEAN NOUVEL, 1987

PARIS, FRANCE

IT WAS THIS BUILDING that won many sceptics over to the pleasures of Modern architecture and excited a generation who had been brought up with Modern design and had no real problem with it. This is a bold claim, yet many observers of the architectural world were aware of something of a sea-change in public sensibilities in the late 1980s. Modern architecture was no longer a demon to wrestle with or something terribly difficult that no one without a doctorate could make head or tail of but something to enjoy, to talk and read about.

Jean Nouvel (born 1941) is a master of the popular, yet ground-breaking building. The Institut du Monde Arabe was one of the famous *grands projets* initiated in Paris by President Mitterand. On a site on the banks of the Seine, it comprises two intersecting blocks, one curved and facing the river, the other rectangular and facing south. Between the two there is a courtyard. Inside, a wide range of cultural activities and a restaurant are offered. Yet what most people long to see is the wonderful south-facing glass wall. Between sheets of glass, exquisite metal diaphragms in the guise of Islamic patterns frame lenses that open and close like the human eye to control the intensity of daylight entering the Institute. This is a brilliant example of how art, architecture and new building technology can work together to enhance one another. A *tour de force.*

Church on
the Water

TADAO ANDO, 1988

TOMAMU, HOKKAIDO,
JAPAN

ANDO CAN DO SO VERY much
with so little. The Church on the
Water relies for its effect and mood
on the changing seasons, beyond
the great glass screen that fills its
east end. The seasons here remain
marked. In winter the snow lies
deep and crisp and even, and the
lake that frames the view through

the window freezes over entirely.
In summer, the skies are clear and
the air warm: then, the screen is
lowered out of sight and services
are held with Nature as a live and
spirited backdrop. Christ's cross
stands here in all seasons to
remind the faithful that he is with
them at all times.

To focus the congregation's
attention in this way makes perfect
sense, and indeed the rest of this
simple concrete container is
without incident. Ando's
architecture never offers more
than it needs to in a structural or
decorative sense. It relies for its

effect and power on the play of
light and shade, on texture, on all
the senses playing together to feel
an architecture rather than to feast
on it with eyes greedy for incident
and sensation.

Very few architects in any
period have been able to get
away with this. No trickery is ever
involved. What is required, as Ando
must have known innately, is a
natural sense of place, of repose,
of human sensitivity to the
slightest change in temperature,
mood and setting. This is
architecture of rare genius, and
is about as timeless as it gets.

La Grande Arche

JOHANN OTTO VON
SPRECKELSEN, 1990
LA DÉFENSE, PARIS,
FRANCE

A MODERN COUNTERPART to
the famous Arc de Triomphe, von
Spreckelsen's huge, abstract and
anonymous gateway terminates the
heroic axis that runs from Place de
la Concorde, along the Champs
Elysée, through Etoile and right
up to La Défense, the terrifying
mountain of offices and corporate

headquarters to the west of Paris.
From the steps of this visually silent
monument, the eye is drawn
straight through to the Arc de
Triomphe. From the top of the
Arche, reached by a lift that
climbs vertiginously up through
the giant aperture, the views of
Paris are stunning.

Although it serves as a
monument – to the bicentenary of
the storming of the Bastille and the
French Revolution – the Arche has
a more prosaic purpose; within its
mighty white Carrara marble-clad
walls are 35 floors of government
offices. Given the design of the
Arche, these look out into its

enormous hollow centre and to
north and south (depending upon
which side you work on), but not
to the east, as if enticing views of
Paris would put bureaucrats off
their stride.

The Arche is basically a
hollowed out 100-metre (330-ft)
cube. The design was chosen in
a competition held in 1982 for
which there were 400 entries.
Von Spreckelsen, a Dane, was very
much an unknown and it is to the
credit of the Mitterand regime
that, in the construction of its
grands projets, it was so willing
to employ architects from elsewhere
in Europe and the USA.

Imagination Building

RON HERRON, 1990

LONDON, ENGLAND

A LITTLE BIT of Archigram (p.393–4) came happily and eventually to life in what was the former lightwell of a five-storey red-brick Edwardian office block in central London. Herron converted the whole building for the design group Imagination but brought it to life with this spectacular and unexpected atrium at its heart. New windows and doors were made in the white-painted internal walls on either side of the atrium and these either look on or lead over a criss-cross weave of high-level, perforated steel bridges. Above these, a voluminous fabric roof billows in the wind. This gives the building the sort of festive air that Archigram had always promised in its drawings. The roof is an entertaining addition to the local skyline. It was engineered to withstand winds of 260 km/ph (160mph). Down below, the atrium boasts overscaled pots of plants, trees, a modern baroque staff restaurant and the sort of genuinely informal atmosphere that architects have long talked of trying to create – for example at Centraal Beheer (p.234) and Hillingdon Civic Centre (p.291) – without succeeding.

In the case of Imagination, it was the client who set the tone; here work was meant to be a pleasure, not a penance. Architect and client got on so well that Herron, working with his two sons, set up shop here.

Neuendorf House

JOHN PAWSON AND
CLAUDIO SILVESTRIN, 1990
MAJORCA, SPAIN

A HOLIDAY HOUSE as artwork for a German art dealer, the Neuendorf House is a masterly composition of walls. No roof is visible from the outside, just a high concrete perimeter wall finished in a sun-burned stucco. The house is reached across fields along a stepped-stone path. This leads to a narrow, 9-metre (30-ft) high slit in the wall which, in turn, reveals an amphitheatre-like courtyard, empty save for simple stone benches flanking two sides.

The courtyard leads into an austere dining room, the heart of the house. There is nothing here save for a stone table designed as part of the architecture and sculpted wooden chairs by the great Danish furniture maker Hans Wegner. The fireplace runs the length of one wall. Other rooms are equally austere, employing the same palette of materials – stone floors, wooden benches, wooden bath tub, stone basins, smooth white concrete walls. Daylight plays through the rooms from slits and chutes and is always restrained.

The overall feeling is that of living either in a modern sculpture or in a latter-day monastery. This is not all that surprising: John Pawson (born 1949) made his name designing Minimalist art galleries and Claudio Silvestrin (born 1954) was to have become a priest or monk before turning to architecture.

Temple on the Water

TADAO ANDO, 1992

AWAJI ISLAND, HYOGO,
JAPAN

ANDO IN ANOTHER magical mood. This Shingon Buddhist temple dug into a hillside overlooking the Bay of Osaka is entered by a long concrete stair that passes down through the centre of a circular lake awash with gorgeous floating lotus plants. From even the slightest distance, the monks look as if they are walking down among the lilies and into the water itself.

This is a lovely conceit and one that visitors never tire of watching. The watchword is simplicity: of both materials and design. On the surface, Ando has done little more, it seems, than to create an entrance. Down below, the temple opens up into a womb-like world of warm red passageways and then into a blaze of colour as the prayer hall itself is reached. This comes as a surprise, particularly for those who know how sparing Ando's palette of colours is. Yet, these are colours – the reds and oranges – that are sacred to Buddhist monks and their rituals; they are not gratuitous.

Ando's temple is a good example of how an architecture of great simplicity and still rooted in the fertile ground of Modernism can be at one with Nature. It is one thing to design a building that mimics and otherwise represents the forms of Nature as in, for example, the works of Bruce Goff (p.96), Herb Greene (p.105) or Imre Makovecz (p.112). It is quite another to set a modern building quietly and respectfully into a natural setting so that the one, Nature, enhances the other, Architecture. The latter is an old and valuable lesson: the Greeks did it at Athens and Ando does it 2,500 years later here near Osaka.

Stein
House

SETH STEIN, 1995

KNIGHTSBRIDGE, LONDON,
ENGLAND

A STRONG REACTION TO the excesses and gimcrack quality – intellectually and aesthetically – of US- style Postmodern design changed the face of youthful British architecture during the last decade of the twentieth century. A young generation of architects wanted a Modern world, but one that was less puritanical than that of Walter Gropius and the Bauhaus and reflected both a world that was once more affluent, more colourful and, somehow, less naive. In this house, tucked away on a formerly semi-industrial site in one of London's smartest districts, Seth Stein (born 1959) shaped a courtyard house that was Modern, had it own distinct identity and yet borrowed cleverly and carefully from a wide range of twentieth-century sources. So, there's a touch of Le Corbusier here, Tadao Ando there; there's more than a hint of the work of Luis Barragán and, then again, references, by way of the courtyard plan, to a way of house building that dates back to Ancient Rome and even earlier.

Confident use of pigmented colour and contrasting materials makes for an experience that is far from puritanical and yet the house has a sense of strength and quietude that the masters of the Modern Movement sought in their most inspired designs.

Richard Attenborough Centre

IAN TAYLOR, 1997

LEICESTER, ENGLAND

OPENED BY THE LATE DIANA, Princess of Wales, the Richard Attenborough Centre for Disability and the Arts captures a particular moment in the story of British patronage: the princess made charities, notably those concerned with the sick or disabled, a fashionable cause. This was good news for this low-key, thoughtful and elegant building that needed the kind of support that Diana was able to give it. The Centre's purpose was to train people with severe physical disabilities to become fully fledged artists. For the blind to be taught to sculpt or those with no arms to paint requires a special building. Ian Taylor provided a design that not once acts in the condescending way so many buildings for the disabled do, if not intentionally. It employs subtle changes of surfaces, acoustics and smell (the corridor lined with Cedar of Lebanon panels is a perfumed delight) to help students move about. There are no patronizing colours anywhere (why people who are disabled should have to look at lurid colours all day is a mystery), while subtle shifts of daylight and shadow are brought into the building through a top-lit atrium. The various spaces are flexible and the building has an enviable sense of determination. It is finished in simple materials and is one of those modest Modern buildings that is far more than the sum of its parts. Cleverness gives way to subtlety here.

Museum
of Rowing

DAVID CHIPPERFIELD, 1997

HENLEY-ON-THAMES,

ENGLAND

DAVID CHIPPERFIELD (born 1954) pursued a determined "homage" to the early Modern Movement having left the office of Norman Foster to set up on his own in the 1980s. Influenced by traditional Japanese architecture, as were many pioneers of Modernism, Chipperfield developed an uncompromising aesthetic that could easily be perceived as being severe and unyielding. This made much sense in the fashionable shops and cafés he designed in Tokyo and London, but outside the new cosmopolis could seem altogether too cold and even aloof.

The Museum of Rowing was one of those happy accidents whereby the sensibility of the architect was seemingly threatened by local planning restraints and yet the result was happy. In this case, Chipperfield was forced to adopt a pitched roof – something he had eschewed to date. However, the roof of this handsome museum is what makes it likeable. The balance between the chaste walls and interiors and their timber roofs is exactly right and the building seems to express something about the nature of the construction of boats and of boatsheds. Planning restrictions have become increasingly tight and architects can no longer expect to pose, to set a compass on the face of the world, but are forced to stop, look, listen and be deft and inventive.

British Library

COLIN ST JOHN WILSON,
1997, LONDON, ENGLAND

COLIN ST JOHN WILSON (BORN
1922) liked to compare this vast
pile of red bricks alongside George
Gilbert Scott's exuberant Neo-Gothic
Midland Grand Hotel to the work
of Alvar Aalto. In particular he
cited Aalto's wonderful town hall at
Säynätsalo (p.191). The comparison
cannot hold. Where Aalto's subtle
work was gentle and natural and
feels at one with its island landscape,
Wilson's exterior is big, cold and
obtrusive and the hard brick looks
as if it has been cut with a cheese
wire. The great redeeming quality
of this gigantic tweed jacket is its
imposing interior, which has some
of the qualities of Aalto but
probably more of the beautifully
crafted town halls, libraries and
railway stations of Sweden and
Finland in the 1910s and 1920s.

The Library took many years to
build, but was clearly designed to
last for hundreds of years. So, oak
desks and chairs (by Ron Carter)
are as solid as the trees their wood
came from, walls are lined in
marble, heavy brass door handles
and handrails wrapped in leather.
The top-lit reading rooms – science
on one side, arts on the other –
are dignified places to study, while
throughout the costly building
Wilson provided ledges, nooks
and corners for readers to meet.

In scale and in purpose, this
curious building – clumsy on the
outside, all glorious within –
resembles a grand medieval abbey
revisited on London's Euston Road.

Garage House

SETH STEIN, 1997

KNIGHTSBRIDGE, LONDON,
ENGLAND

ONE OF THE BEST of a young
generation of born-again white
Modern architects in the 1990s,
Seth Stein makes imaginative
houses that take into account the
new concerns of city-dwellers, like
where to park the car. Car parking
space had become prohibitively
expensive in central London when
Stein squeezed this light and airy

house into a tiny plot in London's
Knightsbridge, not far from the
famous Harrods department
store. Not only did the client want
a parking place, he also wanted
to look at his cars as works of art.
Whether you agree or not, Dante
Giacosa's design of the 1957
Fiat 500 is a lovely sculptural
work. In this house it takes pride
of place and can be raised in
a very swish lift into what is,
when the car is out for a
spin, a living room.

The living room as garage is
an idea that has been explored
by several architects in the past –
notably by Geoffrey Bawa (p.299)

in Sri Lanka who designed the
living room of his house in
Colombo around his vintage Rolls-
Royce – but never in such an
ingenious way. The rest of the
house is as neatly packed and
organized as a small modern car.

The New Modernism of the
1990s was a style, no more and no
less, and carried none of the moral
baggage nor the obsession with
functionalism that characterized
the early Modern Movement.
Stein's tiny house may be a new
form of *existenzminimum*, but
it has nothing to do with the
quest for ideal housing for the
working classes.

Meeting Room

CLAUDIO SILVESTRIN, 1997

HOMBRICH ART
FOUNDATION,
FRANKFURT, GERMANY

BUILT ON THE SITE of a former
NATO missile base in what had
been West Germany until the fall
of the Berlin Wall in 1989, the
Hombrich Art Foundation was the
brainchild of a retired Frankfurt
property developer who was also,
as property developers so often
were in the 1980s and 1990s, a
keen patron and collector of
contemporary art. The Hombrich
Foundation, however, was rather
special. It comprised not just
galleries devoted to the work of
modern artists, but also studios and
workshops, a cloister and cabins to
stay in, a bakery, brewery and an
organic farm. It was meant as a
way of redressing a world that had
been given over to war, a city to
fast-buck architecture and farmland
to agro-chemicals.

At the centre of the Foundation
is this meeting room or place of
contemplation by Claudio Silvestrin.
A simple space, it consists of little
but light falling beautifully onto
warm white walls, a stone floor and
benches. It is the opposite of all the
architecture that has been built in
"Bankfurt", as Frankfurt became
known in the prosperous 1980s.
And in Silvestrin's hands it works:
it is one of those spaces that stops
people chattering and quietens
the human spirit.

Stein
House

RICK MATHER, 1997

HIGHGATE, LONDON,

ENGLAND

RICK MATHER (born 1937) is an
American architect who came from
Portland, Oregon to London and
has worked quietly on the design
of refined white Modern houses,
restaurants, museums and galleries.
His is an approach that has developed
project by project without fuss, drama
or error. A well-known chain of
sophisticated Chinese restaurants in
London and Hong Kong – "Zen" –
made Mather something of a
household name among people who
dined out in fashionable style in the
1980s. His proposals for delicate and
difficult projects, such as the extension
of the historic Dulwich Picture Gallery
by John Soane or the Wallace
Collection in central London, are
models of architectural good
manners. So, too, is this white and
glass family house in north London.

Its precision, clarity and delicacy
of manner are all hallmarks of
Mather's unerring style of elegant
restraint. Here, though, Mather went
that bit further and created a house
that is almost ethereal. It could
hardly be described as a machine
for living for it is as unlike a machine
as a house can be. In this sense,
Mather proved that the language
of early Modernism, refined
through usage and practice over
many decades, had mutated into a
manner of speech very different
from the original strident posturing
of Le Corbusier and the Bauhaus.
Most of all, it was very hushed.

Ruskin Library

MACCORMAC–JAMIESON–

PRITCHARD, 1998

LANCASTER, LANCASHIRE,

ENGLAND

JOHN RUSKIN (1819–1900) was a fiery Victorian critic and seer, famous as the champion of the great English painter J. M. W. Turner and for his books *Modern Painters* and *The Seven Lamps of Architecture*. He wrote like an archangel might, looked like an Old Testament prophet and railed against bad art, poor architecture and a social fabric too thin to provide the working people of Britain with anything like a decent living or education. This handsome white library was built as a kind of entrance gate to the University of Lancaster overlooking the sands of Morecambe Bay and not far from Ruskin's romantic home, Brantwood, in the Lake District.

Its plan is in the shape of an eye (Ruskin was always asking people to look closely, to argue with the eye) and it is designed to be a modern version of the baptistery at Parma or Siena Cathedral in Tuscany. At each end of the elliptical building, tall windows – one an entrance – rise its full height. They reveal the richly coloured "treasury" or holy of holies in which Ruskin papers from previously separate collections have been garnered. The treasury and indeed the whole of the interior are finished in warm and richly coloured materials that contrast powerfully with the white, crystalline walls. It is a happy place to work in on a dark and stormy night.

Walsall
Art Gallery

CARUSO–ST JOHN, 1999

WALSALL, ENGLAND

MANY NEW MUSEUMS opened in
provincial English towns in the 1980s
and 1990s are located either in
cultural ghettoes or else in converted
red-brick Victorian warehouses.
Caruso–St John's Walsall Art Gallery
is a shining exception. And shine it
does, its tall walls clad in various
shades of grey terracotta that sparkle
on wet, sunny days. It shines too in
the sense that it is a brand new
design by a firm of young architects
with ideas very much of their own.
It is sited in the heart of a new
shopping development, and far from
being the arty-smarty shops one
would expect around and about a
gallery, the shops here are branches
of the chain stores Woolworth and
British Home Stores. In Walsall, art
has been brought down from
Parnassus to the market place and
people doing a bit of Saturday
morning shopping in "Woolies"
can go for coffee in the gallery's
rooftop terrace restaurant.

There is nothing precious about
the design of this rigorously
planned building, which owes its
internal logic, and thus the irregular
window spacing, to the nature and
scale of the collections arranged
within it. It has a toughness that
belies the delicacy of much of the
work on show and has clearly been
built to last. The one enjoyable
affectation of the project is the
digging of a canal basin up to the
gallery at one end, a detail that
has more than a touch of the great
gardens of Versailles about it.

Tate Modern

HERZOG–DE MEURON, 2000

BANKSIDE, LONDON,

ENGLAND

TO BUILD a new gallery or convert an existing building. That was the choice the Tate Gallery faced when it set about looking for a second home for its ever-expanding art collection. The problem with building from scratch was the lack of a suitable site in central London and the fact – as the gallery's shrewd director, Nicholas Serota, well knew – that it would take a long time to steer a worthwhile new building through tortuous planning procedures. The redundant Bankside Power Station was an inspired choice. A majestic temple of power, it stands on the south bank of the Thames opposite St Paul's Cathedral. Converting it to the new Tate Modern gallery included making a connection to Wren's great temple by way of a footbridge designed by Norman Foster, the sculptor Anthony Caro and Chris Wise, an engineer from Ove Arup and Partners. An Underground station links the gallery to the West End.

The conversion of the power station was favoured both by conservationists and those looking forward to the pristine galleries designed by the Swiss practice Herzog de Meuron. Jacques Herzog (born 1951) and Pierre de Meuron (born 1951) are well known for a strict yet romantic new Modern architecture relying for its impact on tactile materials that belie the need for conventional decoration.

Reichstag

NORMAN FOSTER, 1999

BERLIN, GERMANY

BUILT TO HOUSE the parliamentary assembly of the Second Reich, the Reichstag (1894) was a heavy-handed exercise in Neo-Renaissance style by Paul Bellot. In February 1933, less than a month after Hitler was voted into power, it burned down in mysterious circumstances. Hitler blamed the Communists and used the occasion to ban all parties opposing his NSDAP (Nazi Party). It would have been demolished if Albert Speer had been able to build his giant domed assembly hall (p.54) here, but it survived both the Nazis and World War Two, during which it was further damaged by bombing. It was patched up between 1958 and 1972 and used as a museum, then dressed up in silver sheeting by the artist Christo in 1996.

In the last year of the twentieth century, the Reichstag reopened as the new seat of a united German government, Germany having been split into capitalist West and communist East from 1945 to 1990, with Berlin firmly back in its role as the German capital. The building was remodelled at great cost by Norman Foster.

Its distinguishing feature is a glass dome over the assembly chamber up which visitors can climb to view the city and to watch that remarkable thing: a democratic German government in action.

The Ark

FUTURE SYSTEMS, 2001

DONCASTER, YORKSHIRE,

ENGLAND

THIS EXQUISITE BUTTERFLY of a building was designed as the heart of the Earth Centre, an ecology park built on the site of former slag heaps in South Yorkshire. Doncaster had, for many decades, been famous for its coal mines and its locomotive works. By the mid-1980s, as Britain gave up manufacturing almost anything

worthwhile in favour of financial services and retailing, Doncaster had all but lost its purpose.

The Earth Centre is an intelligent way of reclaiming land once given over to coal mining and helping to give the town a new focus. The centre's principal activities – research and the dissemination of information about ecological matters to the widest possible public – are contained in a network of pavilions. The most spectacular of these is the exhibition hall, which has been designed by Future Systems. This giant, yet gentle and low-lying building is dug into a hillside

made of compact slag, yet has been designed so that it appears as if it had landed as gently as a butterfly on the site. The three-storey interior was designed to be every bit as "organic" as its sensual exterior, the curved forms evoking those of plants. The plan is designed to be airy and relaxed and the overall impression is of a building that should make ultra-modern design popular.

The Ark at Doncaster is a sensitive riposte to London's Millennium Dome (p.377), and is one of the most eagerly awaited new European buildings of the twenty-first century.

Postmodernism

Here are some of the most colourful pages in this book. "Less is a bore", wrote Robert Venturi (p.283) in his widely read and all too well digested book *Complexity and Contradiction in Architecture* (1966). Venturi might have thought 50 years of Modern Movement architecture a bore, yet the complex and contradictory architecture he proposed as a riposte and way out of the tenacious grip of the Modernist trap proved to be a bigger bore altogether. Architects with a light touch could get away with making outlandish and funny buildings, but there were precious few of them. Freed from the binding corsets of Modernism, most of those who tried on Postmodern dress soon discovered that letting it all hang out was neither seemly nor decorous. On the whole it was plain dumb.

Postmodernism in some form or other was probably inevitable. The Modern experiment had become tired and corrupted in any case; it badly needed a rest. Architects meanwhile were, like anyone else who lived through the 1960s, bombarded with new forms of imagery from Pop culture, advertising, television and new movements in art in which the collage and irony played king and queen. It was not long before buildings emerged that were collages of earlier styles, making knowing references to famous designs. Before too long Philip Johnson

had dressed a Manhattan office block in the guise of a skyscraping Chippendale cabinet (p.297). How we were meant to laugh. Ooh, Philip, you are a wag. And anyone who didn't want to know was simply a bore.

There was, though, another side to Postmodernism that was ultimately more interesting and worthwhile. This stemmed from investigations into history and context by architects in various parts of the world who were struggling to reconcile history and local precedent with Modern designs. The Torre Velasca in Milan by BBPR (p.282) springs to mind as does, much later, such striking monuments to the memory of a specific place as Daniel Libeskind's Jewish Museum in Berlin (p.293).

Such buildings have little to do with the gimcrack excesses of US "Po-Mo", although they are certainly Postmodern. Perhaps a parallel can be drawn here between the Modern Movement as it emerged in Europe – zealous, puritanical, intense – and in the US, as the International Style – chic, amoral and relaxed. Nevertheless there were architects who seemed to be well equipped to play a complex, if outlandish, game, and to score lots of points with buildings of great verve and character that were neither puerile nor kitsch: James Stirling and Michael Wilford's Staatsgalerie in Stuttgart was one example (p.305). Frank

Gehry's Guggenheim Museum in Bilbao another (p.321).

At the very end of the twentieth century, buildings that transcended the early posturings of an architecture struggling to free itself from Modernism, such as those by Gehry and Libeskind, began to emerge. Such architects moved away from the concerns of self-conscious Postmodernists and, if anything, their work was moving in a modern Organic direction. Perhaps, though, labels again proved to be their own undoing; it is just as likely that these designers were simply free spirits whose work was hard to pin down. Whatever, both Gehry and Libeskind proved that late twentieth-century architecture could be highly expressive and play emotional mind-games without needing to be funny or crudely subversive. After all, how subversive can a corporate headquarters be, even if it is clothed in fancy dress?

The fashion for outrageous clothes, however, was ultimately short-lived. It also produced its own reaction. By the early 1990s, young architects the world over were returning to a clean-cut Neomodernism; if this lacked the energy and crusading spirit that the white architecture of the 1920s had had, it was some sort of attempt to sweep the boards clean and to start again after two decades of mostly silly, cardboard cut-out design.

Torre Velasca

BBPR, 1958

MILAN, ITALY

HERE IS A VERY literal expression of the idea of the "High Game of Architecture", or else the beginnings of Postmodernism. The Torre Velasca, a 26-storey office tower in the heart of Milan, can be looked on either as an example of architectural wit, a game played high into the Lombardy sky, or a brave attempt to reconcile the demands of mid-twentieth-century property development with those of traditional design. For, quite clearly, this idiosyncratic building is a modern representation of a medieval Italian tower. With its top eight storeys cantilevered out from the main body of the building and a framework of what look like buttresses, the Torre Velasca distantly echoes the forms of the medieval Castello Sforzesco, one of Milan's principal attractions. Just two years before its completion, BBPR, the team that designed Torre Velasca, had designed a museum installation inside the walls of Castello Sforzesco. The team comprised Gianluigi Banfi (1910–45), Ludovico Belgiojoso (born 1909), Enrico Peressutti (1908–73) and Ernesto Nathan Rogers (1909–69), uncle of Richard Rogers, who formed BBPR in 1932. From early on their concern was to challenge the dogmatic nature of Modernism. For them, architecture needed to be rooted in specific places and to respond to local building traditions: Torre Velasca is the high point of beliefs that were to be taken up widely in the next three decades.

Mother's House

ROBERT VENTURI 1964

CHESTNUT HILL,

PHILADELPHIA, USA

ONE SMALL HOUSE for an architect, but a giant leap for architecture. The Mother's House by Robert Venturi (born 1925) is generally taken as the first knowing step into the choppy seas of Postmodernism. Why? Venturi was the first architect to publish a Postmodern theory of architecture. His book, *Complexity and Contradiction in Architecture*

(1966), was written at much the same time as the Mother's House was built – it really was for his mother; many good young architects with wealthy and adoring mums start this way. Venturi's basic premise was that "less is a bore", a witty riposte to Mies van der Rohe's famous maxim "Less is More". Instead he offered an architecture that took into account all the richness, oddities, quirks and even embarrassments of the world it occupied and tried to represent. So, anything could go, more or less. An architect could drop "quotes" into his buildings whenever and wherever he wanted

to and these could be seen as knowing and amusing. Why shouldn't a Modern architect stick Classical mouldings onto a new building? Why not raid the picture book of history? As a reaction against the puritanical strictures of Mies and the increasing banality of international architecture Venturi's musings made sense. *Complexity and Contradiction in Architecture* was to have a widespread effect, yet the architecture that it gave rise to was never really much fun and rarely inspired.

The Mother's House speaks for itself. Compare it to Le Corbusier's Villa Savoye at Poissy (p.161).

Lincoln Center

PHILIP JOHNSON, ET AL,
1966

NEW YORK CITY, USA

A MIGHTY RENAISSANCE piazza, translated to Manhattan by way of what looks suspiciously like Fascist Italy – it would have fitted well into Mussolini's EUR (p.59) – the Lincoln Center is representative of the "historicist", or early Postmodern approach to urban design and architecture. This rather odd cultural plaza was laid out by the grand Beaux-Arts architect and planner Wallace Harrison (1895–1981) who had previously worked on the Rockefeller Center (p.179) and the United Nations complex on Manhattan's eastern seaboard (1947–50). Harrison designed the rather spookily arcaded Metropolitan Opera House (1966) while Philip Johnson designed the New York State Theatre (1964) and Harrison's partner Max Abramovitz (1908–76) designed the Philharmonic Hall (1962).

The Lincoln Center marked the start of a new formalism in US architecture and the beginnings of a new-found obsession with history and European urbanism. It remains a somewhat cool and aloof space and has never seemed quite at home in Manhattan's busy grid of commercial skyscrapers. It looked at its best in Mel Brooks' movie, *The Producers*, when the stars, Max Bialystock (Zero Mostel) and Leo Bloom (Gene Wilder), hit on the idea of making millions by producing the worst play on Broadway, "Springtime for Hitler"; Brooks could not have chosen a more apt setting.

Port Grimaud

FRANÇOIS SPOERRY, 1969

FRANCE

PORT GRIMAUD is a fantasy seaside fishing port, a playground for wealthy things with yachts and time on their hands. It was the creation of François Spoerry (born 1912) and its make-believe architecture is realized mostly in concrete, although few visitors to this holiday village would guess it. Ersatz creation it might be, yet Port Grimaud works. Spoerry caught the feeling and character of a Mediterranean fishing port with quiet aplomb and reinterpreted it with a sure and gentle touch for those who wanted an escape from the Modern world with all mod cons secretly on tap. Port Grimaud, however, is not alone. Throughout history, architects and their patrons have tried, with varying degrees of success, to design oases of the historical and romantic imagination. Poor, "mad" Ludwig II of Bavaria and his fantasmagoric palaces, Neuschwanstein chief among them, spring to mind.

So, of course, does Walt Disney, who adapted Neuschwanstein for his Sleeping Beauty's castle.

The model, if there was a specific one, for Port Grimaud and its British counterpart – Portmeirion by Clough Williams-Ellis in north Wales – was the picturesque Italian seaside village, Portofino. Portofino became a symbol of the perfect holiday escape for those in love with architecture and an azure sea. Port Grimaud remains hugely popular and has been much copied in spirit, if not in such loving detail, since.

Hyatt Regency Hotel

JOHN PORTMAN, 1974

SAN FRANCISCO,

CALIFORNIA, USA

AN INNATE COMMERCIAL FLAIR has ensured that John Portman (born 1924) has developed and designed some of the world's most significant hotels. Portman wanted to be able to shape both the look and the programme of his buildings, and he has succeeded in spectacular style. His trademark has been the giant hotel lobby, a vast and glittering space shooting up in the far heights of the buildings, animated by glazed "wall-climber" lifts, lit as if part of a funfair, as well as by glittering shops and cafés. In this way, Portman brought the grand drama of the great US railroad stations together with the razzmatazz of Hollywood. These were very exciting places to be when they first raced up in the 1970s, but much belittled by Portman's fellow architects who thought them outrageous. Whether in the design of hotels or shopping malls, they would soon be following in Portman's giant and pioneering footsteps.

Portman was born in Walhalla, South Carolina. He trained at the Georgia Institute of Technology setting up his own architectural practice there in 1953. Success came with his breakaway hotels, and through the 1970s he built very many of them. The Hyatt Regency in San Francisco, is, perhaps, the most dramatic of Portman's hotels.

Piazza d'Italia

CHARLES MOORE, 1978

NEW ORLEANS,

LOUISIANA, USA

A POSTMODERN CONFECTION for the Italian, and more specifically Sicilian, community of New Orleans, Piazza d'Italia is an entertaining urban set design that pokes fun at Classical architecture's pomposity while revelling in its theatrical quality. The centrepiece of the circular piazza is a fountain based on the map of the heel of Italy. From the spandrels of the "ironic" screen above, twin heads – portraits of the architect – spout water. Originally, the scheme was to have been more ambitious, and included a large triumphal arch.

Moore (1925–93) had long worked on subverting the canons of architecture. Born in Michigan and educated there and at Princeton, he set up his own practice in Connecticut in 1970, working as part of a wider team with other offices. Moore had a great interest in breaking down the conventional barriers of internal and external spaces, beginning with the design of his own house in Orinda, California (1962). It was a theme he pursued throughout his career. Whether you find his later work engaging or not depends on your sense of humour. Piazza d'Italia is funny, but the same thing may not be true of a Berlin housing scheme (1980) in which a Disney-like steamboat motif is mixed with clipped, military Prussian Classicism.

Walden 7

TALLER DE ARQUITECTURA,
1975, ST JUST DESVERN,
BARCELONA, SPAIN

A HUGE BLOCK of flats resembling a fairy-tale castle from a distance, Walden 7 is less attractive close up. For many years, the block was surrounded by netting as tiles once attached to the walls hurtled to the ground. This was exciting but rather disconcerting. Walden 7 is interesting for being one of the major stepping stones leading to the extraordinary sequence of prefabricated Neoclassical housing projects designed in France by Ricardo Bofill (born 1939) and his Taller de Arquitectura (p.62–3).

The son of a wealthy Catalan builder, Bofill studied in Barcelona and Geneva before buying an old cement factory near Walden 7 and filling the former silos with fellow architects and with artists, poets, musicians, pets and parrots. It all seemed like a set from a Fellini film, and as surreal in practice as a scene from one of Buñuel's. Remarkably, this iconoclastic practice thrived and especially so when Bofill turned it away from early experiments in Brutalism to a reworking of local traditions – as, supposedly, in the design of Walden 7 – and then to an industrial Neoclassicism. Taller de Arquitectura was certainly fascinating, and not a little infuriating, but what puzzled most was why so many French cities were willing to adopt such crazy stuff.

Best
Supermarket

SITE, 1975

HOUSTON, TEXAS

JAMES WINES (BORN 1932) pioneered a programme of what he called "De-architecture" in the 1970s aided by various members of his design team SITE (Sculpture in the Environment). The idea was quite funny in a *Beavis and Butthead* kind of way. But, once you have sniggered at the artfully tilted and broken façades of no more than three of the Best supermarkets SITE designed, the joke has worn pretty thin. Architecture just isn't very funny (except unintentionally) and Wines was trying a little too hard. What the hell; supermarkets are extremely boring buildings at the best of times and at least the Best buildings raise a smile the first time you see them. Perhaps regular customers laughed too at first, but they probably soon began treating the buildings like any other store. So, while the Best supermarkets appear to be subverting the sacred world of US retailing, they are doing no such thing. In fact, they have done much to promote the chain even to those who will never get to the Almeda-Genoa Shopping Center, Houston, Texas.

Eaton Centre

ZEIDLER ROBERTS, 1977

TORONTO, CANADA

THE MOTHER OF ALL modern shopping malls, the Eaton Centre is also one of the finest and, if you like this sort of thing, among the most convincing. This, perhaps, is because its architecture is more than skin deep. It has integrity, which cannot be said for the plague of shopping malls that ravaged the face of so many countries worldwide in the last two decades of the twentieth century. Mall culture encouraged people off the streets and into a hermetic, safe and, above all, controlled world in which everything is a given and human beings are transformed into zombies, passive machines for shopping. This is not everyone's view, and certainly not if you happen to live in Toronto where the winters are bitterly cold and the only way to survive is to stay indoors. Quite why third-rate replicas of the Eaton Centre are needed in countries with temperate climates is a mystery that archeologists of the future will have to wrestle with as they explore the ruins of these air-conditioned behemoths. The Eaton Centre, however, is a handsome building inside and clearly based on Joseph Paxton's hugely influential Crystal Palace of 1851.

Hillingdon Civic Centre

RMJM, 1979

LONDON, ENGLAND

VERY RUM. A concatenation of bricks and tiles that is somehow meant to represent the friendly face of local government in one of London's western-most suburbs. The upshot is a confused giant of a building that is not quite sure whether it wants to be friendly or not. With its defensive walls and even what looks like a moat, Hillingdon Civic Centre (or what used to be called a town hall or council offices) seems to want to keep its public at bay. Or is it meant to be the Englishman's Castle? Or were the architects trying somehow to knit as many semi-detached suburban houses together to give the appearance of one big and jolly house that everyone would recognize as belonging to an area dominated by avenue after close after cul-de-sac of tweedy brick houses? The answer lies somewhere in the folksy world of what was often referred to as English "Neovernacular" design. In fact, there was plenty that was "neo" in the design of this peculiar building. Behind that tidal wave of orange brick and folksy pitched roofs, there lurks a largely open-plan interior based very much on Herman Herzberger's Centraal Beheer insurance offices in Apeldoorn (p.234).

RMJM (Robert Matthew Johnson-Marshall and Partners) was a prolific architectural practice capable of designing in any number of styles, although inclined, as here, to be tweedy.

St Mark's Road Housing

JEREMY AND FENELLA
DIXON, 1979
MAIDA VALE, LONDON,
ENGLAND

FROM THE TIME of the "oil crisis" of 1973 and the shocking collapse of Britain's economy under the Tory premiership of Edward Heath in the "winter of discontent" (1973–4), the design and construction of high-rise housing and giant prefabricated concrete estates were all but ended. In fact, over the next 25 years, Britain was lucky to see any new public housing of any scale, quality or ambition. Small-scale schemes, however, made a quiet return, as a reaction against "high-rise horrors", as an economic necessity and as architects themselves turned away from the inward-looking estate and, quite literally, came back onto the street. This modest, yet delightful, row of houses in west London showed how it was again possible to design intimate, small-scale homes that had a real character and presence and if gentle were not twee. The architects, Jeremy and Fenella Dixon, had a talent for getting this subtle balance just right. With their endearing mixture of Dutch and pure London details, these houses add to the architectural mix of the street they animate without being loud or showy, even though there are hints of impending Postmodernism in their fashionably "eclectic" façades.

Jeremy Dixon went on to develop the idea further with houses in the same area that drew imaginatively on historical precedent without recourse to pastiche.

Zentralsparkasse

GÜNTHER DOMENIG, 1980

VIENNA, AUSTRIA

WHEN WAS BANKING EVER
FUNNY? Perhaps this bank is
meant to make you laugh; perhaps
its prognathous jaws – just look
at that entrance – are a reminder
of how the bank manager can
chew your head off when you
go too far into the red. Maybe
Günther Domenig (born 1934)
simply wanted to strike a pose
in the polite and rather dull
Favoriten, one of Vienna's central
shopping streets. Whatever, this
is one of those potty buildings
that children adore and which has
inevitably become something of
a tourist attraction in a city that
has too many of these already.
On the surface – and only on
the surface – Vienna is such a
genteel city; no wonder spirited
architects have wished to shake
it up a little. Adolf Loos must
have turned in his grave when this
crazy confection opened in 1980.
The nuttiness does not end with
the scrunched-up metal façade.
Inside and up the stairs of the
six-storey building, pipes and
ducts appear to worm their way
out of bending and twisting
walls as if auditioning for parts
in Terry Gilliam's film *Brazil*. A
gruesome concrete hand reaches
out from one wall as if Roman
Polanski had been asked to help
with the decoration. Although
batty, the bank is finished with
a typically Viennese attention to
detail which somehow redeems
its decorative excess.

Teatro del Mondo

ALDO ROSSI, 1980

VENICE, ITALY

THIS BEAUTIFUL and ethereal tower was built for the 1980 Venice Biennale and, sadly, was broken up long ago. The wooden tower (an iron frame covered with planks) was mounted on a raft and towed along the waterways of Venice where it could be seen weaving its way past the city's magnificent and wobbly monuments before being anchored alongside the Customs' House on the Dorsoduro in the shadow of the dome of Il Salute and across the Grand Canal from St Mark's Square.

The tower was a romantic gesture to one of the world's most romantic cities by an architect always described as a Rationalist. Aldo Rossi (1931–97) may well have been a "Rat", but his was a romantic, aesthetic rationalism, owing more to, say, the haunting townscape paintings of de Chirico than to the scientific rationalism of many contemporary German and US architects. Rossi, born and educated in Milan, was an important theorist. He had worked for the journals *Casabella* and *Il Contemporeano* before designing buildings, and in 1966 he published his manifesto *L'Architettura della Città*. His architecture and his cities were, for the most part, mournful creations, silent monuments, funeral and empty. In certain contexts – the San Cataldo cemetery, Milan (p.304) – this had its place; in others, such as the social housing he designed in the guise of a seemingly infinite and icy arcade in Milan's Gallaratese 2 suburb, it seemed downright spooky. The Teatro del Mondo was the delightful exception.

Garden Grove Community Church

PHILIP JOHNSON AND
JOHN BURGEE, 1980
LOS ANGELES, CALIFORNIA,
USA

ONLY IN AMERICA could you find a building quite like this. Commissioned by a wealthy preacher, the "Crystal Cathedral" is a vast, technologically sophisticated and utterly banal expression of the power of bible-bashing and cult Christian sects. Truly vast – 125 by 60 by 49 metres (410 x 196 x 160 ft) high – Johnson and Burgee's cathedral is based on a plan in the shape of an elongated four-pronged star. From this a technically brilliant, white-coated steel structure rises up at dramatic angles to reach a peak high above the preacher's podium. This frame is then clad entirely in reflective glass: the interior of the building remains as mysterious as God until you enter. Inside, up to 3,000 people can sit in white-marbled splendour. As this is Los Angeles, the car park is as big as the church.

By this stage of his long career, Philip Johnson had experimented with just about every style going. The Crystal Cathedral was a diversion into a kind of Hollywood Hi-Tech, but it was certainly no dead end for the century's most determined eclectic. A few years later, his headquarters for the Pittsburgh Plate Glass corporation was designed as a kind of Barry and Pugin Westminster extravaganza, the whole prickly conceit faced in acres of glass. And as the architect might have said, "You ain't seen nothing yet."

The Atlantis

ARQUITECTONICA, 1982

MIAMI, FLORIDA, USA

FUNNY WHAT A LITTLE sunshine will do. Take one straight up and down 18-storey apartment block. Add bright primary colours, a few zany details and bathe in bright Florida sunshine. What do you get? The Atlantis, a well-known and much liked building that in most other places in the world and without a few key magic touches would simply be a big, bland downtown block of no special interest. Designed by Bernardo Fort-Brescia (born 1950) and Laurinda Spear (born 1951) of Arquitectonica, The Atlantis is a well thought through apartment block that makes the most of the local climate. The north side of the block is faced in reflective glass. The south side is divided into a grid of blue squares, each framing three balconies one above the other on three floors. One of these squares has been hollowed out and replaced by an open air pool shaded by a palm tree, overlooked by a balcony and framed by a bright red spiral stair that climbs the three storeys of the cut out. It is a clever way of bringing a blocky building to life and a feature that, having caught the popular imagination, has been photographed endlessly. Copies of The Atlantis can be found even in China.

AT&T Building

PHILIP JOHNSON AND
JOHN BURGEE, 1982
NEW YORK CITY, USA

WHAT A FUSS this ugly building caused when it was first unveiled. Was it really so very important? Yes and no. Yes, it was the first big-time, ruthlessly commercial Postmodern office block and so brought mega-buck finance into line with the latest architectural fad. No, because it was a bit of a bore. The AT&T building was simply another stack of offices piled high into the sky, but this time clad in pink granite, topped with a mammoth split-pediment and entered via what looked like a huge Venetian window and a lift lobby adorned with a questionable statue of a gilded and naked youth entitled the "Genius of Electricity". Heaven knows where Philip Johnson's genius was the day he signed off the drawings for this overbearing Chippendale cabinet. The building was meant to be witty, but architectural jokes are never very funny and the fact that they are forced, by the nature of buildings, to do the rounds for a century or even more makes them about as funny as a music hall joke circa 1882. Johnson could be a funny man, but the danger of becoming the profession's full-time comedian is that he was expected to come up with more and more outrageous jokes. By the end of the 1980s, Johnson was clearly bored with what was always going to be a cultural dead end.

State Museum

HANS HOLLEIN, 1982
MÖNCHENGLADBACH,
GERMANY

ANY ARCHITECT WHO MUNCHES
his way through the bones as well
as the flesh of a roast pigeon while
dining in the formal splendour of
the River Room of London's Savoy
Hotel has to be interesting.
Hans Hollein (born 1934) is very
interesting. Born in Vienna and
educated there, at the Illinois
Institute of Technology, Chicago

and Berkeley, he enjoyed a rightful
reputation as one of the few
architects truly able to join
together the obsessions of artists,
architects and designers. Close to
many avant-garde artists, he
worked closely with Joseph Beuys,
among others, on the design of
this complex and richly enjoyable
German civic museum.

Here, on the sloping garden of
what was once a monastery, Hollein
built a kind of modern Acropolis,
a dense and rather exquisite urban
landscape composed of pavilions,
steps and piazzas. Together these
various elements were the museum,
a building of many faces and many

parts. The entrance could be
reached from one of three
directions, all of them oblique,
but leading to a pavilion sheathed
in white marble and adorned with
eye-catching chrome pilasters.

From then on in, Hollein
performs a superb balancing act,
keeping visitors guessing as to
what might be around the next
corner – the variety of spaces
here is prodigious – while leading
them on with veiled hints of what
there might be. The variety of
finishes, materials, colours too
are all as prolific as they are
attractive. And the art on
show isn't half bad either.

Parliament Building

GEOFFREY BAWA, 1983

COLOMBO, SRI LANKA

BUILT ON A LAKE like a traditional palace in the region, the Sri Lankan parliament has a magnificent setting. From afar, with its great roofs, it looks to be a very convincing attempt to create a truly regional architecture, one of the concerns throughout the world at the time of its construction and especially in the countries of the developing world. Close up, however, the building is not quite so exciting nor so romantic. This was not the fault of the architect Geoffrey Bawa (born 1919), a Sri Lankan long known for his skill in marrying modern plans to traditional facades, materials and craftsmanship. The building was rushed up by a Japanese contractor forced to use much more concrete and artificial stone than Bawa would have liked. The hectic pace of the project also meant that the normally flamboyant Bawa was very restricted in the use of decoration: where visitors expect elaborately carved screens and other richly carved details, there are none. The assembly chamber itself is impressive if only for its scale – high and spacious to allow the hot air rising from the benches below to dissipate – and for the tented lightweight steel ceiling, a clever piece of decorative engineering. The chamber sits at the heart of the complex and is guarded by four pavilions in the same style.

The importance of the building, aside from its function, is in its attempt to find a language of design that reflected both local values and modern construction. It seemed a hard thing to do and rarely succeeded.

Public Services Building

MICHAEL GRAVES, 1983

PORTLAND, OREGON, USA

IT LASTED JUST a decade, an extraordinarily short working life for a building that was talked about and published worldwide. The Public Service Building put Portland on the map. Big, bold and colourful, it was in many ways the apotheosis of Postmodern architecture. Essentially, it was just a square, 15-storey office occupying an entire downtown block. What made it different was its very superficiality: four sides of bragadoccio "wallpaper" leaden with heavy-handed "jokes". To be fair, the original design was meant to be a lot more fun, with flamboyant statues, swags and ribbons adorning marble cladding. Cuts in the initial budget did away with the frills and the marble was ditched in favour of paint. A host of comic-book Classical pavilions on the roof went too, so the "jokes", with references to Otto Wagner and the Viennese Secession, were rather thin on the façades. Several critics described it as looking more like a biscuit tin than a building, but those who worked here had more than cookies to crumble. They looked out to Portland through tiny square windows arranged to make funny facades rather than to make staff happy. But this was what Postmodernism was about, a rejection of humane, rational values in favour of a few laughs. Michael Graves (born 1934) was Po-Mo's court jester. Once, he was a white Modern, then Postmodern, then he did much of his work for Disney.

TV-am
Building

TERRY FARRELL, 1983,
CAMDEN, LONDON,
ENGLAND

TERRY FARRELL (born 1940)
opened up an English vein of
Postmodernism which, if a little
bloodless when set against the full
US monty, was redeemed in part by
the thoughtfulness of its planning.
TV-am was the first British exercise
in Po-Mo. Farrell converted a garage
alongside the canal at Camden
Lock into a studio and offices for
a company long since melted into
the airwaves of history. He tacked
on a lively façade, bands of brightly
coloured neon and designed an
entrance hall that represented a
journey across the world. The
exterior was animated with eye-
catching paint and its roofline
topped with glass-reinforced plastic
egg cups, a play on the idea of TV-
am's remit: it was a breakfast-time
station. Farrell gave London much
of its Postmodern skyline during
the 1980s, exporting his style
profitably to Hong Kong and
other points east in the 1990s.
He is respected as an intelligent
and subtle urban planner.

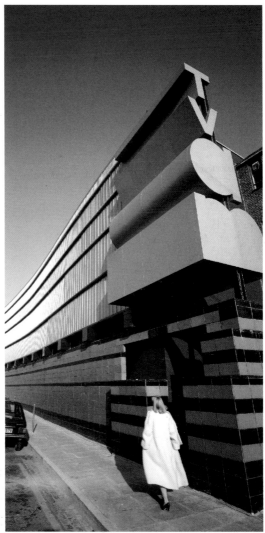

San Juan Capistrano Public Library

MICHAEL GRAVES, 1983

CALIFORNIA, USA

BY THE TIME he designed this "pueblo" public library, Michael Graves was well on his way to becoming one of the principal architects for Disney. Somewhere, over the Postmodern rainbow, the wonderful world of Disneyland and EuroDisney beckoned. This was hardly surprising for, having given up on the white Modernism of his early days as one of the New York Five along with Richard

Meier (p.320), Graves saw in a cartoon-like style of architecture a way of connecting modern architecture to popular sensibilities. The later work for Disney was both over the rainbow and over the top. Perhaps, though, there was a moment when Graves managed a balance between playfulness and worthwhile architecture.

This colourful library with its Spanish–Mexican influences just about gets away with it. It is more or less in keeping with the prevailing style of this sun-bleached sweep of southern California and has a low-key charm that Graves' major

commissions lacked. Even so, the interior is disappointing. The decoration seems to have been applied with a thin brush and the rooms feel more like sets from an exhibition than those you might expect of a public library with its connotations of permanence and learning from the past.

Postmodernism might have given architects the chance to break away from what might have seemed like the puritanical rigours of the Modern Movement, but given what they must have supposed to be freedom, they appeared to have little idea of what to do with it.

Villa Zapu

POWELL-TUCK, CONNOR,
OREFELT, 1984,
NAPA VALLEY, CALIFORNIA,
USA

A HOUSE FOR a Modern fairy tale; if ever Tim Burton's fictional character Edward Scissorhands had decided to give up his Gothic roots and go Modern, this would have been his ideal home. In fact it was commissioned by the Swedish wine grower Thomas Lundstrom as both a home and holiday retreat for guests and as an image-building exercise for his Villa Zapu label. He chose his architects well. David Connor (born 1950) and Julian Powell-Tuck (born 1952) were two Royal College of Art graduates who came into architecture via interior design. They designed the famous Punk shops for Malcolm Maclaren and Vivienne Westwood and wild flats for two of the members of the flamboyant glam-punk band Adam and the Ants. Gunnar Orefelt (born 1953), a Swedish architect, joined the practice, bringing with him a more rigorous approach as well as adventurous clients such as Thomas Lundstrom.

Villa Zapu is built of timber throughout. It comprises a thin, arrow-like house with a tall, detached guest tower separated from the main house by a long swimming pool. Although the villa is a little tricksy, it comes together as a convincing composition and is one of the very best houses of its kind – an expression of the fashion-into-punk-into-graphics-into-architecture movement – that made London such a hotbed of young creative talent from the mid-1980s.

San Cataldo Cemetery

ALDO ROSSI AND
GIANNI BRAGHIERI, 1984
MODENA, ITALY

A LONG TIME in the making, the San Cataldo Cemetery dates from the beginning of the 1970s. It is significant that at this time Rossi had been close to death after a car accident. Perhaps his thoughts on death were refined as a result. Certainly, this is one of the most memorable cemeteries to have been built in modern times, a city of death that moves the visitor to silence. Rossi was to die in a second smash-up in 1997.

The cemetery is a representation of an entire city, but a silent city and one that expresses both the absolute nature of human death and the immortality of the architecture that frames human life. For Rossi, whose buildings were never less than funereal, this was his finest moment. Without the uncertainties of irrational human life to subvert his architecture, he was able to build a city of memory and dreams in which the streets and buildings are inhabited only by the ghosts of our imaginations.

They can be anything we want them to be. A superb sequence of hypnotic monuments etched with deep shadows and set along unyielding axes, the cemetery is built up from Rossi's elemental and mythical "house". "In my house designs", he wrote, "I refer to the basic types of living [or dying] which the architecture of the city has formed through a long process. On the basis of this analogy, every corridor is a street, every court a city square, and a building reproduces the places of the city". At San Cataldo, death has rarely had such a thoughtful and rational dominion.

Neue Staatsgalerie

JAMES STIRLING AND
MICHAEL WILFORD, 1984
STUTTGART, GERMANY

STUTTGART'S NEUE STAATSGALERIE
is one of the few convincing
major buildings realized in a self-
consciously Postmodern manner.
It is a compelling fusion of
Neoclassical and Modern Movement
architecture, interrupted by High-
Tech wizardry, comic book details,
bizarre colours and pedestrian links
that connect the building to
various parts of Stuttgart and
root it to the city. James Stirling
(1926–92) was a bombastic and
original architect who drew on the
vocabulary of twentieth-century
architecture as if it was a game.
In this sense he was the successor
of Sir Edwin Lutyens, another
consummate gamesman. And, like
Lutyens, Stirling's style evolved.
His move into a new Classicism in
the 1980s was bold and original;
his concern, as this gallery shows,
was with integrating colourful
monuments into the existing fabric
of cities rather than with imposing
striking designs on them, as so
many architects tended to do
throughout the century.

National Commercial Bank

SKIDMORE, OWINGS
AND MERRILL, 1984
JEDDAH, SAUDI ARABIA

GORDON BUNSHAFT (1909–90) was, for many years, one of Skidmore, Owings and Merrill's top architects. Here in Jeddah he demonstrated how a modern corporate headquarters could be made to work successfully in the Middle East in both functional and symbolic terms. The offices are set back at an angle within sheer containing walls that have a powerful emblematic presence from any distance while performing the essential role of keeping the heat of the sun under control and shielding windows from glare. The triangular tier of offices can be seen rising through the great rectangular openings cut out of the walls. The openings act as wind funnels and help to cool a form of office accommodation that would make little sense in this climate if designed along the lines of, say, Skidmore, Owings and Merrill's very own Lever Building in New York. The monumentality of the building makes sense given the lack of place here. What is the architect to do, particularly if the client is set on making its presence felt? By offering monumentality in a sea of earlier banality, Bunshaft gave character and order to what was in danger, like so many cities in this region, of becoming a non-place. Even then, a city of striking commercial monuments, no matter how thoughtful or refined, would still be a rather alienating place.

California Aerospace Museum

FRANK GEHRY, 1984

LOS ANGELES, USA

PRANKSTER, FUNSTER, JESTER.
Frank Gehry plays the Fool to
Architecture's aged Lear and gets it
right and wrong in what looks like
equal measures. Gehry (born 1929)
has spent many years pulling
conventional architecture apart
and putting it back together again
in crazy planes and angles. One
of the craziest planes of all is the
F-104 jet fighter he mounted on
one of the zig-zag walls of the
California Aerospace Museum.
This building, rushed up in time
for the 1984 Los Angeles Olympic
Games, comprises an odd
conglomeration of galleries
piled up in front of an older
and conventional building. This
simple yet striking motif imbues
the building with real energy and
makes it unforgettable.

Gehry's mission, rather like
Gaudi's before him, appears to
have been to rip up the rules of
architecture and replace them with
the limits of his own imagination.
The first inkling of what he might
do unfettered was the manner in
which he rebuilt his own house in
Santa Monica (1978). A simple
and rather dreary home was
exploded, with wire, corrugated
fencing and timber extrusions
into a sort of adult playpen or
climbing frame. The house was
just the beginning. With each new
project Gehry stretches his clients
and audience that bit further.
However crazy, Frank Gehry is
always a class act.

Sainsbury Wing

VENTURI, SCOTT-BROWN,
1987, NATIONAL GALLERY,
LONDON, ENGLAND

THIS POSTMODERN-CLASSICAL trifle was the sorry end of a dismal saga in British cultural politics. The National Gallery wanted to build an extension to house its magnificent collection of early Italian paintings and to free up space in its existing Regency building. A developer offered to build a nice gallery sitting on top of lettable offices. He got a long way down the line – this was Margaret Thatcher's money-mad Britain – before a competition was announced for a serious design. It was won by Ahrends Burton Koralek, whose design was described by the Prince of Wales as being like a carbuncle on the face of an old friend and scuppered. Enter Sainsburys, the billionaire grocers, Robert Venturi and a limp-wristed building that tries to be clever and fails dismally until the galleries where the paintings steal the show. You can hang a Bellini Madonna in a garden shed, however, and its ineffable beauty would still shine through.

The Sainsbury Wing is entered separately from the main gallery. The way up to the galleries is obtuse – an ugly stair sheathed in office-style glazing and determinedly off axis. The front is ugly, the back – and this is meant to be funny – resembles the rear end of a London cinema or theatre: in other words, ugly. Was the once iconoclastic Robert Venturi tamed by the cautious British establishment? Or was it just a bad heir day?

Vitra
Museum

FRANK GEHRY, 1988

WEIL-AM-RHEIN, GERMANY

UNDER THE SPIRITED direction
of Ralph Fehlbaum, Vitra became
one of the most adventurous
manufacturers of Modern furniture.
Over the years, the Fehlbaum family
had collected a vast number of
chairs, all the classics and many of
the imponderables or otherwise
unsittables. Where to put them?
Fehlbaum commissioned Frank
Gehry to design a museum in the
grounds of the Vitra factory. It was
a wise choice. Gehry came up with
a design that managed at one and
the same time to be pure and clean,
white, bright and crazy. Walls and
light towers shot, cartoon-fashion,
every which way. But it was also
beautifully built and the plan behind
those provocative façades was neatly
ordered. Inside, the drama comes
from the swoop of the roofs and the
chairs themselves, which are mounted
for the most part on simple white
geometric pedestals and lit, as far
as possible, by the sun. Not only
was the building a delight, but it
was evidence to the effect that a
zany-looking building might yet be
rational, and that strongly sculpted
architecture would draw the crowds,
assuming you wanted them.

Gehry was to be asked to
do this again and again over the
next decade, culminating in his
voluptuous Guggenheim Museum
in Bilbao (p.321). His façades might
seem gimmicky, yet Gehry's plans
are there to remind the sceptical
that, despite the bombast,
everything is in order.

Broadgate Centre

SKIDMORE, OWINGS AND
MERRILL, ARUP ASSOCIATES,
ET AL, 1988
CITY OF LONDON, ENGLAND

A STRANGE – for London that is –
yet successful chunk of urban
planning. Muscular, broad-
shouldered and well fleshed, like a
boxer in a shiny, double-breasted
suit, Broadgate is a spacious pile of
flashy, deep-plan office blocks,
gathered around some fine and
popular new public squares. Nice
piazzas, shame about the
architecture. The problem with the
buildings – their unmitigated bulk
– is the reason they exist. In the
mid-1980s, the City of London
Stock Market was deregulated and,
as if out of the blue, the City needed
dealing rooms by the score. Existing
offices were too old and skinny to
handle these: enter the deep-plan
office. At Broadgate, these
behemoths were dressed in marble,
granite, slate and stone, adorned
with brass, bronze and some
seriously good sculpture. But, they
were Ugly Sisters whatever artists
and architects could do to disguise
their size. The spaces in between,
however, were very welcome: squares
to sit in, steps to sit on, an ice-
skating rink in winter, bars and cafés
galore. All these, plus instant access
to Liverpool Street station, one of
London's most important junction
boxes. The City "crashed" before
Broadgate was completed and no
developer was brave or foolhardy
enough to try anything quite like it
again in central London.

Noe
Building

BRANSON COATES
ARCHITECTURE, 1988
TOKYO, JAPAN

NIGEL COATES (born 1949) taught
for a decade at the Architectural
Association, London, before
commissions for restaurants, bars,
cafés and nightclubs arrived from
Japan. It was a remarkable moment:
an architect who never expected to
build was an overnight star in Tokyo.
The Noe Building – Noah's Ark, but
filled with human beings eating,
drinking and clubbing – was Coates's
first free-standing building. It was
both funny and provocative.

Coates' concerns had long been
with what he called "narrative
architecture", buildings and the
spaces between them that in
themselves told, retold and celebrated
the stories of city life. This meant a
busy architecture full of incident
and detail and one that could be
by turns funny, spiky, cool and even
erotic. Coates did pack much of
this sort of detail into his Tokyo
interiors and the Noe Building, but
it would take another decade before
he was taken seriously enough to
be entrusted with a large building in
Britain. When it came – the Museum
of Popular Music in Sheffield (p.324)
– Coates found himself a major
figure encouraged by the Labour
government of Tony Blair. Coates is
also professor of architecture and
design at the Royal College of Art
and a leading figure in a move to
link architecture not just to other
to other arts, but to contemporary
music and fashion too.

Pumping Station

JOHN OUTRAM, 1988

DOCKLANDS, LONDON,

ENGLAND

A ONE-TIME RAF PILOT, John Outram (born 1934) became one of the most exotic British talents in the last two decades of the century. A Postmodernist, perhaps, he created an architecture very much his own, richly decorated and full of abstruse and colourful meaning. Not that the observer needs to know what Outram means; it is enough to enjoy the energetic and unabashed way in which he took a civic utility like this pumping station on the River Thames and turned it into an architectural occasion, to know that he is on the side of the angels and not just another bandwagon Postmodernist.

The pumping station is a simple box full of powerful and inscrutable machinery. Outram decorated this box with elements drawn from ancient cultures and turned it into a story, should you be able to decipher it, of river gods and goodness knows what. It quickly became a favourite landmark of tourists chugging up and down the river on their way from Westminster or Tower Bridge to Greenwich.

Some years earlier, Outram had worked the same colourful magic with some very prosaic industrial warehouses at two locations in west London. It was fun to see architecture buffs creeping into what for them must have been terrifying factory yards bristling with jeering workers to peep at the latest in picturesque English architecture.

Rooftop Office

COOP HIMMELBLAU, 1989
VIENNA, AUSTRIA

WOLF D. PRIX (born 1942) and
Helmut Swiczinsky (born 1944) are
a couple of live-wire Viennese
architects who like to appear dark
and sinister. The Red Angel
drinking hole they designed at the
beginning of the 1980s in Vienna
was wonderfully menacing. So, too,
this lawyers' office on the roof of a
nineteenth-century city block. The

elaborate rooflight looks as if it has
landed on the roof like some
mechanical bat. The architects
themselves have likened it to a bolt
of lightning. Whatever, it is an
impressive device and one that
does that rare thing – makes a roof
interesting. This was something
that remarkably few architects did
in the twentieth century, as if the
arrival of the flat roof marked the
end of architectural invention
above the cornice line. The great
exceptions were Gaudí – the
roofscape of the Casa Milà (p.75)
is one of the hidden wonders of

twentieth-century architecture and
decoration – architects such as
Gehry or Böhm, for whom the roof
is indistinguishable from the walls,
and Coop Himmelblau in this
small, yet widely published project.
The offices beneath it do not
disappoint although they are not as
quirky as this celebrated rooflight.
The way the roof opens up as if to
bite or swallow the mechanical bat
(or to discharge this bolt of
lightning) is as delightful as it is
the stuff of nightmares. Prix and
Swiczinsky moved on to
international projects in the 1990s.

Pyramid

I. M. PEI, 1989

LOUVRE, PARIS, FRANCE

SUCH WAS THE CONTROVERSY generated over the announcement of plans to erect a glass pyramid in the main courtyard of the Louvre that a fight broke out within these hallowed portals in 1984 between police and protesters. From the vantage point of the end of the century it was hard to know what the fuss was about. Just as Parisians hated the idea of the Eiffel Tower when it was first built, so they took against the idea of the pyramid. They soon got to like it. It was no slavish copy of an Egyptian pyramid, but a very impressive glass reinterpretation of the ancient model. Flanked by two baby glass pyramids and vigorous fountains, the ensemble is as striking as it is memorable and, without doubt, it enhances the bulbous and richly decadent architecture of the famous museum.

The pyramid was designed by the skilful Chinese-American architect Ieoh Ming Pei (born 1917), designer of the East Wing extension of the National Gallery of Art in Washington (1978), a bold and massive abstract composition. The glass pyramid, one of President Mitterand's *grand projets*, was just the tip of an architectural iceberg: Pei's crystalline pavilion was the entrance pavilion that led down to a spacious and refined new lobby, in which visitors were able to orientate themselves before setting out in quest of the Mona Lisa or Venus de Milo. This successful and, ultimately popular, scheme was greatly extended in 1992.

Parc de la Villette

BERNARD TSCHUMI,
ET AL, 1989
PARIS, FRANCE

THIS "DECONSTRUCTIVIST" PARK was one of the (incomplete) architectural surprises of the 1989 bicentennial celebrations of the French Revolution. Neither blatantly monumental nor symbolic, it was laid out over six years and designed to be a delight and nothing else – *folie de grandeur* perhaps, but a

folly nevertheless. Ultimately the park, planted on the site of the former central Paris abattoirs, was to have been overlain with a grid of no fewer than 42 brightly coloured follies, each an enjoyably useless Deconstructivist design by Bernard Tschumi (born 1944) with intellectual input from the hip Deconstructivist philosopher, Jacques Derrida. The follies were, for the most part, painted bright red and slowly, slowly became wrapped around with trees, grass, plants and people. Visitors came here in gradually increasing numbers to see the new science

museums and outsized films in the IMAX cinema housed, secretly to the uninitiated, in the compelling "Geode", a giant mirror-finish ball, by Fainsilber. The follies were meant to frame a rich programme of events, yet, year by year, these never quite seemed to materialize, although one folly now serves as a restaurant, another as a café and a third as a viewing platform. The follies are arranged in a rigorous mathematical sequence and are a rare example of modern architecture without any real or predetermined function.

Judge
Institute

JOHN OUTRAM, 1993

CAMBRIDGE, ENGLAND

THE JUDGE INSTITUTE was a management college designed to train a generation of young British people to manage rather than manufacture. As Britain turned from an industrial to a service economy in the 1980s and aped the United States in business manners, language and culture, so its architectural landscape began to change from one of essential plainness to an increasingly flamboyant and swaggering transatlantic style, based on the florid language of Postmodernism. Perhaps, then, it made perfect sense to house a service economy management course in one of the most florid buildings of its generation. John Outram's temple to budding business executives was an extraordinarily rich conceit, a kind of overbaked Roman basilica stirred into a heady shopping mall stew and spiced with more than piquant decoration. The result was indigestible from any point of view, although the building was carefully thought out in terms of use of space, the organization of its services and its use of energy.

Outram was a pioneer of the British "High Tech" school from the 1950s. The temptation to become ever more decorative, however, seemed only to undermine his essential seriousness of purpose. This was the Postmodern, post-industrial, service economy era and every company and college wanted a distinctive brand. This is what the Judge Institute got.

Supreme Court

RAM KARMI, 1993

JERUSALEM, ISRAEL

THE RESULT of an international competition, Ram Karmi's Supreme Court was an important moment in the long attempt in the last quarter of the twentieth century to reconcile past and present in architecture. Its muscular forms are taken from a romantic view of ancient Israeli architecture, from fortresses, from the architectural legacy of British and Israeli architects working together in what was then Palestine in the 1920s and 1930s and in a modern design that takes fully into account not just history and symbolism, but climate too.

Bibliothèque Nationale

DOMINIQUE PERRAULT, 1995
PARIS, FRANCE

KNOWN LOCALLY AS THE BGV
(*Bibliothèque à Grande Vitesse*), this
massive national library was
commissioned, designed and built
within five years. If that was an
extraordinary achievement, the
building itself is questionable and
in several ways downright perverse.
Perrault (born 1953) arranged the
building, located on the banks of
the Seine, in the form of four giant

open books, made – or so it seems
– almost entirely from glass and
rising from a great stepped podium.
The centre of the podium was
hollowed out into a garden
courtyard around which the reading
rooms were cloistered. The giant
books, one at each corner of the
podium, were the bookstacks. On
paper this was an enjoyable
conceit: the stock of national
learning was there for everyone to
see. The problem was also obvious
for everyone to see: the precious
books were exposed to sunlight. So
the book towers were lined top to
toe with wooden louvres to protect

their cargo. This was an odd way of
doing things, designing a building
as a problem and then spending
considerable energy solving the
problem. The design of the Library
was also criticized for the lavish use
of rare and endangered hardwoods
in many public parts. Nevertheless,
Parisians have long been famous
for moaning about brave new
buildings, then taking them to their
hearts. By the end of the 1990s
there were signs that Perrault's
perverse design was winning
converts. It has a great sense of
occasion and drama and is an
enjoyable and flirty meeting place.

Petronas Towers

CESAR PELLI, 1997

KUALA LUMPUR, MALAYSIA

THE "TIGER" ECONOMIES of Southeast Asia were beginning to lose their claws at the very end of the twentieth century, but for the best part of two decades they terrified the old industrial west as they took to manufacturing like a crispy duck to pancakes and their GDPs (gross domestic product, a standard measure of national wealth) soared. The architectural corollary of this unprecedented economic growth was, as it had been in Chicago in the late nineteenth century, the skyscraper. Southeast Asian nations competed with one another to build the tallest towers. It was hard to say where it would all end, but the tallest to be completed by the century's end were the twin Petronas Towers located in the centre of the Malaysian capital's "Golden Triangle". Such is the importance of the towers to national prestige that a golf course – held in near veneration in this part of the world – had to be torn up to make way for them.

Designed by Cesar Pelli (born 1926), the 88-storey, 451-metre (1,480-ft) towers are joined at the waist by a bridge. They have the appearance of a salt and pepper condiment set, although the profile of the towers is based (very loosely) on those of local Buddhist temples. They might be kitsch, but it would be hard to argue that the early skyscrapers of New York and Chicago were really any different.

Getty Center

RICHARD MEIER, 1997
LOS ANGELES,
CALIFORNIA, USA

A LATE TWENTIETH-CENTURY
Acropolis, the Getty Center sits on
top of a hill high above the
suburban sprawl of Los Angeles as
if dispensing art, culture and
learning to all around. Remote,
chaste and refined, this city within
a city is a remarkable achievement.
A white tram takes visitors up the
hill from a giant car park to a plaza
from which they can wander all day
long from one handsome pavilion
to the next, take in peerless views
of the city, its mountainous backdrop
and the Pacific Ocean, catch the
sun's rays from the Center's many
terraces, bask in its glorious gardens,
eat in its cafés and restaurants and
even take in some art before
making the descent back down to
the crowded freeways and air-
conditioned shopping malls below.

The Getty Center, which cost a
cool one billion dollars, is a
monument to the wealth and oil
exploitation of the Getty family. Here,
art and conservation work carried
out in Getty's name around the
world redeems the spirit of rampant
US capitalism. Or something like
that. The Center comprises a galaxy
of beautifully constructed galleries,
studios, workshops, lecture theatres
and other public functions in
chaste pavilions made of concrete
and clad in travertine by Richard
Meier. It is very impressive, very
detached and an enchantingly
surreal place to spend a day.

Guggenheim Museum

FRANK GEHRY, 1997

BILBAO, SPAIN

ONE OF THE MOST talked about buildings in years, this Basque outpost of the Solomon R. Guggenheim Collection transformed Bilbao's image. Until then this ancient city with its unique language was associated with the ETA (the Basque separatist movement) and violence, its busy port and not much more. From late 1997 it became the focus of weekend breaks for people from all over Europe. And what people came to see was Gehry's madcap museum. ETA did its best to blow up King Juan Carlos when he came to open the building; a bomb was discovered in a tub of flowers which, had it exploded, would have destroyed Jeff Koon's *Puppy* sculpture that stands guard over the museum, the King and at least some of the sensational titanium cladding that distinguishes this acclaimed building. The bombing would have been a mistake, because Bilbao and the Basque country have won more sympathy through the museum than through years of guns and hatred.

The building comprises a central gallery, on several levels with offshoots that include an *enfillade* of classical galleries for the display of intimate artworks, and an elongated gallery for big Pop sculptures, including Richard Serra's *Snake*, three tall sheets of steel winding more than 30 metres (100 ft) along the gallery. Crazy, but wonderful.

No 1 Poultry

JAMES STIRLING AND
MICHAEL WILFORD, 1997
CITY OF LONDON, ENGLAND

THE SON OF A successful London property developer, Peter Palumbo had a dream to commission Ludwig Mies van der Rohe to design an office tower in the City of London. This would replace a pile of pretty, if petty, Victorian offices and shops opposite the Mansion House, official home of the Lord Mayor of London. Palumbo Jr flew to Chicago to visit Mies in 1959. It took another 30 years for Palumbo, thwarted at every turn, not to build one of the very last designs by Mies – it was much like the Seagram Building (p.203). After two public enquiries and despite a team of experts on his side, Palumbo was forced to give up. Instead, he commissioned a polar opposite by Stirling and Wilford, a wilful Postmodern oil-tanker of a building that appeared to be heading on a collision course with the Mansion House. Hardly subtle, this ship of the developer's line took many years to build; it comprises offices, shops, bars and restaurants, a roof garden and an entrance to Bank Underground station. Big, brightly coloured, perhaps it is meant to be witty, but Po-Mo jokes have never worn well, assuming they were ever funny. Palumbo, however, was unabashed and seemingly oblivious to criticism. A collector of buildings in many different styles, he owns, among others, Mies van der Rohe's Farnsworth House (p.186) and Le Corbusier's Maisons Jaoul (p.198).

Jewish Museum

DANIEL LIBESKIND, 1999

BERLIN, GERMANY

A LIGHTNING BOLT zig-zagging beside the old Berlin Museum, the Jewish Museum is one of the most powerful and extraordinary buildings of the twentieth century. Its plan is rooted around a central void that connects the many galleries in this zinc-clad building. The void expresses the absence of the 250,000 Jews who lived in

Berlin at the beginning of Hitler's Third Reich: those who were able abandoned the city they loved; those who stayed were slaughtered. Yet, although this atonal building has all the power of Schoenberg's unfinished opera *Aron and Moses* – a work that Libeskind (born 1946), a trained musician, turned to over and again during the design of the museum – this is not a memorial to the Holocaust. Rather, it is a reflection and a celebration of a people, a way of life and a culture that was quite literally taken out of the city and murdered.

The nearby S-Bahn links Wansee at one end of the line (the Wansee conference of 1942 set a seal on the Final Solution) and Orianenberg at the other, where the headquarters from which Heinrich Himmler ran his concentration camps with such infamous zeal are now local council offices.

The ghosts of Berlin have yet to be exorcized fully. Libeskind's brooding museum, with no entrance that you can see from the street, is the architecture of memory writ as large and as powerful as it has ever been.

Museum of Popular Music

BRANSON COATES
ARCHITECTURE, 1999
SHEFFIELD, ENGLAND

TEENAGERS AND POP MUSIC were mid-century phenomena. By the end of the century they had a long history and many of the early pop idols had passed into the great gig in the sky and the first teenagers were grandparents. Perhaps they would be zimmering their way up to Sheffield in 1999 to recapture the shakin' and shimmerin' days of their youth at the rather pedantically named Museum of Popular Music. This is designed in the guise of four steel drums, symbolizing the driving beat that accompanies virtually all pop music and paying homage to the city of Sheffield still, despite Britain's feverish attempt in the 1980s and 1990s to abandon every last bit of its heavy industry – with trade

unions and working-class radicalism meeting the same fate – a centre of steel making.

The plan is a satisifying one in that it allows visitors to walk straight to the heart of the building and to orientate themselves before deciding on what they want to see rather than trekking aimlessly through galleries in a stupor which has been all too often the fate of gallery-goers in the late twentieth century. The architects were able to build a miniature inflatable prototype of the museum (1998), which was erected in Horse Guards Parade in London and housed "powerhouse::uk", a government-sponsored exhibition of British design creativity and a symbol of New Labour's "Cool Brittania".

Boilerhouse Wing

DANIEL LIBESKIND, 2001

VICTORIA AND ALBERT

MUSEUM, LONDON, ENGLAND

IN STANLEY KUBRICK'S epic *2001: A Space Odyssey*, the near future was presented as one in which humans attempted to stamp a rational design on the universe. This was expressed in their clothes, furniture, spaceships, computers and conversation. Yet, despite their best attempts, they were undermined by the forces of unreason, chaos and interference by ineffable forces from somewhere on high. Architects throughout the twentieth century fought a battle between the rational and the irrational, between romance and reason, order and disorder. Who could say who won? In fact there were no winners. In London, as a new century approached, Daniel Libeskind's spiralling design for new galleries at the Victoria and Albert Museum represented the tussle between these opposite forces. It is as if his proposed building was twisting and turning between the forces of reason and chaos or being pulled askew by the magnetic attractions of polar opposites. The building was designed to pack a lot of varied space into a confined courtyard site. Libeskind's idea was a sequence of galleries corkscrewing its way up, adding to the eccentric and colourful skyline of South Kensington's batty and much-loved Victorian museums. The Boilerhouse Wing was to be clad in terracotta tiles, giving it a truly crystalline and enduring appearance.

The nineteenth century saw the development of new types of building and structure designed by engineers. While architects fought battles of style – should they dress the frames of their masterpieces in Gothic copes, Classical togas or be terribly daring and try both together? – engineers, and a few wide-eyed architects it must be said, explored the possibilities of new materials and structures. As they finally got to grips with

style themselves. By the late 1970s and in the hands of Richard Rogers, Renzo Piano and Norman Foster, this had become an art form in its own right. The style, for it was one, was nick-named Hi Tech, although the intriguing thing about it was that the best of these buildings, far from being naked engineering structures, were highly finished artefacts that required an extraordinary amount of sophisticated

These include the various communications towers and centres shown in this section as well as the former *Financial Times* printing press in London's Docklands by Nicholas Grimshaw (p.364) and the beautiful satellite receiving station at Affleur, Austria, designed by Gustav Peichl (p.359). Such impressive structures could hardly help impressing themselves on the sensibilities of architects who came to prominence in the age of mass communication and sophisticated technology. Second, there is a long tradition of brutally functional yet attractive buildings designed to cover as much space or to reach as high into the sky as possible without any attempt to make light of the fact. These include the John Hancock Tower in Chicago (p.353) and the outsized geodesic dome Buckminster Fuller built for the Union Tank Car Company in Baton Rouge, Louisiana (p.343).

Robotic

MACHINES FOR LIVING IN

these at the turn of the century, the vast majority of architects felt they had to dress them up. It seemed impossible to them that such structures were more beautiful naked. Yet very often they were. Up until, and even beyond, World War One, this batty division between what was architecture and thus Art (no matter how hideous) and what was engineering and thus Science (and often extremely beautiful) struggled lamely on. And then the dam burst. Airship hangars (p.330), factories (pp.329, 331, 333, 348, 361) and even coastal defences (p.340) proved to be works of high art in their own right even if a world apart from the Classical orders and all forms of decoration. Ultimately, the tables were turned and architects began to design in an engineering

craftsmanship to complete. They were celebrations of structural engineering as seen through the eyes of architects, and in a sense their highly polished and refined exhibitions of steelwork, pipes and ducts were as much a form of decoration as Classical columns and swags of plaster fruit. These were ostentatious buildings and designed, perhaps, to prove that an architecture that owed nothing to convention could be very glamorous indeed. Richard Rogers' Lloyds Building (p.363) was every bit as refined and custom-designed as Josef Hoffman's Palais Stoclet (p.26).

There were, however, at least two other strands of Robotic buildings. First, there were those that were first and foremost machines and not for normal or regular human habitation.

The most satisfying of these machine-like buildings, however, are either the most pure, or those that fuse the talents of engineers and architects seamlessly. Look at the airship hangar at Orly (p.330) or the aircraft hangar at Orbetello (p.338). Perfection. Or else consider the magnificent new airports at Kansai (p.370) and Hong Kong (p.373). These are machines for flying from and have an openness and honesty about them that architects working in other Modern traditions found difficult to achieve.

Fuller
Building

DANIEL BURNHAM, 1902

NEW YORK CITY, USA

KNOWN FROM ITS BEGINNING as
the "Flat Iron" because of its
distinctive footprint, the 20-storey
Fuller Building is an early
masterpiece of downtown high-rise
design. Burnham made the most of
a potentially awkward street corner
site to create a building with a
highly distinctive and memorable
profile. It marked the emergence of
the true "skyscraper": all the available
technology needed to reach for the
sky was now available. Elisha Otis
provided the passenger elevator as
early as 1857; the great Chicago
fires of 1871 and 1874 encouraged
the development of iron and steel
frames for buildings; foundations
were developed that would take the
weight of these secular towers of
Babel; and techniques for cladding
iron and steel frames with brick and
stone panels had become practical
and reliable. Within five years of
the completion of the Fuller
Building, New York "skyscrapers"
had topped 152 metres (500 ft)
and the sky was truly the limit.

Climbing high above Manhattan,
the Fuller Building followed the
principles enshrined in Louis Sullivan's
famous essay "The Tall Office
Building Artistically Considered"
(1896), in which the ideal office
building was composed on the lines
of the façade of an ideal Palladian
house or a Classical column, with a
base containing shops and lobby, a
middle section containing any
number of office floors and a top
floor in the guise of an attic storey.

Fiat
Factory

GIACOMO MATTÉ-TRUCCO,

1923, TURIN, ITALY

"WE AFFIRM", wrote the poet
Filippo Tommaso Marinetti in his
Futurist Manifesto, "that the
world's magnificence has been
enriched by a new beauty: the
beauty of speed." That was in 1909
when cars were not exactly fast and
just six years after the Wright
brothers had proved that powered
flight was possible (at 20 kph/12
mph). In 1920, Giacomo Matté-

Trucco (1869–1934) began work
on the construction of the new
Fiat Factory at Lingotto, not far
from the centre of Turin. It was, as
any building could be at the time,
a symbol of Futurist ideals.
Dedicated to the speedy and
efficient production of cars, it
boasted a parabolic test track on
its elongated roof. Images of Fiat
cars speeding around the top of
this imposing factory have long
been used to capture an era in
which the machine was king (or
dictator) and speed his mistress.
Even so, the factory is a concrete
heavyweight and, test-track aside,

is fairly far removed from Futurist
ideals which looked not just to
speed, but to a fundamental
lightness of structure and being.

The vast complex no longer makes
cars. It has since become, very
gradually, a major exhibition complex
and cultural centre, remodelled
sympathetically by Renzo Piano. As
an image of the brave new machine
world opening up to architects,
engineers and designers after the
brutal experimentation of World
War One, it remains forever that
famous concrete race-track buzzing
like an angry wasp above a city
drawn into the Future.

Dymaxion House

BUCKMINSTER FULLER, 1927

BUCKMINSTER FULLER (1895-1983) was an intellectual jack-in-the-box, a brilliant US inventor with the gift of the gab; anyone who ever sat through a Fuller lecture wondered where on earth those four or even five or six hours went. His one great obsession was to create lightweight structures and to achieve the greatest technical performance with the least expenditure of energy and materials. In this, he could certainly be said to have been well ahead of his times.

Fuller's first project was the Dymaxion House ("Dynamic plus maximum efficiency") prototype of 1927. This was a literal interpretation of Le Corbusier's dictum that a house was a machine for living in. Its lightweight structure comprised six triangular rooms suspended from a central structural core that also housed the main services (kitchen, bathroom, plumbing etc). With a diameter of 15 metres (49 ft) and a height of 12 metres (29 ft), the house weighed just 2,227 kg (4,900 lb) and could be dismantled and transported with the greatest of ease. The trouble is that no one really wanted to live in a machine like this, and in any case the traditional North American balloon-framed timber house was also easy and cheap to build and could be moved from one site to another too. The Wichita House he built in 1946 was a more sympathetic development of the Dymaxion House, although it still looked more like a Martian spaceship than an American home.

Van Nelle Tobacco Factory

MART STAM, JOHANNES
ANDREAS BRINCKMAN,
ET AL, 1930
ROTTERDAM, THE
NETHERLANDS

THIS GRACEFUL FACTORY was largely the work of the Mart Stam (1899–1987) who spent two years in the office of Brinckman (1902–49) in the mid-1920s. Martinus Adrianus Stam was from early on a dedicated socialist; having worked with Hans Poelzig and Max Taut in Germany in the early 1920s, he went to the fledgling Soviet Union where he worked with the revolutionary Soviet architect El Lissitzky (Eliezer Markovich, 1890–1941) in Moscow before transforming the Van Nelle project into one of the iconic designs of the early Modern Movement.

The factory was housed in one handsome extensively glazed block with a cafeteria perched on its roof like an airport control tower. An ancillary three-storey block curving away from the factory housed offices, a library and a café for white-collar workers. Aside from being much lighter and airier than most contemporary factories, the all-embracing design kept the site free of clutter and makeshift buildings. It was much visited by factory owners and architects from around the world and became a model for the look as well as the physical organization of the modern industrial plant. Stam went on to teach at the Bauhaus in Dessau, while Brinckman began work on the Bergpolder housing block, Rotterdam (1934), one of the very first residential buildings to stand on stilts.

Chrysler Building

WILLIAM VAN ALEN, 1930

NEW YORK CITY, USA

POSSIBLY THE BEST LOVED high-rise building in the world, the Chrysler Building is a masterpiece of engineering skill and Art Deco showmanship. Designed by William van Alen (1883–1954) to be the tallest building in the world (320 metres/1,048 ft), it held this record for just a year before the Empire State Building (381 metres /1,250 ft) on New York's Fifth Avenue broke it. Even so, the Chrysler Building is generally considered to be the prettier of the two. The architect Rem Koolhaas has famously illustrated the rival Manhattan skyscrapers as a pair of lovers in bed together enjoying a post-coital rest: he depicted the Empire State Building as male, the Chrysler Building as female. The technology to build this high (in steel) was tried and tested by the late 1920s, yet the Chrysler Building stretched the capabilities of the US construction industry to literally new heights. The chief attraction of the building, however, lies largely in its flamboyant stainless steel decoration; the lantern or "crown" that caps the tower is exquisite. The skyscraper was commissioned by the Chrysler Corporation, which explains the name and the many automotive references in the building's extensive decoration, but Chrysler was never to occupy the building. Van Alen himself was accused of various financial improprieties during the construction and rather disappeared off the architectural map after 1930.

Empire State Building

SHREVE, LAMB AND
HARMON, 1931
NEW YORK CITY, USA

PHENOMENON, icon, movie star
and tourist attraction, the Empire
State Building has been one of the
world's most famous buildings
since it opened just in time to meet
the real impact of the Wall Street
Crash of 1929. It is not a building
much discussed in architectural
histories as it is seen as an over-
the-top example of Art Deco styling
wrapped around a stock steel frame.
This is unfair. Aside from being the
world's tallest building for more
than 40 years, the Empire State
Building acts as a magnificent
fulcrum on the Manhattan skyline.

Its appearance is elegant and its
cladding of limestone and granite,
decorated with a minimum of Art
Deco flourishes, is stylish rather
than flashy. In urban terms the 380-
metre (1,250-ft) tower – 450-metre
(1,472-ft) if you count the
communications tower added to the
roof in later years – performs its
role well. From the sidewalk
nothing more than the eight-storey
base can be seen: the tower is set
back and can be seen only from a
distance. The base is cut through
with a noble arcade with shops,
services and cafés. The Empire
State is a very public building.
Since 1931, about 120 million
visitors have been up to its viewing
galleries. The architects were
Richmond H. Shreve (1877–1946),
William Lamb (1883–1952) and
Arthur Loomis Harmon (1878–1958).

Giovanni Berta Stadium

PIER LUIGI NERVI, 1932

FLORENCE, ITALY

EXTENDED AND SLIGHTLY SPOILT in recent years, Pier Luigi Nervi's (1891–1979) communal stadium at Florence was this great engineer's first triumph. The design is simple – an oval of concrete stairs and 35,000 seats with one section covered by a concrete shell grandstand that has the appearance of a giant pair of jaws. The design owes as much to precedents set in ancient Rome as it does to a new, plastic use of reinforced concrete.

Nervi was born at Sondrio, Lombardy and studied engineering at Bologna University. He set up his own firm in 1920. He ranks with Freyssinet (p.330) and Maillart as an engineer who was also an artist, a designer who could turn logical calculations into a form of poetry realized in modern materials. In his many writings, Nervi insisted that the process of creating form was the same for engineers and architects as it was for artists. It depended as much on intuition as it did on logic and mathematics. His first built project was a cinema in Naples in 1927; within a decade he had become one of the world's most impressive and expressive structural engineers. He summed up his wide-ranging thoughts on the subject in a number of important books, among them *The Art and Science of Construction* (1945), *The Architectonic Language* (1950) and *New Constructions* (1963).

Empire Tower

THOMAS TAIT AND
LAUNCELOT ROSS, 1938
GLASGOW, SCOTLAND

TAIT WHACKED THIS Russian-inspired Constructivist tower up to its full height of 76 metres (250 ft) in just nine weeks. Not bad considering it featured a fully operational restaurant as well as a viewing gallery. And, by night, the tower was lit up. The tower could be seen from up to 130 km (80 miles) away. The occasion for its unheralded design was the Empire Exhibition of 1938. The tower was the structural anchor of the show that was held at a time when Glasgow, now a city better known for its nightclubs and fashionable bars, was the home of British engineering and shipbuilding at its very best. Great liners and railway locomotives were launched from its shipyards and rolled out from its workshops. Tait's tower was an impressive example of what Glasgow could do. The speed of construction was made possible by Tait's choice of steel angles, rivetted together and clad in the corrugated steel that Glasgow manufactured for export around the world. The net effect was remarkable: here at last, in Glasgow of all places, a Soviet Constructivist tower had been erected, in record time. The tower was demolished soon after the exhibition. A sitting duck for Lutfwaffe bombers, it would have been a miracle if it had seen out World War Two as Glasgow was badly hit.

Aircraft Hangar

PIERO LUIGI NERVI, 1940

ORBETELLO, TUSCANY, ITALY

THE ITALIAN FASCIST DICTATOR, Mussolini, once said "I am a reactionary and a revolutionary according to circumstance". Nowhere was this statement more true than in the architectural policies encouraged and pursued by Il Duce from the 1920s until his fall in 1943 when the German army seized Italy before losing it to the Allies. Right till the end, Piero Luigi

Nervi was designing and building a sequence of a dozen or so magnificent and revolutionary aircraft hangars in pre-cast concrete. Here was proof – sad in a way – that sabre-rattling and war itself can stimulate some of the most inventive and beautiful design and engineering. The hangar at Orbetello (destroyed) was perhaps the finest of Nervi's sequence. Here a cat's cradle of a roof – a latticework of prestressed concrete members, or bones – was supported on six delicately curving concrete buttresses. The roof measured no less than 102 metres (336 ft) by

36.5 metres (120 ft) and was covered with asbestos-cement sheets. The effect was one of cathedral-like Gothic beauty, belying the savage purpose of the machines of war gathered under this peerless vault. Nervi, unlike many engineers, never denied that he was seeking beauty in his designs: his quest for filigree and lightweight concrete structures was as much to delight the eye as it was to push forward the boundaries of structural engineering. For Piero Nervi, the quest of the artist, architect and the engineer was one and the same.

Wolf's Lair

TODT ORGANIZATION, 1940

KATSZYN, POLAND

ADOLF HITLER railed against the decadence of Modern architecture, yet for most of World War Two the Führer ran his blitzkrieg campaigns from the bowels of some of the most radical concrete structures yet built. Deep in Poland's Mazurian Forest, the Todt organization (named after the engineer who built Hitler's autobahns) built the Wolfsshanze (Wolf's Lair), 27 acres of bombastic concrete buildings and bunkers. This is where Colonel von Stauffenberg failed to assassinate Hitler in 1944 and where the Führer walked his pet German Shepherd, Blondi, before morning briefings. The complex included a casino and sauna, fortified houses for Hitler, Goering and other heads of staff, together with officers' quarters and barracks for no fewer than 3,000 personnel. Hitler's own gargantuan bunkers looked disturbingly like the architecture of the so-called Brutalists of the 1950s.

The SS wired the buildings up so as to self-destruct in the event of the Wolf's Lair being overrun by the Red Army. Eventually the Soviets arrived and the complex was blown up; yet, such was the quality of Todt's reinforced concrete that it was all but impossible to destroy the Wolf's Lair. At the end of the twentieth century it survives as a monument to Hitler's flawed ambitions and as proof of the great strength and enduring qualities of concrete construction.

Post Office Tower

ERIC BEDFORD, ET AL, 1964
LONDON, ENGLAND

THE POST OFFICE TOWER
symbolized the "white hot
technological revolution" the Labour
government (1964–70), led by
Harold Wilson, promised the people
of Britain. Where Germany, Japan
and Italy were all modernizing
rapidly from the mid-1950s, Britain,
by and large, continued to enjoy an
after-lunch nap and was still very
much living in the 1930s at the
beginning of the 1960s. The Post
Office Tower, soaring more than
180 metres (600 ft) into the
London smog, beamed microwaves
across the North and South Downs
and the Chiltern Hills rising
above the London basin, taking television
and radio broadcasts and countless
telephone calls with them. The
pencil-thin concrete tower, which
rose from an eight-storey base, was
clad in steel and glass to make it
look more polite than it would have
been in naked concrete. Although it
looks as if there are offices rising
the height of the tower, this is just
an illusion. However, because the
Post Office was keen to show off
its leap into the white, hot future,
Eric Bedford and his team at the
Ministry of Works designed public
viewing galleries and a revolving
restaurant at the top of the tower.
Though hugely popular, these were
sadly closed to the public after an
IRA bomb shattered them in 1971.
They have never reopened, although
the restaurant is now a hospitality
suite for the management of British
Telecommunications.

Northern Aviary

LORD SNOWDON, CEDRIC
PRICE AND FRANK NEWBY,
1965, REGENT'S PARK ZOO,
LONDON, ENGLAND

WHAT LOOKS TO BE an outsized cat's cradle overlooking Regent's Canal turns out to be an ethereal structure alive with birds both exotic and homely. Sparrows, pigeons and other winged cockney urchins fly into this near-invisible structure to spend a day with more colourful relatives who wouldn't last very long outside the likeable confines of this giant birdcage. A rectangular base with pools is spanned by a zig-zag concrete bridge (for human visitors) and these are covered by a mesh of anodized aluminium supported by tension cables attached to four tetrahederal frames. The birds nest wherever they can and have room to spread their wings and fly. For these facts alone, Snowdon (born 1930), Price (born 1934) and Newby (born 1932) deserve a special mention in zoological as well as architectural despatches. The London Zoological Society had long championed intelligent design, from as far back as the 1830s when Decimus Burton (1800–81) built the handsome brick Camel and Giraffe Houses, and a century later with Berthold Lubetkin's Penguin Pool (p.171). Until the construction of this aviary birds were confined to iron cages in which they were unable to fly. The soft structure of this radical birdcage allows the birds to fly, ensuring that if they crash into the walls they will not hurt themselves.

Reliance Controls Factory

TEAM 4, 1965

SWINDON, WILTSHIRE,
ENGLAND

THIS COOL, CLEAN, clinical industrial machine – no more and no less than a finely detailed steel envelope containing the maximum possible amount of clear, brightly lit, neutral space – is one of the first important designs of Norman Foster (born 1935) and Richard Rogers (born 1933) together with their first

wives Wendy (1938–89) and Su (born 1940).

Foster, born and trained in Manchester, teamed up with Rogers, who had trained in London, while a postgraduate student at Yale University. They returned to London and set up in practice together, working on a number of projects that took as their starting point the building as a smooth-skinned shed or elegant machine with materials and details drawn from the very latest palettes and portfolios. Their work was quickly labelled "Hi-Tech", a tag that was to stick. Both architects went on to become major players on the

international stage in the 1980s, having made their name with buildings that were glamorous and sophisticated yet cheap, easy and quick to build.

Many light industrial buildings and the architecture of Britain's first US-style business parks had something of the look of the Reliance Controls factory about them. Swindon, once famous for the Great Western Railway locomotive works (the town grew up around the railway), was to become the heart of Britain's "Silicon Valley" as the computer industry and its Hi-Tech headquarters surfed this way.

Vehicle Assembly Building

MAX URBAHN AND ROBERTS
AND SCHAEFER, 1966
CAPE KENNEDY, FLORIDA,
USA

A TWENTIETH-CENTURY PYRAMID of sorts, standing in relation to the NASA settlement at Cape Kennedy much as the Egyptian pyramids once did to Memphis, the Vehicle Assembly Building (VAB) was, at the time of its construction, the largest building in the world. It needed to be: this is where the giant *Saturn* rockets that, in July 1969, lifted the *Apollo 11* mission on its way to the first Lunar landing, were pieced together. As tall as cathedrals, the rockets were a development of the *V2* rockets, designed by the precocious young Nazi scientist, Werner von Braun. Designed by Max Urbahn (1912–95), the architect-planner and engineers Roberts and Schaefer, the steel-framed monster made no overt concessions to style, yet had a monumental magnificence all of its own and a notably Classical layout. To give some sense of its herculean scale, the main doors are 150 metres (500 ft) high and 20 metres (70 ft) wide. The building was designed to house four *Saturn V* rockets, which were moved in and out of the VAB on mobile launch-pads. The VAB was an important monument in humankind's quest for the stars, just as the Egyptian pyramids had been some 4,000 years earlier: the big difference was that rocket fuel, computers and a wing and a prayer had replaced the power of prayer alone.

Yamanashi Press and Broadcasting Centre

KENZO TANGE, 1967

KOFU, JAPAN

ALTHOUGH IT HAS never been completed and never will be – the open-ended nature of this powerful building is also the essence of its form – Tange's hugely impressive communications centre feels somehow right. Set against a backdrop of hills and mountains, it has the quality of a medieval castle, lacking only the turned-up gable

ends and the intricate, filigree decoration of ancient and ritualistic Japanese architecture: it could easily be the home of a brotherhood of modern Samurai. The massiveness of the structure is implied by the 16 hollow concrete tubes that support the deep-plan floors (housing television studios, a newspaper printing plant and a radio broadcasting station) and carry the services needed to run this modern fortress. The conceit of the structure is that it can be extended almost indefinitely. The conceit of the architecture is that it

has no end, no beginning, no façade and is all but indeterminate. And yet, for all this, it has an imposing presence and is one of the greatest buildings in modern Japan. It also represented Kenzo Tange, then in his early fifties, at the height of his powers. As he competed for more and more international projects, so his special magic appeared to be undone: that magic had been his bringing Modernism to Japan as it reinvented itself after World War Two and developing a recognizably Modern Japanese language of design.

Television Tower

D. BURDIN, L. BATALOV,
N. NIKITIN, 1967
OSTANKINO, MOSCOW,
RUSSIA

MOSCOW'S TELEVISION TOWER
rockets 533 metres (1750 ft)
towards the Moon. It is a thrilling
and dizzying structure that,
beneath its aerial, contains
panoramic viewing platforms and a
three-storey restaurant. There are
also eleven floors of mechanical
plant and technical gubbins galore.
The superb tower rises from a multi-
storey podium made up of four
floors of television studios topped
with a multi-storey office block. Not
surprisingly, the base of the tower
is immense and the sky-piercing
structure is a blatantly heroic example
of what concrete can do. It is also
a symbol of the way in which the
former Soviet Union devoted huge
resources to scientific enterprises
both as a way of trying to raise
living standards and to show the
capitalist world that Communism
really did work. The Soviets were
the first to put a satellite into orbit
around the Earth and Yuri Gagarin
was the first man in space. For a
while it looked as if the USSR really
was overcoming what many
observers saw as inherent structural
weaknesses in its economy and its
society. In the end they proved to
be right. Even so, hopeful symbols
like the television tower at Ostankino
remain to show what the Soviet
Union wanted to be: a triumphalist,
one-party state with lashings of
highly-visible high technology.

Elgin Estate

GREATER LONDON COUNCIL
ARCHITECT'S DEPARTMENT,
1968, MAIDA HILL,
LONDON, ENGLAND

IMAGINE SEEING a television set being hurtled from the twenty-second floor of a plastic-clad tower block. Imagine watching the Fire Brigade putting out a savage blaze on the eighteenth floor of its twin and being told that this was just a routine "chip-pan blaze". Built with such confidence in new technology, the twin plastic towers of the Elgin Estate were soon to become a "sink" for the most disadvantaged of west London families. Local authority architects believed they were doing their best not only to solve London's perennial housing shortage, but also to create a new type of city home for the age of instant technology. The result was a pair of towers that looked too much like refrigerators and washing-machines for comfort. They were quick to build, taking just ten months, yet speed was certainly no guarantee of decent homes. There was no pleasure to be had from not being able to open a window beyond a minimal angle. This was the sort of sad housing block that conservationists, who once had eyes only for Georgian terraces and Victorian churches, wanted to preserve at the end of the century. They had obviously never had to live in or near the Elgin Estate. The blocks were finally pulled down in the 1990s and replaced by low-rise homes.

John Hancock Center

SKIDMORE, OWINGS AND
MERRILL, 1970

CHICAGO, ILLINOIS, USA

AS THE SKYSCRAPER became ever taller and more complex, so the engineer came to play an ever-increasing role in its design as well as its construction. Although nominally designed by a team led by Skidmore, Owings and Merrill's Bruce Graham (born 1925), the hugely impressive John Hancock

Center – a black hole appearing to suck all available light into its dark immensity – owed its dramatic exposed structure, and thus its entire character, to the brilliant engineer Fazlur Khan. Khan developed a way of cross-bracing a skyscraper with steel beams on the outside of the building: this method can be seen in the huge X-braces that criss-cross their way up this Chicago behemoth. The net result was office floors free from the interruption of structural columns. This was a revolution in building design over which property

developers must have wept with delight: from now on, the net-to-gross ratio of office space to building structure was all in favour of the renter. Fortunately, the John Hancock Center is not just a sky-high filing cabinet for office workers. Inside what appear to be countless floors – there are exactly 100 – are 670 apartments as well as shops, restaurants and garages. The roof, about 300 metres (1,000 ft) above the sidewalks, is topped by antennae that have always looked rather disturbingly like missiles. Not a building to be messed with.

Nakagin Capsule Tower

KISHO KUROKAWA, 1972

TOKYO, JAPAN

WHAT LOOKS LIKE a large scientist's model of a molecular structure turns out to be a cheap, overnight hostel for workers in the Ginza district of Tokyo. The tower is made up of 140 prefabricated "living capsules", each looking like a washing machine and slotted into a concrete climbing frame in a complex and lively manner. This is the sort of architecture that can be made in basic Lego sets and, like Lego bricks, its construction is simple but very clever. Living space is always at a premium in Tokyo, which is why the "living capsule" made sense here, but the tower was also a vivid expression of ideas that had been floating around the globe concerned with the the creation of instant cities. The idea that "living capsules" could be added when needed was appealing at a time when technology became available to realize the dream.

Kisho Kurokawa (born 1934) set up his own office in Tokyo in 1961, having worked with Kenzo Tange. He was much influenced by the science-fiction-like housing at the time and the "living capsule" idea was one that caught the imagination of the media worldwide. How could anyone live in such small spaces for even one night? Only the Japanese could do so. Of course, this wasn't true. Within 15 years of the building of the Nakagin Tower, Europeans were checking into hotels built alongside motorways along the same principles, but without the ingenious architecture.

Hopkins House

MICHAEL HOPKINS, 1975

HAMPSTEAD, LONDON,

ENGLAND

A ONE-TIME PARTNER of Norman Foster, Michael Hopkins was a keen exponent of Hi-Tech design before he changed course some time in the 1980s and began to pursue a tweedy architecture that appealed to conservation bodies, planners and government agencies without the slightest whiff of controversy. Before he developed this diplomatic style, his buildings were noted for their industrial strength and rigour and for a particularly clean and satisfying use of factory components. In this sense, his own home in a beautiful leafy street near Hampstead Heath went one step further than even the Eames had done in the 1940s (p.202). Those brought up in the house remember its noisiness and lack of privacy, and probably it made better sense as a summer pavilion than as an all-year family house. Even so, it was a brave attempt to strip the family house of its protective façade and to display it warts and all. Not that you find anything so unpleasant in an English architect's house. They are nearly always neat and trim, reflecting the very suburban values they appear to want to escape.

Hopkins went on to design a fine Hi-Tech factory for the Greene King brewery in Bury St Edmunds, Suffolk, and the inspired research laboratories for Schlumberger on a greenfield site outside Cambridge (p.360) before he had what appeared to be a change of heart and style.

Sony
Tower

KISHO KUROKAWA, 1976

OSAKA, JAPAN

A FORERUNNER OF Lloyds of
London (p.363) and the Pompidou
Centre (p.358), the Sony Tower
deserves to be better known outside
Japan. What Kurokawa built here
was a 72-metre (235-ft) tower off
which were slung steel-clad toilet
capsules and up which ran lifts
inside a largely transparent tube.

The floors in which Sony displayed
its latest electronic goodies were
entirely free of columns or other
spatial intrusions. The building is
rather like a spaceman who clips
oxygen tanks and other life support
systems to his Hi-Tech suit. Or the
tower can be seen as a kind of exo-
skeleton. Whatever, it is one of the
triumphs of the "Metabolist"
movement of which the young
Kurokawa was a leading light.

If the Metabolists had a clear-
cut programme, it had much to do
with bridging the gap between

private and public space.
Traditionally in Japan, every
building was separated from the
next, if only by the width of a
hand. The private realm was
defiantly distanced from the public.
Kurokawa's reaction to this idea (it
was not always quite so true in
practice, not, at least in the
twentieth century), was to make his
connections loud and clear:
plugged-in, slotted together in a
powerful display of the possibilities
and strange poetry offered by new
materials and technology.

Sainsbury Centre

FOSTER ASSOCIATES, 1977

UNIVERSITY OF EAST
ANGLIA, NORWICH,
NORFOLK, ENGLAND

ONE OF THE HANDSOMEST sheds in Christendom – or anywhere else in the world – the Sainsbury Centre for Visual Arts is an exquisite aircraft hangar in spirit conjured by Norman Foster's magic into one of the most glamorous of all art galleries. Commissioned by wealthy grocers, the Sainsbury Centre is a part of the University of East Anglia and fine arts students get to study in its shimmering interior. The design is simple. A white steel truss is sheathed in what were once silver and are now white panels, and all the services needed to run the building are tucked in between these two elements. At either end, the structure is glazed from floor to ceiling. And that's about it. However, this simple description of an essentially simple building tells only half the story: not only does this shed sparkle on the outside, but its interior is quite breathtaking and remains so even after several visits. Inside, this art hangar is all but one great space, superbly lit and animated with beautiful tribal sculptures and other exotic works of art. A gallery floor contains lecture rooms and offices.

An extension dating from the early 1990s, also by Foster, has been dug underground at one end of the building. Here, the patron's paintings are held in a store that is a curious cross between a Hi-Tech bank vault and a pharaoh's tomb in the Valley of the Kings. The Sainsbury Centre is also a machine for teaching in: both a gallery and an academic institution.

Pompidou Centre

RENZO PIANO AND
RICHARD ROGERS, 1977
PARIS, FRANCE

BOMBASTIC. Iconoclastic. Bowellist (it wears its insides on the outside). Think of any more or less suitable term you can to pin down this explosion of a building and you will still be struggling to make sense of it. The Centre Georges Pompidou is one of the most exciting, wilful, eccentric and popular of all twentieth-century buildings. Most remarkable of all, it was commissioned by a right-wing French president and designed by a gang of rather left-wing architects and engineers led by the ebullient and charming Renzo Piano (born 1937) and Richard Rogers.

The team did not expect to win the international competition; it entered at the very last moment in 1970 when the design was very much a loose concept. With a great deal of help from Peter Rice, up went this vast assembly of brightly coloured pipes and ducts and tubes. The result is not quite as wilful as it seems. What you are looking at is a vast art centre designed so that it has the maximum amount of uninterrupted floor area. Even the lifts and famous escalators – rising in glass tubes up the side of the building – are on the outside. The result is a busy machine on the outside, an adult climbing frame, with what might have been calm spaces for the contemplation of art inside. No such luck. The building quickly became a tourist attraction and one that rivalled the Eiffel Tower in popularity. It was always crowded, and by the late 1990s was exhausted. It was closed and refurbished in time for a new Millennium re-opening.

Ground Signal Station

GUSTAV PEICHL, 1980

AFLENZ, AUSTRIA

GUSTAV PEICHL (born 1928) has a particular genius for creating sculptural, artful buildings from scientific functions and public utilities that are normally framed in dreary, all too functional sheds. Peichl's aesthetic has been very much his own. Radio stations in Graz and Eisenstadt, Austria, a phosphate treatment plant in Berlin and this ground signal station at Aflenz, Austria, are wonderful designs rooted in a kind of late twentieth-century Baroque, and yet distinctly Modern too. No Postmodern irony here, just one man's highly individual eye at work on buildings that deserve to be celebrated rather than hidden. Peichl's decorative vocabulary – shiny pipes, portholes, gantries, gangways, ladders – is clearly drawn from ships, and his buildings sail, fully rigged, as if through designed landscapes.

The ground signal station is the most restrained of his gleaming architectural machines. It had to be. Scientists found that the best place for the satellite signal receiver was in the middle of a nature reserve. As a result, Peichl dug his buildings into the ground. The result is deeply satisfying, with offices, receiving station and laboratories grouped around two interconnecting circular courtyards. In summer, these are surrounded with lush grass and meadow flowers; in winter, they are capped with snow. The quality of finishes here lives up to the beauty of the surrounding landscape.

Schlumberger Research Laboratories

MICHAEL HOPKINS, 1981

CAMBRIDGE, ENGLAND

THIS IS HOPKINS' finest effort, a building that is exciting, yet gentle and animates a flat stretch of countryside on the Bedford Plain at Madingly, just beyond Cambridge. It has lost some of its lustre over the years, yet the basic idea was excellent. Instead of a solid and intrusive technical building, Hopkins came up with what, from a distance, looks like the tents of either a travelling circus or else a Hi-Tech Bedouin caravan. Beautifully lit at dusk, the three tents are held up by a concatenation of tall steel masts and tensile cables. The laboratories are housed in extensively glazed, steel-framed structures below.

Hopkins was one of many architects to have become intrigued by the possibilities of fabric roofs at the beginning of the 1980s and was to use them to subtle effect in, among other designs, the much admired Mound Stand at Lord's Cricket Ground, London (p.259).

Fabrics were available that were lasting, weatherproof and strong. They played a valuable role in softening the over-mechanical Hi-Tech style that British architects excelled at, but which was always in danger of becoming a cliché. Schlumberger proved to be an energetic patron committed to investment in some of the most sane architecture of the 1980s, notably its new centre in Paris and the Menil Collection in Houston, Texas (p.256), both by Renzo Piano, master of the "Soft Tech" approach explored here by Hopkins.

INMOS Research Centre

RICHARD ROGERS
PARTNERSHIP, 1982
GWENT, SOUTH WALES

HIGH UNEMPLOYMENT and cheap labour were staples of life in South Wales for most of the twentieth century. At least two attempts involving some of Britain's most radical architects were made to inject new jobs and creativity into the area. The first was the Brynmawr rubber factory (p. 189) by the Architects Co-Partnership shortly after World War Two; the second was another government-backed scheme, the INMOS factory and silicon-chip research centre designed by the Richard Rogers Partnership.

Standing like some exotic insect in the Welsh countryside, the Rogers' building is magnificent, and quickly caught the attention of advertising agencies as well as architecture critics. Its construction really did appear to herald a new era for this profoundly depressed region, famous for its lack of decent modern design. The building is simple, yet held together by a gloriously complex system of masts. The masts held cables that supported an extensive roof on either side of a central service corridor. All servicing for the building was mounted above the corridor and within the brightly coloured frames of the masts. This bravura show of structural wizardry was as satisfying to gaze at as a fully rigged sailing ship. It was almost fetishistic in its obsessive detailing and all the more enjoyable for being so.

Financial Times Printworks

NICHOLAS GRIMSHAW, 1988

DOCKLANDS, LONDON,

ENGLAND

THE FINANCIAL TIMES commissioned this sleek printing plant, but sold it on again almost before the presses were warm. This was not a criticism of Grimshaw's confident Docklands landmark, but a sign of how fickle and fast-changing the newspaper industry had become: today's building, yesterday's headline. In fact it was noteworthy that any London-based newspaper that was printing in the capital after the Fleet Street diaspora of the mid-1980s prompted new forms of electronic publishing. Yet, for a while at least, the "pink 'un", as the FT was known for the colour of its paper, was printed in the East End and in great style. Grimshaw's building was really little more than a very smart tin box fronted with one of the most adventurous windows yet made. The biggest available sheets of glass were supported by a finely-wrought web of modern steel tracery that enabled the whole of the big printing press to be seen in one sweep of the eyes. The sight of the newspaper being printed at night was, for that short while, one of the least known but finest spectacles in London. The pink paper could be watched as it coursed at great speed around the vast web, the building lit up in a way that made sure you could best enjoy the action.

Grimshaw (born 1940) worked long and hard on the details of his buildings, so much so that he even put them on show in regular travelling exhibitions. For an architect fascinated by engineering, it was important to be able to work up his own details where and whenever possible. In one sense, these details are Grimshaw's architecture.

Canary Wharf Tower

CESAR PELLI, 1991

DOCKLANDS, LONDON,

ENGLAND

CANARY WHARF TOWER was for a brief while Europe's tallest building. Clad in sun-catching stainless steel, 245 metres (800 ft) and 50 floors high, it dominates views of London at almost every turn of the head and can be seen up to 32 kilometres (20 miles) away from the principal approach roads from all points east into central London. The tower, designed by Cesar Pelli (born 1926), is the focal point of Canary Wharf, a titanic development of offices, shops, hotels and apartments in the old London docks. Every building in this unlikely slice of Chicago-shipped-to-London in the late 1980s by the Canadian developer Reichmann was built on a megalomaniacal scale and in a heavy-handed Postmodern style. The enigmatic tower is perhaps the only building here with any real presence. It has become well known as the offices for several national newspapers including the *Independent*, *Daily Telegraph* and *Daily Mirror*. In all other respects it is conventional and even old-fashioned. A giant lift lobby gives access to racks of dreary offices, enlivened here and there by some of the sparkier tenants (Live TV boasts a floor decorated by David Connor). Few of those working here get to enjoy the spectacular views which make the whole reason to be here – cheap rents aside – spurious.

Barcelona International Airport

TALLER DE ARQUITECTURA,
1992

BARCELONA, SPAIN

THE DEATH OF THE DICTATOR
General Franco not only restored
the monarchy to Spain but brought
new-found prosperity to the
country and a great deal of
autonomy and democracy to
regions such as Andalucia and
Catalonia, of which Barcelona – an
anti-Franco city always – is the
fiercely independent capital. The

1990s added more major events to
Spain's resurrection: Expo '92 at
Seville and, in the same year, the
Olympic Games in Barcelona. The
Olympics prompted far more than
major investment in Barcelona, they
prompted the city to rebuild itself
on a heroic scale. This heroism
began at the international gate to
the city, the airport.

The new terminal, by Ricardo
Bofill's Taller de Arquitectura, was a
grandiloquent work. It boasted one
of the longest internal axes ever
seen and had a hard, almost
militaristic logic that appeared
somewhat at odds with Barcelona's
new-found freedoms and rising

prosperity. Franco would have
loved it. In fact the new terminal
was surprising in other ways too.
First, it was a stylistic turn-about
for the Taller, which had for more
than a decade made its name with
its own brand of prefabricated
Neo-Classical design: now, the
Taller had gone International
Modern, with undertones of the
monumental Fascist architecture of
the 1930s. Second, unlike Rafael
Moneo's airport at Seville, which
echoed regional architectural
identities, Barcelona airport was
defiantly "neutral". Reflecting the
city's role as a major port, its
architecture was of the world.

Waterloo International Terminal

NICHOLAS GRIMSHAW, 1993

LONDON, ENGLAND

A NEW GATEWAY to continental Europe from London, Waterloo International has been highly acclaimed. Not only is it determinedly modern, but it also harks back, without any stifling feeling of nostalgia, to the great train sheds of Victorian Britain, notably that of York station with which it shares a gently curving roof. The great glazed roof, held up by a lattice work of blue steel, curves around the exceptionally long platforms and reduces both in height and width as it stretches away from the concourse. The result is a station that appears to squeeze the Eurostar trains from its southern end like toothpaste from a tube. Interestingly, Grimshaw's original proposal envisaged the terminal – it was called "terminal" rather than "station" because, at the time, Britain's railways, on the verge of being flogged to private enterprise, were keen to pretend they were airlines – as a very regular rectangle. It was the railway engineers and local planners who insisted it follow the established curve of the tracks as they snaked out of Waterloo. Grimshaw rose magnificently to the challenge. The one sadness here is that the beautiful roof is largely wasted on the passengers, who are required to hang around in the lounges beneath the train shed and so only catch glimpses of the roof as they hurry to find their seats. The bulk of the terminal is hidden below, but well lit and thoughtfully planned.

Satolas TGV Station

SANTIAGO CALATRAVA, 1993

LYONS, FRANCE

CALATRAVA (born 1951) is an engineer, architect and designer who brought a new excitement to bridges and railway stations in the 1990s. His forms are organic, challenging and often very beautiful. This station, built to link Lyons airport with the expanding French high-speed rail network, is one of his most bombastic designs

and is as unforgettable as it is satisfying for passengers to use. The site, some way from Lyons itself, was anonymous and empty, an emptiness that appeared at the time of the station's construction to stretch away for as far as the eye could see from the airport. This encouraged the Spanish engineer to create a monument that would be unmissable by travellers, by rail, road or air: the station is very much on view from the windows of planes landing at Satolas airport. The great, bird-like arch – a wing in flight, a beak, a talon –

reminiscent of the work of Eero Saarinen (p.104), forms the concourse that gives on either side and under impressive concrete portals to the long platforms below. The sense of occasion engendered here as the shark-nosed TGVs slide menacingly into and out of the station is something rail travel had been lacking for very many years. This station may seem a little over-the-top, yet its role is to make rail travel exciting and desirable and to make its presence felt in the subtopian landscape of the airport.

Communications Tower

NORMAN FOSTER, 1994

BARCELONA, SPAIN

A TRULY THRILLING structure that brought architects and engineers together at their best. Foster's design was engineered by Ove Arup and Partners, who from the 1930s had been the handmaidens of modern British architecture and, thankfully, are still an enormous and greatly inventive international outfit.

If a city is to be dominated by a communications mast – and communications technology was an obsession of the 1990s – then that mast ought to be worth looking at. This one is. As tall as the Eiffel Tower, the Barcelona tower was erected on very different principles. Instead of the main body of the structure carrying its own weight, this is taken up by long cables that hold the slim, central mast of the tower in place. It looks like a daring balancing act, and it is. High up, the mast boasts a 14-storey structure containing all manner of technical and electronic gubbins as well as offices. This was constructed off site and on the ground, assembled as one piece and hoisted in eight hours from the ground up to its lofty nest where it was bolted into place. It was an extraordinary feat and made the construction of the mast that much easier and safer than it would have been if it had been built in the sky. Foster's design was highly successful in turning a need into a thing of beauty and excitement.

Kansai International Airport

RENZO PIANO–BUILDING
WORKSHOP, 1995

OSAKA BAY, JAPAN

YOU CAN BELIEVE MEN can fly
when you witness a Jumbo Jet take
to the sky, but are you ready to
give credence to the idea of an
international airport floating on
water? This is more or less what
Kansai Airport does. This giant
terminal stands like an elegant,
gigantic insect on a purpose-built,
man-made island in the Bay of
Osaka. Japanese authorities were
neither willing to expend valuable
coastal land on the construction of
a new international airport, nor
willing to accept the noise that
would follow in its wake. The result
is a mind-boggling feat of civil
engineering upon which Renzo
Piano (born 1937), has designed
one of the world's finest air
terminals. Aside from its fluid, soft,
organic form, the terminal is a
crystal-clear device that allows
passengers to move very easily from
bus, train or taxi from the mainland
to their aircraft; the process is
seamless and the aircraft are always
in view. Despite its vast size, the
building allows people to feel
rooted and comfortable inside as
the scale of interior spaces is varied
and designed to create intimacy
from enormity.

Renzo Piano trained as an
engineer before becoming an
architect, which at least helps to
explain the aesthetic of his rational,
yet romantic, designs in which
engineering forms are never
allowed to run wild and for
appearance's sake alone as they do
in the work of so many so-called
High-Tech architects.

American Air Force Museum

NORMAN FOSTER, 1997

DUXFORD, CAMBRIDGESHIRE,
ENGLAND

NORMAN FOSTER was the perfect choice for this shrine to US warplanes. A keen pilot, his buildings have long drawn from the imagery and technology of aircraft. Here though he allowed the warbirds on display full rein. They are the stars and theirs is the design and detailing people who come to this outpost of the Imperial War Museum want to see.

The building takes a back seat, framing the aircraft in a subtle wash of daylight and allowing people to walk around them from both the ground and on high, using a ramp that curves up and around the exhibits. The impressive concrete roof wraps around this ramp – the entrance to the museum is at its apex – and then curves like a shell high above the aircraft, some of which hang from its vaults, to end in a vast window that allows visitors to look out to Duxford's runway, often the scene of historic warplanes taking off and landing. The roof digs down into a grass mound away from the runway. The intention here was to make Foster's concrete hangar as unobtrusive as possible – it is overlooked by houses presumably lived in by people who dislike historic aircraft, which seems a little odd – and to insulate the structure. The building is really little more than a glorified hangar, but this is its strength, and if it is just a hangar, then it is the handsomest of them all. Foster's genius was to transform plain designs into the stuff of memorable poetry.

Commerzbank

NORMAN FOSTER, 1997

FRANKFURT, GERMANY

THE TALLEST BUILDING in Europe at the century's end, the Commerzbank is far more subtle than the runner-up, Canary Wharf Tower (p.365) in London. The problem with very tall office buildings is that they have tended to be little more than elongated filing cabinets. Workers shoot up in swish lifts only to be presented with another identical floor. Those who have to make do with desks or "workstations" as they became known from the 1970s – are not even allowed to enjoy the views. Foster attempted to solve this in Frankfurt by designing the Commerzbank as a spiral of offices climbing up a central shaft. This arrangement allowed for four-storey atria, facing in different directions, to rise with the height of the building. The result is a skyscraper with a powerful and humane logic driving both the way it looks and the way it works. This is in sharp contrast to the towers shooting into the sky at the same time in southeast Asia which have little or no internal character.

Foster attempted a further development of the idea of the skyscraper as hanging garden in the design of a "Millennium Tower" for the City of London (1996). It was to have risen from the site of the old Baltic Exchange, which was destroyed by a massive bomb planted by the IRA in 1993. It would have been welcome, as a symbol of confidence, but planning permission was refused.

Chek Lap Kok Airport

NORMAN FOSTER, 1998

HONG KONG, CHINA

A BREATHTAKING ACHIEVEMENT, Chek Lap Kok Airport is the world's largest of its breed and the largest construction project of its era. And it is destined to grow even bigger. Just six years before, the site had been a range of hills rising out of the sea off the South China coast. These 100-metre (300-ft) peaks were flattened in the process of the creation of an artificial island

measuring 6 kms (4 miles) by 3.5 kms (2 miles). Everything needed to build the airport was delivered by boat and at the peak of construction the workforce totalled 21,000. It was planned to be the world's busiest airport, acting as an immense junction box for travellers passing through or flying to southeast Asia. The terminal building, shaped like a giant aircraft, is stupendously big – 1.27 km (½ mile) long – yet its lightweight structure and clarity – a development of Foster's earlier air terminal at Stansted in Essex – makes it remarkably relaxed and easy to use. Passengers are never

confused as to where to go to catch their plane nor are they diverted as they were in so many contemporary airports, and notably in Britain, through labyrinths of duty-free and other shops. Nevertheless the Hong Kong Sky Mall is the largest shopping area of any airport. Over all this Foster placed a lightweight steel roof in the form of a sequence of shallow vaults supported by the building's exposed concrete structure. Along with Kansai (p.370), Chek Lap Kok raised the standard of airport design at the end of the century immeasurably.

Press Pavilion

FUTURE SYSTEMS, 1998
LORD'S CRICKET GROUND,
LONDON, ENGLAND

THE WORLD'S FIRST monocoque building, the Press Pavilion at Lord's Cricket Ground was assembled off-site in a boat-builder's yard, transported in sections, lifted up onto concrete supports and bolted into place. It was designed in this way to minimize disruption to the game and completed during two winter recesses. In the first year the support columns, incorporating lifts, stairs and services, were erected while the main body of the building was being assembled elsewhere. In the second year, the pavilion was placed on its pedestal.

The pavilion is an egg-like structure sheathed in aluminium panels and designed to be as light as possible to offer the press uninterrupted views of the famous pitch. It includes a restaurant and bar and is remarkable for its compact nature, its lightness of being, its sophistication and quiet nature. Future Systems, Jan Kaplicky (born 1938) and Amanda Levette (born 1955), is a practice dedicated to forward-looking architecture and came into its own in the 1990s. The time was right because an audience had developed that, tired of Postmodern tricks and keen on the New, were looking out for modern design that was fresh, intelligent and easy to warm to. Perhaps to their own surprise, Future Systems fitted the bill.

Stade de France

MICHEL MACARY, AYMERIC
ZUBLENA, MICHEL
REGEMBAL, CLAUDE
CONSTANTINI, 1998

PARIS, FRANCE

EIGHTEEN TEAMS of architects and builders battled it out in the course of 1994 to win the important commission to design what was intended to be the most impressive sports stadium in the world. Its real debut was the 1998 World Cup football competition. The winning architectural team, who beat Jean Nouvel to the post, set to work in 1995. The 80,000-seat stadium was designed not simply as a sports venue, but as the focal point of a major urban regeneration scheme in an old industrial quarter of St Denis. As such it was always meant to be beautiful, which it certainly is.

The distinguishing feature of this distant ancestor of the Colosseum is its elliptical roof, a kind of halo, surrounding the stadium 43 metres (140 ft) above ground level. This lights up at night and can be seen glowing softly at the heart of St Denis from many viewpoints and over a considerable distance.

By the late 1990s, sports buildings had again become the great works of civic art and engineering they had been both in ancient Rome and at the zenith of the Modern Movement

The twentieth-century city grew and grew and grew. This brought with it enormous problems of health, transport and crime, of housing, energy and pollution. These concerns were there at the start of the century and just got bigger all the while. Architects and planners addressed these issues with a bewildering variety of schemes, many left on the drawing board (thank God) and many others built. Few of these brand new cities in the heart of the countryside. The Garden City (p.380) was an English invention, but it was soon exported around the world. At heart it was suburban in outlook, envisaging the laying out of small urban settlements that lacked the vibrancy and creative energy of, say, London and Paris, Berlin and Vienna, Chicago and New York.

The garden city idea maintained its grip throughout

Cities

SHAPING THE HUMAN ZOO

were anything like successful. The problem of the city is one that refuses to go away: when it thrives it expands and threatens to veer out of control. A healthy city from the point of view of finance and jobs is often chaotic. The most dynamic of all, such as Hong Kong, Shenzen and Tokyo, late in the century, saw buildings pulled down even before they were completed as land values rose and more profitable projects were hatched. And yet it is this economically healthy chaos that has disturbed the tidy minds of architects and planners who have in their mind's eye ordered streets lined with handsome, unchanging buildings.

The best answer progressive architects and designers could come up with in the early years of the century was to make a break from old cities and lay out

the century, manifesting itself as far afield as Canberra and New Delhi. Rival ideas included those driven by Le Corbusier who believed that the country could be brought into the heart of the city if traditional streets were razed and high rise apartment and office blocks could take their place standing on stilts above verdant parkland. Few city authorities, however, felt able to put such iconoclastic plans into action. They did happen, though, but not for the best after European and Japanese cities were blitzed during the course of World War Two. Here, at last, was the chance Modern Movement architects and planners had to put their ideas into practice. Away with old-fashioned streets and squares, rows of eighteenth-century houses and roadways too narrow for the car. The car was the

future. It was given priority at all costs. Pedestrians would have to avoid it by walking along concrete gangways in the sky. Their homes would be in the clouds too, but built down to low budgets and imbued with none of the grace let alone the gardens and generously lit rooms proposed by Le Corbusier. The pattern was repeated worldwide. It was very sad. Hitler had given architects the chance to damage their cities more effectively than the combined efforts of his Luftwaffe, rockets and tanks. If this sounds unfair, then ask those who had to live in them.

This destruction of the traditional city led soon enough to an increasingly intense global study of how to weave its fabric back together again, of how to find ways of coping with the car, of redeveloping at a pace and on a scale that people could keep up with and make sense of. It was a slow and exhausting process and there was no sign that it would let up as long as people chose to live in cities and as long as cities continued to be the engine of social wealth and the heart of art and culture.

At the end of the century the fastest growing cities were in Southeast Asia – especially in China; yet while the Chinese spawn cities with precious little regard to environmental concerns, Europeans and Americans struggle to contain the excesses of urban growth. The imbalance between these two approaches can only become further out of kilter in the twenty-first century.

Letchworth Garden City

RAYMOND UNWIN, ET AL,

1903

HERTFORDSHIRE, ENGLAND

LETCHWORTH was the first Garden City and the source of much fun for critics and cartoonists at the time. "Visitors are requested not to tease the citizens," was one notice that appeared in a cartoon doing just that. Why? Because the citizens of Letchworth must have seemed an odd bunch at the time. The first Garden City, an idealistic fusion of town and country set apart from the modern, industrial world in rural Hertfordshire, was initially a haven for all sorts of arty-crafty cranks and eccentrics. In the new roughcast Voysey-style cottages with their limewashed walls, oak furniture and tapestries lived an unprecedented generation of hatless, gloveless Theosophists, socialists and vegetarians. The men wore smocks and sandals and espoused such quixotic causes as Esperanto. Day trippers from London came to laugh at them. Letchworth was truly a human zoo. Planned by Raymond

Unwin (p.22), it was a direct result of a close reading of two powerful books by the polemicist and planner Ebeneezer Howard (1850–1928) *Tomorrow: A Peaceful Path to Real Reform* (1898) and *Garden Cities of Tomorrow* (1902). Letchworth was constituted in 1903, its team of eminent architecture consultants including Richard Norman Shaw (1831–1912), W. R. Lethaby (1857–1931) and Halsey Ricardo (1854–1928). Unwin's plan for the heart of the new city was based on Wren's 1666 plan for the City of London, but, like the original, never got off the ground. Cosy with its Arts and Crafts cottages and Neo-Georgian civic buildings, Letchworth was nicely built, thoughtful and, after the novelty wore off, rather dull. However, at the end of the century British planners were responding anew to Letchworth as they sought ways of building millions of new homes.

Plan
Voisin

LE CORBUSIER, 1922

PARIS, FRANCE

THIS IS THE PLAN that, in so many ways, helped to give the Modern Movement a bad name. One look at this early plan by Le Corbusier to knock down a vast chunk of Paris north of the Seine and to replace it with high-rise concrete apartment blocks towering into the sky was enough to confirm the worst suspicions of those who thought Modern architects little more than crazed megalomaniacs with a mission to destroy historic cities. Le Corbusier loved Paris. It seems very unlikely that even if he had been given the power to do so he would have put the Voisin Plan into action. It was more an idea of how Modern citizens might live in the future. The idea is crystal clear, dogmatic and a reproach to the Garden City and Garden Suburb movement that had taken root in England and which was spreading its mimsy gospel across Europe. Corbusier believed that the country could be brought into the heart of cities in the form of urban parkland and that densely occupied, but light and airy, apartment blocks would rise above them. This way it was possible for citizens to live densely while enjoying fresh air, sunlight and good health that the city of the Industrial Revolution had denied them. The city would be zoned, so that only the professional classes would live in this Modern splendour. What about the workers? They would live further out, connected by road and rail links. The Plan Voisin was clearly not meant to be the harbinger of the high-rise working class estates of thirty and forty years on.

Berlin

ALBERT SPEER, 1937

GERMANY

ALBERT SPEER'S North–South axis plan for the new Berlin, or Germania, that was to be built after Germany's victory at the end of World War Two, was truly the stuff of nightmares. Thankfully, and for many other more important reasons, Hitler's Nazi war machine was stuffed by the Allies and Speer was imprisoned for 25 years. When he was released from Spandau Prison on the edge of Berlin in

1966, he was driven to the airport along part of what would have been this, the mightiest street ever conceived. In a flash of inspiration, Speer saw "what I had been blind to for years ... our plan [his and Hitler's] completely lacked a sense of proportion."

He wasn't kidding. The scale was hard to believe. The grand processional avenue began at the Grossehalle (p.53), passed under a victory arch twice the size of the Arc de Triomphe – its architect was Hitler himself – and then passed ranks of engorged Neoclassical monuments. These would have included palaces for Goring and

Hitler, an SS high command complex that looked like the Shell Centre built on London's South Bank in the 1950s seen through a magnifying glass, a monument to Mussolini as big as Bernini's arcade in front of St Peter's Rome and a university capped with a skyscraping tower. In between there were to have been muscular hotels, enormous cinemas and many boring ministry buildings. Speer had made a study of Daniel Burnham's 1909 plan for Chicago as well as Lutyens's plan for New Delhi, but the effect in Berlin was very much his own. Very little of Germania was built and very little of it survives today.

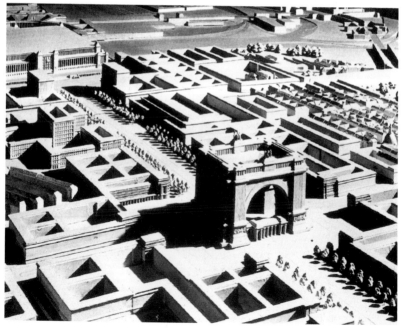

Milton Keynes

MILTON KEYNES
DEVELOPMENT
CORPORATION, 1962
BUCKINGHAMSHIRE,
ENGLAND

MILTON KEYNES was a new kind of Garden City, modelled in part on the free form of Los Angeles and in part on an older English tradition. It was the first city to be heavily marketed. An advertising campaign extolling the virtues of a new city where there were far more trees than people ran for many years.

The city slowly came to life and by the end of the century it had the feeling of a well-ordered suburb on a very large scale. However, it also had the feeling of having no real centre except for the railway station whose trains ferried its citizens backwards and forwards to London to work some 70 km (45 miles) to the south. Otherwise there is an elongated shopping mall and a square of routine Modern offices and shops leading off from this along fairly featureless avenues. Houses, designed mostly in a modern "vernacular" style – lots of bricks, stained timber and pitched roofs – are loosely arranged in clumps a good way from the shops and station. A car is very much a

necessity for many people living here and the city was designed around it. To an outsider the sheer number of roundabouts guiding traffic from one anonymous area to another can be baffling. It is easy to get lost as there is no sense of place or of a centre to head to as visitors do in historic or more conventionally planned cities. The saving grace is the design of nearly all roads as tree-lined avenues.

By the last decade of the twentieth century these had matured and are very beautiful for most of the year. They also add to the deeply ingrained suburban character of this city as a marketing dream.

IIT Campus Project

REM KOOLHAAS–OMA 2000
ILLINOIS, USA

IT IS ALWAYS A BRAVE if chancey, move to re-address the work of an architect considered to be one of the all time "greats"; yet this is what Rem Koolhaas, the Dutch architect did when he announced a new masterplan for the campus of the Illinois Institute of Technology in 1998. The character of the campus had been established by Mies van der Rohe (p.197), during his tenure there as a teacher. To Mies the institute owes the ethereal yet commanding Crown Hall.

Koolhaas's scheme is very different from that of Mies. Where Mies went for a purist, Modern Movement reinterpretation of the idea of an ideal Greek city, Koolhaas's plan represents a very different line of thought: here is a university campus at the end of the twentieth century, designed with the complexity of a new world of apparently endless choice in mind.

For Koolhaas and the Office of Metropolitan Architecture (OMA), the modern city is a thing of vibrancy, narrative and endless connections and possibilities, a place of uncertainty, choice and casual encounter. So here there are to be no absolutes, neither in terms of paths through the campus nor in the design of new buildings. The idea that a building or the plan of a campus or even a city, should be a little like the internet – choose where you want to go, what you want to find from an almost infinite network of paths and sources – was still radical at the end of the century. Can the city and architecture survive without certainty? That is the question Koolhaas, among other architects, has posed; it is not an easy one to answer much less face up to.

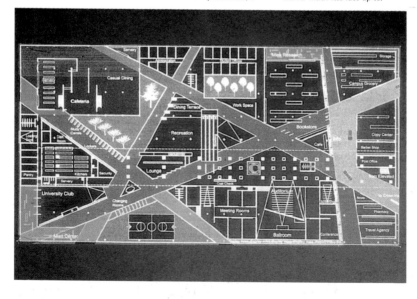

Millennium Village

RALPH ERSKINE, ET AL,

2000

GREENWICH, LONDON

RALPH ERSKINE was eighty-four when he unveiled this competition-winning plan for the Millennium Village at Greenwich in 1998. The proposal is for a "green" or "ecologically sustainable" urban development – mostly housing – to be built on reclaimed industrial land on the Greenwich peninsula. This faces the icy cold winds that scythe across East Anglia from Siberia and the Arctic and stands in the great shadow of the Millennium Dome designed by the Richard Rogers Partnership.

Erskine's proposal is for a mix of modest 12-storey towers that will, with trees, form a windbreak with low-rise flats and houses sheltering behind along curved avenues. The houses would be designed so that they can be expanded or contracted as families grow or shrink. This would be done by building them with demountable internal walls. The homes would be insulated to the nth degree, linked to a central computer (for information, communication etc) and generally reflect contemporary concerns to do with the use of energy and so on. The upshot is a new way of looking at the English garden suburb. In this sense the scheme, although thoughtful and well-mannered is a bit of a disappointment. It appeases a deeply ingrained suburban mentality, but does little to develop ideas about what a modern urban development might be at the beginning of the twenty-first century. It is Hampstead Garden Suburb without the drama of Lutyens.

This section is really the start of another book which is why it has been short-changed. It is a huge subject and one that exercised the minds of architects around the globe and down through the century. What will the future be like and how could they have helped to shape it? Of course there are those who have wanted to hinder it, to slow change down or even to reverse it. This was true of certain Arts and Crafts, Classical and

computers and ultimately a combination of the two.

Speed, energy, progress. These words were at the heart of the twentieth-century journey into the future. Just look at how excited the Italian Futurists were by them at the time of World War One. It is not difficult to understand why they longed for change. The world they inhabited was stifling, corrupt and probably as sick as they imagined it to be. World War

them at various times in the course of the century. The images are taken from films as well as architects' own projects because the twentieth century was the century of the mass-produced and globally circulated image. From now on all people with access to cinemas and then television and, in the 1990s, the Internet, received and consumed the same images. This did not necessarily mean that one day in the future all architecture would be the same, because people in different parts of the world have different ways of looking at it. It did raise, however, the possibility that one day architecture might die and be replaced by simple containers on which people could, with the aid of new technology, project whatever image they wanted. There would be no more style wars: all styles could have a place. Equally, this deluge of images and gamut of technology might well encourage a reaction against all too visible high technology. Certainly, there were signs by 1999 that more people wanted their homes to be beautiful, simple and – yes – Modern escapes from the busyness of the world. They might not want to run away from it altogether, as thinking people with a bit of money had at the beginning of the century, but they would learn how to separate Architecture – Le Corbusier's masterly, magnificent play of light on surfaces – from Building.

Futures

BRAVE NEW WORLDS

Organic architects. Whatever they believed or wanted, however, the world spun, taking a dazed and confused society and an increasingly eclectic architecture with it.

In the early days of the century and up until World War Two, many Europeans and Americans, and increasingly people from all over the world, were enthralled by the notion of progress. The world could become a better place if only airplanes could fly higher and break the sound barrier, if cars and trains could race along at ever greater speed along guided expressways and tracks, if buildings could be taller, sleeker and kitted out with more and more gadgetry. And then we would fly into space, served increasingly by intelligent machines, robots at first, then

One tore it apart. Now progress was possible, and although the global economy was wobbly, and even disastrous, all the way between 1918 and 1939, progress seemed to be a reality. The fast planes and trains and cars really did arrive as did Modern architecture. World War Two, however, rocked the notion of human progress. If the Germans could really do what they did to the Jews and if all the other atrocities were taken into account together with the physical destruction of cities, then who could ever believe again that the twentieth century was the century of progress and that a golden age lay not so very far off in some technological future?

This section shows a few of the dreams that inspired architects or were drawn by

Airport/Railway Station Fantasy

ANTONIO SANT'ELIA, 1913

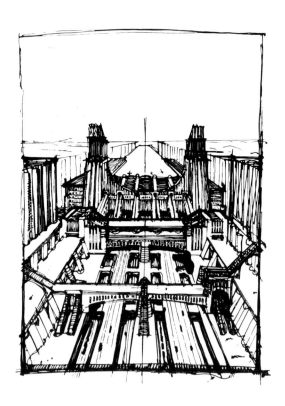

ANTONIO SANT'ELIA (1888–1916) burst onto the architectural stage in 1914 with a display of heroic, imaginative schemes for a radical city of the future. The venue was the first *Nuove Tendenze* exhibition in Milan. Two years later, Sant'Elia, who had volunteered to fight in the Italian army, lay dead somewhere near Monfalcone. His influence, however, simply grew and grew, affecting generations of forward-looking architects from Matté-Trucco, architect of the Fiat Factory (p.329) one of the few Futurist monuments built, to Richard Rogers in the 1970s and 1980s with buildings such as the Lloyd's Building in London (p.363). Sant'Elia studied in the school of architecture at Como, the Accademia di Brera, Milan and the Scuola di Belle Arti in Bologna, graduating in 1912. He teamed up with the iconoclastic Futurist movement of poets, writers and artists founded by the charismatic Filippo Tommaso Marinetti, who championed the cause of unbridled speed and technology. He worked feverishly on the creation of an imaginary "Città Nuova" (future city), which included designs such as this one for a combined airport and railway station. Every line in the drawing suggests energy and speed driven by an overpowering and imperative technologia. The ideas were taken up by Fritz Lang and used in *Metropolis* (p.392). Sant'Elia's memorial to the war dead was the one structure he designed that was built – posthumously.

The Cabinet of Dr Caligari

ROBERT WIENE, 1919

TO SPEND TOO MUCH EFFORT trying to make head or tail of this surreal film would be a mistake. Best to sit back and enjoy the way it looks. It is famous for the topsy-turvy world it created, full of crazy angles and strange lighting. The sets seemed to borrow something from the radical design movements afoot in the newly born Soviet Union and from the German Expressionists. They also presage, and had some influence on, both the short-lived Punk approach to architecture witnessed in Britain around 1980 and the work of the Deconstructivists of a decade later.

The film is a bizarre mixture of horror and early science fiction about a mad doctor who gets what look like the walking dead to do his strange business.

Plug-in City

PETER COOK, 1966

PETER COOK'S Plug-in City was one of the best things to come out of Archigram. It was a dream of a future megopolis in which hedonism blended happily with ultramodern technology. At first glance, Cook's urban utopia looks very much like the Pompidou Centre (p.358) by Renzo Piano and Richard Rogers (1977) or Norman Foster's unbuilt design for a new civic centre and transport interchange at Hammersmith in west London (1979). This shouldn't be surprising as Rogers and Foster were both influenced by Archigram and Rogers, in particular, was excited by the notion of a liberating technology that would help people to enjoy themselves in city centres rather than threaten them in a "Big Brotherish" or *Metropolis* manner.

Plug-in City was topped with cranes to show that it was in a state of constant flux: if someone wanted to move their living capsule or pleasure pod, or whatever, they could. Cook's architectural ideas were premised on the idea of people having a good time but within the context of a new and highly responsive architecture. Plug-in City was influential, but it will have to remain on paper until cities are built in space and a clip-on, plug-in way of building communities will make sense. After Archigram, Cook designed many fantasy projects, yet few, if any, had the vital impact of Plug-in City.

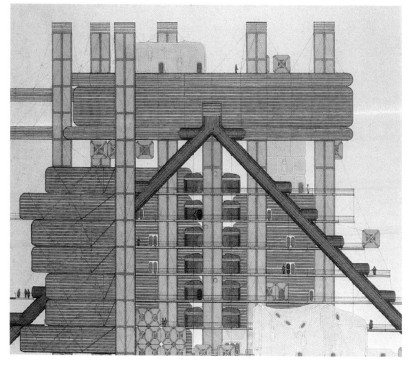

Cardiff
Opera House

ZAHA HADID, 1995

CARDIFF, WALES

UNBUILT FOR ALL the wrong reasons, the Cardiff Bay Opera House was one of the finest unrealized projects of the 1990s. Its fate was a small tragedy for Wales, a country that has never been famous for the quality of its architecture and which seemed determined to behave in a small-minded way over this superb design. The idea was that a new opera house would become the cultural hub of the reclamation and urbanization of Cardiff Bay that forms the seaside hem of this city in South Wales. An international competition was held, drawing many of the world's finest architects. It was won by Zaha Hadid (born 1951), an outspoken and fiercely distinguished Iraqi-born architect who had the disadvantage of being a woman, an Iraqi (the West had been at war only two years before the competition with the Iraqi dictator Saddam Hussein) and at the very edge of the avant-garde. Shafted by narrow-minded local business interests and crusty chaps at the Millennium Commission (a national body set up to spend Lottery money), Hadid's masterpiece vanished yet remained unforgotten.

Hadid's style, often best represented in her striking paintings, is a fusion of the obsessions of Russian Constructivists, modern Deconstrucitvists and her own powerful aesthetic of dynamic, acutely angled forms. In 1998 she won a competition to design a new museum of contemporary art in Cincinnati, Ohio and was, at long last, able to prove that her architecture had what it took to re-energize the image of a city.

Index

Acknowledgements

The publishers would like to
thank the following sources for
their kind permission to
reproduce the pictures in this
book:

Akademie Der Kunste 163
AKG London 5tr, 34, 50, 53, 54,
85, 87, 382, 391/Hilbich 108
Allsport/D Rogers 375
Alvar Aalto Museum/M. Holma
169/M. Kapanen 191
Tadao Ando Architects &
Associates 117, 249, 261, 265
Arcaid/Alex Bartel 52, 71, 79,
111/Richard Bryant 4br, 5bl, 6,
8, 9, 18, 27, 28, 74, 76, 80,
102, 106, 174, 226, 239, 240,
251, 253, 254, 255, 256, 259,
260, 262, 264, 268, 270, 272,
274, 275, 291, 299, 301, 305,
309, 312, 315, 317, 319, 322,
323, 344, 357, 363, 364, 365,
366, 369, 371/Stephen Buzas
110/David Churchill 65, 122,
172/Niall Clutton 308/Peter
Cook 263/Stephane Couturier,
Archipress 314/Nick Dawe 162,
173/Colin Dixon 257/Malcolm
Dixon 101t/Barry Edwards 228,
247/ Richard Einzig 227,
245/Mark Fiennes 25bl, 44, 90,
178, 283, 292/ Scott Francis
152, 335/Scott Francis/ Esto
176/Derek Gale 25r, 142, 218,
271, 358, 360/Chris Gascoigne
171/ Dennis Gilbert 125, 217,
318/Michael Halberstadt
166/Martine Hamilton Knight
167, 316/Martin Jones 215/
Ian Lambot 372/Lucinda
Lambton 11, 15/John Edward
Linden 4tr, 4bl, 33, 43, 73,
267, 320, 367, 370/Joe Low
68/Bill Maris 185/Peter Mauss/
Esto 297/James Neal 83/Robert
O'Dea 72r/Paul Raftery 2, 3,
75, 101b, 126, 321, 368/Ezra
Stoller/Esto 104, 183, 194,
203, 231, 244, 252, 353/
Natalie Tepper 157, 188, 222,
307/ Richard Waite 59, 170,
303, 310
Architectural Association 205,
333/ Archigram 5br, 393,
394/Valerie Bennett 36,
132/Stephan Buerger 200/Alan
Chandler 137, 141/G. Clarke
190/Etienne Clement 195/
Peter Cook 24, 298/Sandra
Denicke 155/Taylor Galyean
287/Gardner/ Halls 95,
160/John T Hansell 193/ Seki
Hirano 112/Peter Jeffree 177/
Philip Keirle 77/Rik Nijs

93/Andrew Mincyin
295/S.Mintz 96/Michael
Pattrick 192/Tim Street-Porter
105/ David Smith 247/D.
Tinero 206/ Bob Vickery
234/Dennis Wheatley 346,
246/Tony Weller 361/Nathan
Wilcock 138/Peter Willis 232/F.
R. Yerbury 148, 154
Architectural Review 143
Archivio Storico Breda 98
ASAP/Daniel Reiner 214
Bastin & Evrard 13, 84
Behnisch & Partner 258
Bennetts Associates Architects/
Peter Cook 269
Bildarchiv Preussicher Kulterbesitz
78, 82, 113, 133, 156
Maria Ida Biggi 294
de Bijenkorf bv163
Helene Binet 266
Peter Blundell Jones 86, 147
Ricardo Bofill/Taller de
Arquitectura 62, 63
Branson Coates 311, 324
British Cement Association 336
William P. Bruder Architect 118
Buckminster Fuller 332, 343
Carson Pirie & Scott 127
Caruso St John Architects 276
Castelvecchio Museum/Maurizio
Brenzoni 213
Catedra Gaudi Barcelona 81
Central Milton Keynes Shopping
Management Company Ltd 383
Martin-Charles 41, 45, 56,
135, 161
Chicago Historical Society 197/
Hedrich-Blessing 187, 223
City of Newcastle upon Tyne
Council 243
Prunella Clough/Irongate Studios
153
Coop Himmelblau/Gerald
Zugmann 5tl, 313
Corbis/Paul Almasy 220, 230/Peter
Aprahamian 165/Dave Bartruff
107/ Bettmann 38, 328/James
P. Blair 57/ Stephanie Colasanti
285/John Dakers; Eye
Ubiquitous 354/MacDuff
Everton 29, 385/Eye
Ubiquitous 207/ David
Forman;Eye Ubiquitous 103/
Lynn Goldsmith179/Robert
Holmes 224/Angelo Hornak
211/Jeremy Horner 35/Hulton-
Deutsch Collection 51/Harold
A. Jahn; Viennaslide
Photoagency 40/Andrea
Jemolo 150/ Karly-Mooney
Photography 286/ Charles &
Josette Lenars 288/ Philippa
Lewis; Edifice 236/Dennis
Marsico 238/Kevin R. Morris

55/ Michael Nicholson
151/Michael St Maur Sheil
379/Paul Thompson;Eye
Ubiquitous 114/UPI 36/Patrick
Ward 296/Nik Wheeler
290/Michael S. Yamashita
58, 284
Maria Elisa Costa 181
Country Life Picture Library 16,
19, 47
Cuban Embassy 106
James Davies Travel Photography
115
Daniele De Lonti 304
The Earth Centre 279
English Partnerships 387
Eye Ubiquitous/Frank Leather 61/
P Thompson 281
Fiat UK Ltd 329
First Garden City Heritage
Museum, Letchworth 380t
Fondation Maeght/Claude
Gaspari 216
From the Collections of Henry
Ford Museum & Greenfield
Village 331
Foster & Partners 278, 348, 373
Future Systems 374
Roberto Gabriele 49
Gio Ponti Photo Archives 204
J. Glancey 37, 40, 42, 66,
339, 380b
Glasgow School of Art Collection,
endpapers
Ronald Grant Archive 327
Michael Graves Architects
300, 302
Nicholas Grimshaw & Partners
376
W.G. Habel 88
Zaha Hadid 395
Robert Harding Picture Library 22,
26, 60, 221, 347, 334
Hartill Art Associates 139,
146, 248
Hedrich Blessing 186
Adriano Heitmann Fotografo 235
Eduard Hueber 242
Hulton Getty 341, 342
Timothy Hursley 120
The Image Bank 1, 94, 116,
225, 282
Yasuhiro Ishimoto/Kenzo Tange
Associates 199
Kida Katsuhisa 121
Leon Krier 384
Lucien Kroll 241
Sir Denys Lasdun 210
Geleta Laszlo 119
Makona 119
London Metropolitan Archives
352
Millennium Jason Shenai
109/Richard Glover 277, 355
Osamu Murai/Kenzo Tange

Associates 345, 350
Museo Nationale de Arte Romano,
Merida 64
National Film Archive 392
Michael Nicholson, 4tl, 21
Novosti (London) 351
Office For Metropolitan
Architecture 386
Frank Den Oudsten 134
PA News/Andrew Stuart 377
Panos Pictures/Daniel O'Leary 201
Gustav Peichl 359
Carlo Pozzoni 175
Jean Christophe Pratt 198
Andrew Putler 325
RCHME/Peter Behrens 168
RIBA 12, 14, 17, 31, 46, 48, 89,
97, 128, 129, 130, 131, 145,
149, 159, 189, 219, 293, 330,
337, 338, 356, 381, 390
Roger-Viollet 140
Yutaka Saito 100
Science Photo Library/NASA 389
Scotland In Focus/A.G. Firth 92
Shokokusha Co. 209
Julius Shulman 99, 144, 182,
184, 202
Henry Pierre Schultz Fotografie
123
Claudio Silvestrin 273
John Simpson & Partners 67
SITE 289
Skidmore, Owings & Merrill LLP
362/ Wolfgang Hoyt 306
Jose de la Sota 212
South African High Commission
39
Margherita Spiluttini 158
Tim Street-Porter 7, 136,
196, 229
Hisao Suzuki Fotografo 237
Tempere Tourist Office 23
Ticino Turismo 250
Curtis Trent 233
TRH Pictures 340
Aldo Van Eyck 208
Marco Verona 91
Westminster Cathedral, The
Administrator 72bl
Jenny Wood 69
Silvia Zenobio Nascimento 180

Special thanks to Lynne Bryant,
James Neal and Lucy Waitt at
Arcaid; Deborah Fioravanti and
everyone who kindly supplied
images for this book.

Every effort has been made to
acknowledge correctly and
contact the source and/copyright
holder of each picture, and
Carlton Books Limited apologizes
for any unintentional errors or
omissions which will be corrected
in future editions of this book.